Routledge Revivals

Rural Land-Use Planning in Developed Nations

This edited collection, first published in 1989, provides a detailed analysis of rural land-use policies on a country-specific basis. Case studies include analyses of planning and legislation in Britain, The Netherlands, Japan, the U.S.A. and Australia. Alongside a comprehensive overview of the concept and application of rural land use from Paul Cloke, environment issues, resource management and the role of central governments are topics under discussion throughout. At an international level, this title will of particular interest to students of rural geography and environmental planning.

Rural Land-Use Planning in Developed Nations

Edited by

Paul Cloke

First published in 1989
by Unwin Hyman Ltd

This edition first published in 2013 by Routledge
2 Park Square, Milton Park, Abingdon, Oxon, OX14 4RN

Simultaneously published in the USA and Canada
by Routledge
711 Third Avenue, New York, NY 10017

Routledge is an imprint of the Taylor & Francis Group, an informa business

© 1989 Paul Cloke and contributors

All rights reserved. No part of this book may be reprinted or reproduced or utilised in any form or by any electronic, mechanical, or other means, now known or hereafter invented, including photocopying and recording, or in any information storage or retrieval system, without permission in writing from the publishers.

Publisher's Note
The publisher has gone to great lengths to ensure the quality of this reprint but points out that some imperfections in the original copies may be apparent.

Disclaimer
The publisher has made every effort to trace copyright holders and welcomes correspondence from those they have been unable to contact.

A Library of Congress record exists under LC control number: 88016973

ISBN 13: 978-0-415-71566-9 (hbk)
ISBN 13: 978-1-315-88057-0 (ebk)
ISBN 13: 978-0-415-71563-8 (pbk)

Rural Land-Use Planning in Developed Nations

edited by
Paul J. Cloke

London
UNWIN HYMAN
Boston   Sydney   Wellington

© P. J. Cloke and contributors, 1989
This book is copyright under the Berne Convention. No reproduction without permission. All rights reserved.

Published by the Academic Division of
Unwin Hyman Ltd
15/17 Broadwick Street, London W1V 3FP, UK

Unwin Hyman Inc.,
8 Winchester Place, Winchester, Mass. 01890, USA

Allen & Unwin (Australia) Ltd,
8 Napier Street, North Sydney, NSW 2060, Australia

Allen & Unwin (New Zealand) Ltd in association with the Port Nicholson Press Ltd,
60 Cambridge Terrace, Wellington, New Zealand

First published in 1989

British Library Cataloguing in Publication Data

Rural land-use planning in developed nations.
1. Developed countries. Rural regions. Land use. Planning
I. Cloke, Paul J.
333.76'17'091722
ISBN 0-04-711025-2

Library of Congress Cataloging-in-Publication Data

Rural land-use planning in developed nations / edited by Paul J. Cloke.
p. cm.
Bibliography: p.
Includes index.
ISBN 0-04-711025-2
1. Land use, Rural—Planning. I. Cloke, Paul J.
HD108.6.R87 1988
333.76'17—dc19
88-16973 CIP

Typeset in 10 on 11 point Bembo
and printed in Great Britain by
Billing and Sons, Worcester

Acknowledgements

The editor would like to offer special thanks to the following: Roger Jones of Unwin Hyman for his sustained support over a number of publishing ventures; Maureen Hunwicks, whose skills of speedy efficiency have been so vital in producing manuscripts; Philip Bell, without whom conversation in Lampeter about rural planning would mean talking to yourself; our friends, Caroline and Philip Swain, Ros and Mike Scriven, and Gwyn and George Pegram, who have offered strong support to the Cloke family in recent times; and lastly Viv, Elizabeth and William for their constant love and patience.

PJC
Lampeter
March 1988

Contents

1 Planning and rural land use: concepts and
  applications *Paul Cloke*   1

  Introduction   1
  Land use: in search of concepts   3
  The market and intervention   5
  The role of planning in its state context   9
  The aim of this book   15
  References   16

2 Land-use planning in rural Britain   18
  Paul Cloke

  Introduction   18
  The countryside and its interests   20
  The 1947 Act: collectivizing the development decision   24
  Planning rural development   26
  Conservation by designation   29
  The Thatcher Era I: voluntary management   33
  The Thatcher Era II: the politics and policies of ALURE   38
  Conclusion   42
  Notes   45
  References   45

3 Rural land-use planning in The Netherlands:
  integration or segregation of functions?   47
  Leo M. van den Berg

  Introduction   47
  Land-use trends in the countryside   48
  Agencies, guidelines and interest groups for rural planning   58
  Land development   61
  Dilemmas and solutions in two complex land-development
  projects   65
  Conclusion   72
  Acknowledgements   73
  References   74

Contents

4	Land-use planning in rural France *John Aitchison*	76
	Introduction	76
	L'espace rural français	77
	Plans d'occupation des sols and *chartes intercommunales*	79
	Agriculture, forestry and the landscape	83
	Landscape and nature conservation	89
	Le littoral	94
	La montagne française	97
	Conclusion	100
	References	101
5	Rural land-use planning in West Germany *Brian J. Woodruffe*	104
	Introduction	104
	Land-use trends	105
	Land-use issues in the agricultural landscape	107
	Village renovation schemes (*Dorferneuerung*)	117
	Issue in conserved landscapes	120
	Conclusion	126
	References	127
6	Rural land-use planning in Japan *Michael Hebbert*	130
	Introduction	130
	The land of Japan	133
	The forest	136
	Agriculture	139
	Urban land	142
	Land conversion between uses	143
	Land planning	146
	Acknowledgements	150
	References	151
7	Rural planning in the United States: fragmentation, conflict and slow progress *Thomas L. Daniels, Mark B. Lapping & John W. Keller*	152
	Introduction	151
	The federal role: federal lands management, environmental laws and spending programmes	153
	Federal development spending programmes	160
	Agricultural land retention	164
	State forestland planning	167
	Developments of regional impact	169
	Three examples of state planning for rural areas	170
	Conclusion	175
	References	176

8	Rural land-use planning in Canada *Christopher R. Bryant*	178
	Introduction	178
	Rural land use and land-use planning	180
	The rural land base	182
	Rural land-use conflicts	185
	The principal issues	186
	Emergence of conflicts into the political arena	188
	The planning of rural land use	190
	Rural land-use conflicts: examples	191
	Amenity and natural environment issues	198
	Conclusions	199
	Acknowledgements	201
	References	202
9	Rural land-use planning in Australia *Geoffrey T. McDonald*	207
	Introduction	207
	Australia's land resources and their use	210
	Land-use issues	214
	Institutions	219
	Planning and plans	222
	Conclusion	233
	References	234
10	Sectoral and statutory planning for rural New Zealand *Warren Moran*	238
	Introduction	238
	Local and regional statutory planning	242
	The role of central government agencies	244
	An appraisal of rural planning in New Zealand	251
	Acknowledgement	260
	References	260
11	Land-use regulation in deregulatory times *Paul Cloke*	264
	Introduction	264
	Rural land-use problems	267
	Policies for the regulation of rural land use	272
	The changing political context	280
	Planning regulation within state deregulation	285
	References	287
	Index	288

1 Planning and rural land use: concepts and applications

PAUL CLOKE

Introduction

Rural land is regarded as important for a number of reasons. It represents the space and resource base for timber and food production, and so becomes an essential component in the political discourse over the strategic need for agricultural self-sufficiency, and over the economic necessity in the case of some nations to reproduce an export capacity in agricultural produce under rapidly changing trade conditions. It also comprises a major spatial constituency for outdoor recreation and is therefore subject to the necessary discussions about access, facility-provision and management which accompany both multiple land use and specific recreational schemes on rural land. Recreation is in turn predicated on landscape quality (at various scales) and often also on the factor of heritage which is attributed to the rural environment, again both in part and as a whole. Recognition of the value of landscape in its heritage context and in ecological terms has given rise to an expanding interest in the conservation of rural land and landscape, whereby an attempt is made to express a format of common interest in maintaining particularly threatened or precious elements. Conservation has become important, not only in deep rural areas but also on the urban fringe. Paradoxically in these areas of conflict over the transfer of rural land to urban use, often for housing development, the influx of adventitious rural residents gives a boost to the conservation cause, which has been characterized (somewhat cruelly) as groups of people wanting to ensure that they are the last to be permitted to move into – and thereby spoil – these rural environments.

These various functions of rural land are potentially conflicting, but not inevitably so. The scale and distribution of rural land in different nations is sufficiently varied that caution is necessary in any generalized view of rural land-use conflict. There does, however, seem to be mounting evidence that the scientific and technical changes in the second half of the 20th century, when allied with the changing nature of world trade and economy, do constitute prompters of accelerating conflict. For example, changes in agricultural production have made significant impacts on rural landscapes both visually and in terms of downstream pollution. Mechanization has been accompanied by the economic desirability of large improved fields, unencumbered with landscape features such as hedges, trees, wetland areas, and so on. Chemical fertilizers, herbicides, pesticides, all necessary for 'modern' agricultural production, have turned some parts of rural land into what Goldsmith & Hildyard (1986) have termed 'an industrial wasteland'. Neither is it those industries traditionally viewed as 'rural' which are the only polluters, as emissions from urban-based power stations contributing to international flows of acid rain on rural land have shown (Park 1987). It is the economic imperative of increased productivity which has led to the low priority given to some parts of the rural land base.

The conflicts between agriculture and other industries and concern for conservation of the rural environment are not the only components of the accelerating turbulence over rural land-use issues. Where priority is given to recreation and tourism, potential over-use of some rural sites can lead to environmental damage and psychological pollution of previous wilderness experiences. The deconcentration of industry and housing which have accompanied the counter-urbanization phenomenon (see Fielding 1982, Cloke 1985) has also had a considerable visual impact on rural environments. The disposal of urban industrial waste in rural locations and the siting of potentially polluting industrial establishments such as nuclear power stations in remote rural sites are adding significantly to rural land-use problems, as is mineral exploitation in some cases.

These conflicts are with us now, but there are others which are not far off according to the view of some futurists relating to post-industrial society. For example, there is a body of opinion (see, for example, Robertson 1978) which suggests that the movement towards 'alternative life-styles' which has been apparent in many rural areas over the last twenty or so years represents a precursor to a much more significant back-to-the-land trend in the the post-industrial future. Whatever the prejudices about post-industrial theory – and there are many – it is possible to foresee an increasingly technological mode of production linked with increasingly technocratic labour markets resulting in higher rates of redundant labour than are experienced now. Society has yet to face up to how it will cope with the support of the unneeded workforce, but some argue that there will be a return to a more simple land-based lifestyle in rural areas. Were this to happen at any scale, a further laminate of use would be required from rural land – a use which might lead to a higher degree of environmental consciousness but which could be out of tune with many existing landowners and land users in the areas concerned.

Rural land-use issues, then, have become an important facet of late capitalist nations, and are likely to become more so. In rational terms, the role of planning in the mediation of conflict might be thought to be equally important. Planning itself, however, is also changing with the new political regimes which have accompanied the economic restructuring taking place in many nations. It is therefore necessary briefly to examine the context, purpose and type of planning through which intervention occurs in rural land uses.

Land use: in search of concepts

Sandy Mather, in his book *Land Use* (1986), uses a biblical illustration of a fundamental contrast in attitudes to land. In the book of I Kings, Chapter 21, is told told the story of Naboth's vineyard. Ahab, King of Samaria and personifying wealth and power at that time, wishes to purchase Naboth's land as an extension to his own property – as Mather points out, Ahab regards land as a commodity to be bought and sold. Naboth, however, places a different value on his land since it is an inheritance from his family and he is merely a steward over it, so he refuses Ahab's offer. Mather (p. 2) uses this conflict to outline two fundamental concepts of land:

> On the one hand, land is simply a form of property that may be traded at will. On the other, land is much more than just personal private property, and its possession is not (just) a matter for market forces to determine. In this second concept, a sense of stewardship attaches, and land is a form of common property, either in the sense of succeeding generations or, by extension, in the wider sense that the community has an interest in it.

These issues of how land is conceptualized may be seen to be at the root of wider issues of how and why landowners can or should be controlled in the use of their own property (Clark 1982).

It would, however, be foolish not to take note of the ending of the Ahab–Naboth dispute. With Queen Jezebel urging him to act in a manner which benefited his power status and wealth, and having Naboth put to death over some trumped-up charge, Ahab took possession of the land he coveted. This serves as a stark reminder that contests over land usage are fought in the arena of existing power relations and so the settling of conflict will often not be through a rational mediation of issues but rather according to the power and influence of competing land users. Following the biblical theme, there is a clear illustration of what should be expected in these circumstances:

> If you see the poor oppressed in a district, and justice and rights denied, do not be surprised at such things; for one official is eyed by a higher one, and over them both are others higher still. The increase from the land is taken by all; the king himself profits from the fields.
> (Ecclesiastes 5.8–9, New International Version)

These attitudes to land, and the power relations which underlie land-use conflicts, are emphasized here because any discussion of the *planning* of rural land use requires a focus around which to weave its analysis. It would be easy to go along with Patricios (1986) emphasizing that because land use is influenced by history, institutions, politics, technology, society and economy, and because each of these factors differs in different nations, there is therefore a 'bewildering number of variety of themes' for land-use analysts to consider. However, such an approach is not particularly helpful in breaking down the parochialism of land-use planning studies. It suggests that we can perhaps know about planning in other nations but we can only understand that planning in the context of the particular circumstances of that nation.

Neither is it useful to replace the 'bewildering variety' with over-simplified generations whose perceived utility is in achieving some link, however spurious, between land-use issues in particular places. For example, Fabos (1985) describes four common characteristics of land-use issues:

(a) they present or generate one or more uncertainties
(b) they can be perceived as both a problem and an opportunity
(c) they have a supply and a demand aspect
(d) they can be dealt with in one of two ways, either systematically or conceptually

But it seems unlikely that these characteristics can be translated into a cogent, theoretically informed view of the planning of rural land use. Indeed, they merely beg further questions: how and for whom are uncertainties reduced; how are 'problems' and 'opportunities' distributed amongst the various interest groups involved; does the mechanism of the market place regulate supply and demand, and if so what impacts result; and where do political factors enter into either systematic or conceptual approaches for dealing with land-use issues? As Healey (1986) has argued, identifying outcomes is not enough; we have to look at the different ways these outcomes can be evaluated.

One way forward here is to focus on the idea of regulating land-use conflicts. Dawson (1984) and others stress first that land (unlike other factors of production such as labour and capital) is in (almost) fixed supply, and second, that it is specifically located such that its value is closely interrelated with the activities being pursued nearby. Pollution from adjacent land uses will reduce land value whereas value-adding improvements to neighbouring land will sometimes benefit land values despite the fact that in both cases the land in question has not itself changed in character or use. Dawson (p. 3) suggests that

> the market fails to allocate the costs and benefits of such operations accurately; and, because this is the case, there has been an increasing tendency for governments to restrict the rights of private owners to use their land as they wish, in the interests of society at large.

Two issues arise from these contentions. First, in what ways is market-place regulation of rural land use deemed to be inefficient; and second, how are 'the interests of society at large' interpreted and implemented? These themes are pursued through an analysis of the *reasons* for planning intervention, and through a discussion of the *role* of planning within its state context.

The market and intervention

Why has it been necessary to plan rural land use? If land-use decisions were made merely by landowners alone, then not only would there be a potentially random intermixture of uses but also there would be no protective mechanism against wholesale changes to existing cherished landscapes or to strategically necessary land

Planning and rural land use

uses. There has therefore arisen a series of traditional wisdoms as to why planning systems have been generated which provide a framework for the decisions of landowners and land users. Held and Visser (1984), for example, advance four roles for land-use planning, which infer in each case market inefficiencies or injustices:

(a) to discourage certain uses which would be incompatible with existing uses
(b) to achieve greater efficiency in the use of land resources in the area
(c) to reduce or eliminate certain hazards
(d) to preserve or to protect desired elements of the existing environment

and Dawson (1984) adds three more at the meso- and macro-scales:

(e) to control the aggregate allocation of land among alternative uses
(f) to achieve particular levels of output, particularly in agriculture
(g) to control the intermixture of uses to provide a pleasant and safe environment.

This kind of listing of roles for land-use planning fits worthily into the rational decision-making view of the planning process. Society identifies potential inefficiencies and inequalities arising from market-led land-use decisions; politicians design planning procedures which permit the regulation of decisions by landowners; and planners implement those decisions, unswervingly being able to recognize the 'common good' when they see it. Indeed, this whole approach is based on this premise of there being a common good. As Held and Visser (1984, p. 4) conclude:

> Their [land-use plans] primary purpose is to protect a substantial common or public interest which, if left to individual private decisions, would not likely be protected, or where without action supporting a concern of the community, uses would be made of the land which would constitute a threat to the health, safety, or general well-being of the community.

Accordingly it is possible to outline various forms of rural land-use planning which have been pursued for the common good. First, land can be controlled by the imposition of laws and ordinances on landowners so as to restrict the use of their land.

In the UK, for example, town and country planning legislation restricts the transfer of farmland to urban uses (see Hall 1974, Ratcliffe 1978, Cullingworth 1985), whereas in many other parts of the world zoning ordinances are used to control the type and intensity of land use in a particular area (Carlson *et al.* 1981). Secondly, land can be controlled by bringing it into public ownership, or maintaining its 'crown' or 'state' status. Most national park areas in the developed world are controlled through ownership. Thirdly, less direct control can be exerted through fiscal measures of various kinds, for instance grants and subsidies to promote particular forms of agricultural production. Fourthly, indirect control of land use can be achieved through the control of land ownership and occupancy, with many states in the USA, for example, prohibiting the corporate ownership of farmland so as to protect family farmers (see Reimund 1979).

This combination of roles and mechanisms provides a well-established basic framework for rural land-use planning. However, the vigorous debates of critical planning theory (see Healey *et al.* 1982, Cooke 1983, Hanrahan & Cloke 1983, Cloke & Hanrahan 1984, Reade 1987, amongst others) would clearly suggest that this view of rural land-use planning as some kind of neutral and almost apolitical arbitration service between competing rural resource bidders is both artificially simple and politically naive. This theoretical debate has partly arisen from the sheer practical difficulties of attempting to research 'real life' planning against the background of this simple rationalist model. Crucially such research has concluded that both the land development process and the system of planned intervention in land-use changes are far more complex than is conventionally assumed. Barrett and Healey (1985) have analysed this complexity in the context of the operation of different mechanisms in the process of land conversion, and their conclusion (pp. 350–1) is worthy of extended note:

> Whilst it may be relatively easy to describe the 'ingredients' or resources to be assembled for development to take place, it is more difficult to find a way of describing the development *process* itself that encompasses the interaction of the different activities, the range of agencies involved in the process and, particularly, the complexity of their interrelationships. Conventional descriptions of the development process either categorise the functions involved, or adopt a 'pipeline' approach, listing the stages involved in the conversion of land from one state to another . . . In practice the functions are combined and performed in different

ways for different sectors by a range of agents including land owners, local authorities, developers, builders, investors and financial institutions, occupiers and professional advisers.

Another factor underlying the increasing acceptance of critical planning theory relates to the notion of the 'common good' mentioned above. The assumption that planning at either national or local levels actually reflects the common good (however defined) is increasingly criticized by evidence from studies of power relations since it assumes the free rein of *pluralist* power, in which any individual or group can gain access to public policy and the state does not generate consistent biases towards any special interests. Such a view ignores other more powerful and realistic concepts of decision-making power: *elitism/instrumentalism*, which suggests that minority elite groups hold power and that the activities of the state (including planning) are structured so as to serve the interests of these groups; *managerialism* which indicates key professional managers who through technical expertise and the manipulation of decision-making machinery are able to influence policy in favour of their own interests and world-view, or of those of their peers; and *structuralism* which promotes the viewpoint that class relations represent the only real disaggregation of society which can inform the analysis of power and policy-making. The state thus favours the current balance of class interests in its planning and policy-making. Within the latter three broad approaches, the 'common good' represents a legitimation of particular class or sectional interests that have achieved dominance in power relations. It should not be assumed from these concepts that powerful groups always get their way in every land-use decision – that too would be a gross over-statement of how land-use planning happens – but they do help to explain both the broad direction of change, the exemption of certain land-use changes (for example, from one agricultural use to another) from accepted planning processes, and the strength of lobbies for compensation or betterment, when negative decisions have to be accepted.

What begins to emerge here is the need for much more complex and politically informed concepts of both the overall constraints on land-use planning in its context as a state activity (and therefore deriving from power relations between and within the state and society) and the more practical complexities of bargaining, negotiation and action which occur in the continuum between policy and action in the implementation of planning (Barrett & Fudge 1981). Furthermore, it should be stressed that these interrelationships do change over time, perhaps with shifts in power relations between different fractions of capital or class, or perhaps as the ideological momentum of particular governments mediate to an extent the structures inherent in the wider state.

A clear example of temporal changes in planning is provided by Garner (1985) in the British context. He describes the 1947 Town and Country Planning Act as giving complete control to local authorities of the use of land, and the design and appearance of buildings in that area. Then he describes how holes have appeared in this fabric of control. Five such holes are emphasized:

(a) the designation of *enterprise zones* where outline but not detailed control of land is maintained
(b) the proposed *simplified planning zones* which will replace detailed development control with broader zoning mechanisms in rural areas (although not in National Parks or Areas of Outstanding Natural Beauty)
(c) the *General Development Order*, where with increasing tolerance planning permission can be granted without formal application
(d) the *Circulars* from central government which have frequently dictated policy to local authorities, influencing, for example, green belt policies
(e) the use of *Section 52 Agreements* where planning permission is granted in exchange for concessions from the developer ('planning gain') which can often be worth millions of pounds.

A rational view of planning might suggest that these changes have occurred for the 'common good' but it seems far more fruitful to investigate the influence of interest groups who have gained most by these decisions. This can only be pursued by a closer examination of the state context in which planning operates.

The role of planning in its state context

This broad and complex conceptual area can only be given cursory treatment here, and is discussed in more detail in Cloke and Little (1987, 1989). It is important because of one fundamental premise; namely that planning and policy-making are undeniably integral aspects of state activity and as such are subject to the context and constraints of all state activities. By looking in isolation at what planners and policy-makers achieve, there is a danger that our analysis will blame them for deficiencies and failures which are due to factors beyond their control and traceable back into the machinery and role of the state. Therefore the context of the state appears to be a crucial area of investigation for understanding the constraints within which the complex procedures of bargaining and negotiation in planning take place. It is not suggested that theories of the state can provide a monolithic top-down explanation of rural (or any other kind of) planning. Rather, they serve as insights into the constraining context within which the 'visible' decision-making processes of planning and policy-making operate.

It would be a truism to suggest that there is no one theory of the state. However, it is useful to review briefly a few of the main conceptual strands which both highlight some of the assumptions which underlie current analyses of rural planning and provide alternative theoretical foundations for ongoing study. Use is made here of Clark and Dear's (1984) division of the state into three layers:

(a) *form* – the structural link between society and the state
(b) *function* – the roles which are necessary to reproduce that form
(c) *apparatus* – the instruments through which functions are performed.

Form

The relationship between society and the agencies of government, law, judiciary and administration which make up the state is complex, multifaceted and value-laden in ideological terms (see Dunleavy 1980, Urry 1981, Cooke 1983, Ham & Hill 1984). Nevertheless, there are clear issues of theoretical divergence according to which, the analysis of planning and policy-making will vary enormously. One such issue is mentioned here in order to demonstrate the importance of state theory in the context of rural land-use planning.

The traditional viewpoint of the form of the state adopted (often implicitly) in rural planning studies is that the state can be represented by an amalgam of its institutions. The state can thereby be investigated, in surrogate, by research focusing on particular departments of government or specific institutions within the bureaucracy, and it follows that it can often be assumed that power is vested *in* these institutions. Such an assumption conditions the ensuing research agenda which concentrates on the activities of these agencies and tacitly accepts the state's own definition of which agencies are of 'relevance' to rural planning. In this way, the departments of the central state dealing with agriculture and the environment, and the local and regional government agencies dealing with rural constituencies have been the major foci of investigation.

Some state theorists, however (see Poulantzas 1973), offer an alternative to this viewpoint, recognizing the state as a condensate of class-based social relations. Thus power is not vested *in* government institutions, it is exercised *through* those institutions by the dominant social fractions which underlie the state. Such a view of state form would, if accepted, change the way we seek to understand why and how rural policies come about. In particular, inter-institutional and trans-institutional approaches will be generated which seek to acknowledge that institutions are merely a reflection of a state whose form is dictated by class relations. These concepts also tie in with the notions of power relations mentioned above. Pluralist ideas of power relations are incompatible with the concept of the state as a condensate of class-based social relations. Equally, acceptance of structuralist forms of power relations precludes the assumption that state power is vested in (rather than exercised through) government institutions.

Although these brief descriptions grossly over-simplify the theoretical discourses concerned, it is nevertheless evident that the way in which rural planning is understood will differ significantly according to which of these assumptions is adopted.

Function

Theoretical deliberations over state form inevitably shape those relating to state function, and it is again the case that the theoretical assumptions about the functions attributable to the state will reflect directly in the roles of planning and policy-making and thereby set the hidden agenda of objectives for these specific parts of the state machinery.

Again the conceptual debate over state function is too complex and vast to reproduce here. One issue, however, serves to illustrate the kind of assumptive decision which has to be made by those seeking to understand rural planning in its state context. Mandel (1975) describes the function of the state as being to protect and reproduce existing social structures and social relations of production. A key issue for our understanding of the role of planning is how these functions of protection and reproduction relate to current power relations. Do they occur in an *aggregate* way such that all groups can potentially benefit, or in a *selective* way, favouring elites, managers, or dominant class and capital interests?

An assumption of pluralist power relations exercised in the institutions of government would lead to an aggregate view of state function. The state would be seen as in but not of the capitalist structures which surround it and therefore the functions of the state (including planning) would not be dominated by those capitalist structures. Clark and Dear (1984) provide examples of such functions:

- the regulation or deregulation of the market for the public good
- the arbitration of competing bids for resources
- the adjustment of the market to the state's normative goals through social engineering
- the guarantee of freedom of individual decision-making.

Alternatively an assumption of elitist or structuralist power relations leads to a selective view of state function. Either the state functions in favour of elites (and to an extent managers) within the bounds of discretion set by class and capital interests, or we are dealing with a specifically capitalist state, determined by the current balance of social relations. Clark and Dear also envisage a suite of state functions in this context, including:

- a parasitic or superficial role
- an instrument of class rule
- a system of political domination
- a means of legitimation.

The adoption of either of these polar viewpoints is likely to lead to an over-simplification of the role of the state. While it is apparent that the state derives much of its power from the economic and political imperatives of capital, it also seems that the state can generate energy and power on its own account as well as being a channel for the exercise of external power. We are therefore faced with the prospect of accounting for the state being contemporaneously founded in the social relations of capitalism and able to generate authoritative power of tis own accord.

Saunders (1978, 1982) has acknowledged this dualism in his distillation of state functions into two levels of intervention:

(a) the *corporate* level, at which the state intervenes in areas of production on behalf of capital interests

(b) the *competitive* level, at which services are provided for dependent populations.

The corporate level of intervention appears to be integral to the capitalist state, with its outcomes being selectively dependent upon power relations which show consistent bias. The competitive level of intervention is the result of some autonomy of decision-making within the state, but such discretion usually seems constrained by the need to prioritize the corporate functions of the state. Analyses of rural planning and policy-making achievements tend to reflect the idea that corporate intervention for production has been given far higher priority in most states than competitive intervention for consumption.

Apparatus

It is at the level of apparatus that rural planning mechanisms are most familiar. Yet the analysis of apparatus is constrained by the assumptions previously made concerning the form and function of the state. Traditionally rural planning apparatus has been treated as one discrete part of the machinery of government, but the above brief discussions of state form and function would suggest that this unisectoral description is misleading. Clark and Dear (1984) discuss four main areas of apparatus:

(a) *consensus* – securing participation in the processes of society, politics and law
(b) *production* – securing conditions for capital accumulation, for example, by regulating social investment and consumption
(c) *consumption/legitimation* – a mixture of the promotion of well-being and securing the allegiance of society to the dominant social contract through the provision of welfare services
(d) *administration* – ensuring the smooth running and compatibility of the other apparatus.

Viewed in the light of these four categories, rural planning apparatus cannot be thought of as unisectoral. Land-use planning has been part of the *production* apparatus, particularly in its varying support for the agricultural and construction sectors of capital; it has been part of the consumption and legitimation apparatus, through the provision of recreational facilities and conserved amenity; it has performed a *consensus* role through public participation procedures; and it has an important *administrative* role, particularly in seeking compatibility with other instruments of state policy. In many ways, then, planning constitutes a loose collection of mechanisms which derive from different functions of the state, and which receive different levels of priority in terms of the needs of state power.

So what?

This brief discussion of key issues within the theory of the state has highlighted some of the alternative theoretical assumptions which underlie rural planning in its political context, but there will doubtless be some who will question the validity of this unwelcome incursion into the cosy world of practical apolitical planning. One major answer to the question of 'so what?' lies in the rather rational notion of planning as a response to problems. Even those who are entrenched in a rationalist view of planning with their assumptions of logical and neutral decision-making processes, have begun to recognize the severe limitations in the ability of rural planning to respond to the conflicts of rural land use. Such a recognition should then lead to an interest in exploring the nature of the state's response to changing circumstances, for if planning and policy-making are state activities, it follows that they will be intertwined with the wider matter of how the state responds to problems.

The state's response is neither static nor monolithic. Rather there is a continuous process of response and counter-response between state and society. However, the beneficiaries of these interactions have been rather more constant in that the state's response appears to be much more to the needs of dominant capital interests than to the needs of other groups. If this is the case, then previous attention to the minutiae of rural planning in practice needs to be widened. Rural planning activity needs to be seen in the context of overall state functions and against the background of the purposes which the apparatus of the state is designed to fulfil. Specific rural land-use problems should be integrated into this spiral of response and counter-response between state, capital and society. In so doing, there might be a greater understanding both of the hidden agenda of roles which rural planning performs, and the political economic constraints within which rural policies are made and implemented.

The structure and the agency of planning for rural land use are inextricably linked. Thus far, our understanding of planning and its impacts has skewed towards agency, and by making use of the theorization of the state that imbalance can be redressed. This theme is mirrored by Healey (1986) and by Barrett and Healey (1985) whose fourfold agenda for research in land policy encompasses both local detail and structural constraint in the policy process. They suggest four topics for future research:

(a) land supply, land ownership and land markets
(b) roles and interests in the development process
(c) purposes and types of state intervention in land, its use and development
(d) the internal organization of the state as it relates to land questions.

It is against this background of information and research needs that these accounts of rural land-use planning in various nations have come together.

The aim of this book

This introductory chapter has sought to highlight a number of different themes. Albeit briefly, it has outlined the potential conflicts in rural land use, it has discussed various integrating themes for rural land-use studies, it has looked at the conventional wisdoms of interventionary rural land-use planning 'for the common good', and it has attempted to place such planning in the important contexts of power relations and the form, function and apparatus of the state. Inevitably the chapters that follow address these themes only partially, as much more specific research is required to answer some of the questions raised here. Nevertheless, these chapters are collectively aimed at breaking down the currently parochial nature of rural land-use planning studies.

Although the book is only a starting point in terms of theoretical advancement it does aim to provide a major contribution to the knowledge and understanding of the planning of rural land use at an international scale. Inevitably, developed nations approach the planning of rural land very differently according to scale, the available budget of rural land, the political acceptability of planning intervention, and the relative strength of major rural land-using groups (particularly the agricultural lobbies). It is to be expected that underlying trends of economy and land use will attract diverse responses in different nations according to these various factors, but it will also be interesting to see whether common factors in rural land-use planning emerge such that elements of the theory of the state are illustrated in transnational comparisons.

To these ends, each author has been asked to address an agreed range of issues, including:

- major land-use conflicts
- landscape conservation
- rural land budgets
- the nature of planned intervention at various scales
- central–local state relations and activities
- rural political climate.

In this way it is hoped that the book will be founded on complementary themes, while exposing the interesting idiosyncracies of individual nations.

References

Barrett, S. & C. Fudge (eds) 1981. *Policy and action*, London: Methuen.

Barrett, S. & P. Healey 1985. Priorities for research in land policy. In *Land policy: problems and alternatives*, S. Barrett & P. Healey (eds). Aldershot: Gower.

Carlson, J., M. Lassey & W. Lassey 1981. *Rural society and environment in America*, New York: McGraw-Hill.

Clark, G. Rights, property and community. *Economic Geographer* 15, 120–38.

Clark, G. & M. Dear 1984. *State apparatus*, Boston: Allen & Unwin.

Cloke, P. 1985. Counterurbanisation: a rural perspective. *Geography* 70, 13–23.

Cloke, P. 1987a. Policy and planning in rural areas. In *Rural planning: policy into action*, P. Cloke (ed.). London: Harper & Row.

Cloke, P. 1987b. Policy and implementation decisions. In *Rural planning: policy into action*, P. Cloke (ed.). London: Harper & Row.

Cloke, P. & P. Hanrahan 1984. Policy and implementation in rural planning, *Geoforum* 15, 261–9.

Cloke, P. & J. Little 1987. Policy, planning and the state in rural localities. *Journal of Rural Studies* 3, 343–52.

Cloke, P. & J. Little 1989. *The rural state*. Oxford: Oxford University Press.

Cooke, P. 1983. *Theories of planning and spatial development*. London: Hutchinson.

Cullingworth, J. 1985. *Town and country planning in Britain*, 9th edn. London: Allen & Unwin.

Dawson, A. 1984. *The land problem in the developed economy*. London: Croom Helm.

Dunleavy, P. 1980. *Urban political analysis: the politics of collective consumption*. London: Methuen.

Fabos, J. 1985. *Land use planning: from global to local challenge.* New York: Chapman & Hall.
Fielding, A. 1982. Counterurbanisation in Western Europe, *Progress in Planning* 17, 1–52.
Garner, J. 1985. The decline of planning control. *Journal of Planning and Environmental Law*, Nov., 756–8.
Goldsmith, E. & N. Hildyard (eds). *Green Britain or industrial wasteland?* Cambridge: Polity Press.
Hall, P. 1974. *Urban and regional planning.* London: Penguin.
Ham, C. & M. Hill. *The policy process in the modern capitalist state.* Brighton: Wheatsheaf Press.
Hanrahan, P. & P. Cloke 1983. Towards a critical appraisal of rural settlement planning in England and Wales. *Sociologia Ruralis* 23, 109–29.
Healey, P. 1986. Emerging directions for research on local land-use planning. *Environment and Planning B13*, 103–20.
Healey, P., G. McDougall & M. Thomas (eds) 1982. *Planning theory: prospects for the 1980s.* Oxford: Pergamon.
Held, R. & D. Visser 1984. *Rural land uses and planning.* Amsterdam: Elsevier.
Mandel, E. 1975. *Late capitalism.* London: New Left Books.
Mather, A. 1986. *Land use.* London: Longman.
Park, C. 1987. *Acid rain: rhetoric and reality* London: Methuen.
Patricios, N. (ed.) 1986. *International handbook on land use planning.* Westport, Conn.: Greenwood.
Poulantzas, N. 1973. The problems of the capitalist state. *Power in Britain.* In J. Urry & J. Wakeford (eds). London: Heinemann.
Ratcliffe, J. 1978. *An introduction to town and country planning.* London: Hutchinson.
Reade, E. 1987. *British town and country planning.* Milton Keynes: Open University Press.
Reimund, D. 1979. Form of business organization. *USDA Agricultural Economics Reports* 438, 128–33.
Robertson, J. 1978. The politics and economics of the SHE. *Built Environment* 4, 266–74.
Saunders, P. 1979. *Urban politics: a sociological interpretation.* London: Hutchinson.
Saunders, P. 1982. Why study central–local relations? *Local Government Studies*, March/April, 55–66.
Urry, J. 1981. Localities, regions and social class. *International Journal of Urban and Regional Research* 5, 455–73.

2 Land-use planning in rural Britain

PAUL CLOKE

Introduction

> Land-use planning in Britain – and in most other countries as well – has been built on the extremely shaky and insecure foundation of illusion rather than that of reality.
> (Best 1981 p. 184)

Robin Best's sentiment is one which can be agreed to by most researchers interested in rural land-use planning in Britain, but often for quite different reasons. Best himself had particular myths in mind:

(a) a vast expanse of the country is sterilized by urbanization at wastefully low density
(b) urban sprawl is continually engulfing good quality land, and before long all our precious countryside will be built over
(c) urban take of agricultural land is on a large scale, particularly in South-East England
(d) agricultural output is threatened if continuing losses of farmland are not substantially reduced
(e) Britain's small size and high levels of urbanization make it unique so far as land-use patterns and the severity of land competition are concerned

and proceeded to expose each of these as illusory, concluding his book with a most optimistic statement: 'With sensible decision-making and an appropriate strategy of land use, as contained in county structure plans, we could achieve all of our land-use objectives' (p. 191). In many ways, Robin Best's analysis of urban use of agricultural land has been proved essentially correct, yet his hope for the achievability of all land-use objectives may well turn out to be illusory.

For example, from the point of view of *rural* land use it has been argued by Newby (1980 p. 288) that until recently planning has been:

> virtually a by-product of a system designed to cope with urban growth, partly because the countryside was regarded as a bucolic backdrop to life in urban areas and partly because the idea of a planned countryside was, to influential public opinion, anathema . . . only in the last decade or so, therefore, has rural planning not proceeded by default.

According to these sentiments, to talk about 'all our land use objectives' is an uncomfortable if not dubious task since the objectives of some will presumably not match the interests of others. Urban–rural tensions, *influential* public opinion (as opposed to other opinion) and the bucolic idyll for some, set against the deprived living and working environment of others (McLaughlin 1986) all suggest the idea of fundamental divisions of interests and intentions which are wrapped up in rural land-use planning. Newby still offers us the note of optimism, however: 'only in the last decade or so'. Have contemporary planning processes, therefore, proceeded with a clarity of purpose towards land-use objectives which have somehow specified a 'common good'?

Not so, according to Ambrose (1986), who traces the progress of planning from the wartime committees of Barlow and Uthwatt through to the present reign of Thatcherism. He concludes that 'the post-Uthwatt retreat from a strong state interventionary role in land development, a retreat interrupted by brief advances in 1946–8, 1965–70 and 1974–7 has now by the mid-1980s become a rout' (p. 64). He refers to the current orientation towards market forces of government in Britain which he describes as 'a small-minded government to whom the whole idea of collective caring and shared social responsibility is anathema' (p. xi).

So are we achieving all our land-use objectives, have we developed a scheme of planning which is at last not operating by default, or are we experiencing the last throes of a retreat from laudable interventionary aspirations to deregulation and a market-led free-for-all?

This chapter does not attempt a full sequential treatise of land-use planning legislation and techniques in Britain, for such analyses are freely available from the existing work of, for example, Blacksell and Gilg (1981), Blunden and Curry (1985) and Davies (1986). Rather it seeks to highlight certain key themes in the history of postwar land-use planning which illuminate both the evolving balance of power amongst rural interests and the backdrop against which current important changes to land-use planning are being played out.

The countryside and its interests

Much of Britain should be viewed as one of the most densely populated areas of the developed world. For example, England and Wales cover an area of 15.1 million hectares and in 1981 had a population of some 49 million. The resultant density of 3.24 persons per hectare is topped only by The Netherlands (Best 1981). Even when the lower density area of Scotland is added so as to give a figure for Great Britain, the density level is 2.24 persons per hectare. Despite this apparent overcrowding some 77% of the land area of England and Wales is used for agriculture, and a further 7.5% for forestry, and so the vast majority of the land mass is perceived to be 'countryside' and therefore subject to rural land-use planning.

During the postwar period British agriculture has been transformed (Countryside Commission 1987). The volume of output has doubled in the space of 40 years, and home-produced foodstuffs now cover more than 80% of domestic needs. Through a potent mix of technological advance and government subsidy, these changes have been accompanied by a radical restructuring of farm structure and labour. The current figures of 195 000 full-time farmers and 260 000 farm holdings in the UK represent more than a one-third decrease from the immediate postwar position. Small farms have become less important, while larger units have become crucial to the total agricultural output, with the largest 12% responsible for more than half of the total production. The restructuring, and specifically the replacement of labour by capital, has caused the loss of more than 300 000 farm jobs in the postwar period, and the Ministry of Agriculture, Fisheries and Food's *Annual Review of Agriculture* for 1987 estimates that the current loss of full-time farming occupations stands at about 9000 per annum.

Britain is therefore an agricultural nation in terms of its land, but not in terms of its people. The rise of employment first in the manufacturing sector and then in the service sector has sustained the employment needs of the nation (apart, of course, from the 4 million or so unemployed, whose labour is currently surplus to the requirements of capital). The point to be emphasized is that rural Britain is not synonymous with agricultural Britain other than in terms of land. This situation gives rise to a series of conflicting interests in the way in which the countryside should be planned. For farmers, rural land represents their factory, the location of their business and their way of life. It is to be preserved from the meddling of uninformed and dangerous outsiders who know little of the seasonal and weather-dependent vagaries of the agricultural life. There are more than enough problems in coping with unanticipated or uncertain conditions of open-air production without having to contend with other interests telling you what to do with your land. Because of the density of settlement and population, however, the farming environment is overlain by the residential environment of increasing numbers of people whose rural interests are non-agricultural. The countryside here represents the scenery for a stage dictated often by architectural, space and fashion standards. The rural environment is often perceived as some kind of birthright which can be purchased in the housing market and must henceforth be maintained pure and unadulterated (until perhaps inner-city living becomes fashionable again). This birthright can also be rented by urban residents through periodic recreation and tourism in rural areas. Collectively these interests might be characterized as supporting the view that 'the countryside stands for all that is important in Britain; it is the expression of the good life away from the stresses and strains of the city and the symbol of everything which is considered truly British' (Best & Rogers 1973 p. 20). As such, these interests have increasingly been ranged against farmers and in favour of conservation and protection of the rural environment.

In this way (albeit over-simply described here), strong and often conflicting interests emerge in the arena of rural land-use planning. First the interests of landowners and farmers are vocally and powerfully advanced. Members of the landed aristocracy and gentry, each owning at least 500 hectares and usually much more, collectively control about 30% of Britain's land, with companies, charities and trusts (notably property and insurance companies and the pension funds) controlling a further 7% or so (Massey & Catalano 1978). It is not surprising that such groups should display fixed attitudes towards rural land:

> Both are strongly opposed to the taxation of land values or of betterment,[1] and, in so far as most of their holdings are rural,

have a strong interest in the prosperity of farming and forestry. It is hardly surprising that they are hostile to the suggestion that planning permission should be extended to agricultural land use.
(Dawson 1984 pp. 61–2).

Equally unsurprising is that such groups are well represented in both houses of Parliament, and have traditionally wielded considerable political influence both centrally and locally. Less explicit, but just as significant in terms of assessing the balance of power of various interest groups, are the more subtle aspects of land ownership and social control. As Norton-Taylor (1982 p. 22) has pointed out:

> There is an interesting conundrum whereby if you own land, you presume – and are presumed – to be better fit to rule, to hold power and responsibility, while if you have successfully climbed the political and industrial ladder, then you should own land . . . Meanwhile the aristocracy and landed gentry enjoy that added appeal, peculiar to Britain, of a paternalistic Whiggism, a kind of enlightened, though frequently arrogant, belief that they are the backbone of Britain.

Often allied to this landowning interest is the agricultural producers' interest group – the National Farmers' Union (NFU). Here, too, there is a remarkable track record of successful lobbying. Not only have threats of planning intervention in matters of changing agricultural land use been successfully staved off, but concessions have been won from government such that if land is designated for conservation purposes and is thereby rendered unimprovable, compensation payments are granted to farmers 'as of right'. This same lobbying machine has consistently won both high guaranteed prices from government and exemptions or relief from central and local taxes, notably from local rates. The NFU has very close links with the County Landowners' Association (CLA), and together they have mounted a very well organized campaign to persuade governments of their point of view.

The political influence of the farming lobby has been a predominant influence in land-use planning in postwar Britain. All governments have had to support agriculture, first because of the need for strategic self-sufficiency, and then because of the enmeshment within the Common Agricultural Policy of the EEC. The Conservative Party in particular has been doubly supportive, because rural areas, and the landowning figureheads within them, have traditionally been their major political constituency. It should be noted, however, that not all farmers have received equal benefit from the lobby's success. Conventionally the distinction has been drawn between corn and horn, denoting the pre-eminence of the large-scale grain farmers in these organizations. Perhaps less evident, but equally pervasive is the distinction between landowner and tenant, with the latter group often the poor relation when farming needs have to be prioritized.

The other major fraction of capital which has maintained a consistent interest in rural land use is that represented by the construction and house-building industries. These, too, have exerted a powerful lobbying influence on governments, seeking the release of land under conditions where profit can be reaped without undue intervention or taxation (in any of its various forms). Ball (1983) has calculated that 60% of construction is undertaken by only 3% of house-building firms, and that 40% is accounted for by only 1/2% of firms. All of these giants are part of large construction groups or multi-purpose conglomerates (Ambrose 1986) and this construction sector has again been a regular beneficiary of government favour. Indeed, Blowers (1987 pp. 290–1) has argued that such benefits have accelerated as the emphasis on private sector development has found increasing ideological favour:

> Through their influence at central and local levels, the big developers have been able to encourage the reshaping of the planning process to suit their interests. The system became effectively transformed to propagate a national policy of land releases and development through the local authorities. The location, form and timing of development was dictated by developers, not by the planning system. Indeed, many local authorities were seduced by the 'sweeteners' in the form of roads, community facilities and other projects offered by developers in return for planning permissions. Such 'planning gains' were, in effect, a form of betterment, provided through private profit rather than, as formerly, through the taxation of development values.

The farming and construction groupings provided two very visible targets for the third major rural interest sector – that of the environmental lobby (Lowe and Goyder 1983). Amenity and conservation groups are numerous and often less than fully co-ordinated. They range from the well-established and often middle-class-dominated groups like the National Trust, to more radical and cross-class organizations such as Greenpeace and Friends of the Earth. Collectively, however, the environmental movement has gained momentum and demanded an audience, such that political parties have had to busy themselves 'greening' their policies (Flynn 1986).

The influence of these various interests has varied enormously over time in postwar Britain. Agriculture has been very powerful until the mid-1980s. The house-builders have been somewhat restricted but nevertheless have gained handsomely in some areas of government policy (notably but not exclusively the New Towns strategy) and have exerted increasingly important influence under the market ideologies of the Thatcher government. The environmental lobby has achieved the status of not being ignored by dint of a long period of steady growth in support through the 1970s and 1980s. In a sense, postwar governments have played some interests off against others, with party politics favouring particular groups. The Thatcher government is in one sense *too* popular, in that its political constituency includes agricultural, house-building and environmental interests at a time when consensus is difficult to forge. This has led to the potential for radical changes to the land-use planning system in Britain. To understand such changes, however, we must briefly take note of the historical disposition of power within the postwar planning era.

The 1947 Act: collectivizing the development decision

The 1947 Town and Country Planning Act acted as midwife to the organization of radical postwar planning in Britain. During wartime, furious discussion and political bargaining had been taking place. Planning, it was thought, could alleviate inequality, create opportunity and ensure a better Britain through postwar reconstruction. The social direction of development, however, raised hugely important issues for both landowners and construction capital. Those landowners denied the opportunity to profit from the sale of their land at inflated prices for development were to demand *compensation* for this loss of profit. Those who gained in the same way because planning permitted development demanded the right to keep the profits from this *betterment*. Others argued that because betterment was caused by the activities of state planning it should be taxed, particularly if funds for compensation payments had to be found.

The wartime Uthwatt Committee looked into these matters. It suggested that land needed for reconstruction be compulsorily purchased at 1939 prices (so as to avoid price speculation), a move which would have completely undermined the flourishing speculative trade in bomb-damaged land. Further, they reasserted the notion that the rights to develop land should be collectivized, even where land remained in private ownership. The final report from the Committee was politically toned down (Cullingworth 1975) but collectivization remained, and betterment was to be taxed at a 75% level.

As Ambrose (1986 p. 51) has noted 'there was enough here to offend virtually every private interest connected with land development' and the postwar Labour government was faced with heavy pressure to dilute Uthwatt's proposals. Nevertheless, its 1947 Act did collectivize the right to develop land although it also included provision of compensation to landowners who could prove that their land had some unrealized development value. Equally, the Act did introduce a 100% levy on betterment, although any compulsory purchase was to be at existing, not 1939, prices.

Postwar land-use planning might subsequently be analysed in terms of persistent attempts by powerful interest groups to claw back the losses suffered at the hands of the 1947 legislation. Admittedly with the focus on redevelopment there had been no attack on the rights of farmers to change the use of their land *within* the exempted categories of farming and forestry use. This issue only arose subsequently with the recognition of the landscape damage caused by farm 'improvements' (Shoard 1980). But the basic capitalist principle of the right to use and profit from owned land had been breached, and pressure was immediately exerted for repeal.

With the return of the Conservative government in 1951, this pressure bore fruit: the tax on betterment was removed, although at the price of drastically reducing the circumstances in which a refusal to develop could be compensated by payments from government; and where compulsory purchase of land was thought to be appropriate it was to be at market prices. Apart from the requirement for planning permission, therefore, the conditions for capital accumulation by landowners and developers were more or less restored. The 1964 Labour government reintroduced the betterment levy (at 40%) and compulsory purchase powers for their new Land Commission, and in 1975 the then Labour government's Community Land Act reintroduced taxation on land dealing and permitted compulsory purchase at less than market value for the facilitation of preferred developments (see Barrett *et al.* 1978). However, both moves proved to be chaotic and only short-lived advances against the retreating tide of pressure for relaxation of planning restrictions.

Planning rural development

The basic planning system introduced in 1947 has survived into the 1980s. Originally, county councils were to produce *development plans* which set out the preferred location of development, and were augmented in some cases by plans for individual rural settlements. In 1968, new legislation amended the system so that the county authorities were enabled to produce more flexible broad-scale strategies in their *structure plans*, while the new district councils had the task of devising detailed development control manuals in their *local plans*.

Much has already been written concerning the details of these various plans and their implementation in rural areas (Cloke 1979, 1983). The concern here is to present a brief summary of how the outworking of this planning apparatus reflected the interplay of political and sectoral interests in rural land use. First, it should be reiterated that agricultural and conservation interests were not seen as conflicting at this stage and so the agricultural sector was given a politically 'safe' pre-eminence in rural policy. As Newby (1980 p. 233) notes:

> Since . . . it was assumed that the conservation of the countryside could safely be left in the hands of those *in situ* and there was no wish to pick a fight with either the NFU or the CLA, from the outset 'the use of any land for the purposes of agriculture and forestry' was excluded from the provisions of the Act.

Moreover, there was established a broad presumption against development on good quality agricultural land. With agricultural support policies also being put in place at this time the national interest was assumed to be served by preserving as large a stock of agricultural land as possible.

The need to protect agricultural land was neatly allied with the radical planning fervour of the 1930s and 1940s to check the spread of urban areas. Both objectives could therefore be used to justify the fundamental land-use planning devices which emerged: the creation of New and Expanded Towns, the imposition of green belts, the channelling of development in rural areas into key settlements and the restriction of development elsewhere (except where needed specifically for the agricultural or forestry workforce). These nationally derived policies should not be viewed as the blueprints of a deterministic top-down planning system entirely dominated by the central state. Rather they represent the policy context within which local negotiations took place – negotiations which not only were shaped by the local balance of power but which also reflected national interests. As the needs of these various national and local interests changed, so too did the outcome of the land-use planning machinery.

Analyses of these changing interests and outcomes in rural Britain vary considerably. Perhaps the conventional historical viewpoint is that adopted by, for example, Davies (1986) who describes three phases of postwar planning:

(1) 1947–63: a period of traditional land-use planning when development plans were prepared under assumptions of low population growth and so devices such as New Towns and green belts could be implemented without undue conflicts of interests between agricultural and development capital.
(2) 1963–74: assumptions about future growth were having to be rapidly upgraded and planning was concerned with providing for a growing population and rising standards of development. Developer pressure on planning increased markedly during this period.
(3) 1974 onwards: the property boom collapsed and planners worked in the context not only of economic recession but also of diminishing expectations about levels of future growth. Their concern was to implement policies despite the erosion of local authority intervention through expenditure cuts and despite the depressed state of capital investment in industry, commerce and housing.

The implications of these phases are fleshed out rather more by Blunden and Curry (1985) who discuss some of the tensions arising over planning issues during the periods of 'growth' and 'no growth'. For example, the growth era led to tremendous pressures on containment policies. With the Ministry of Housing publicly expressing the need for land on which to house 2 1/2 million more people, and with developers craving the opportunity to supply homes for those whose voluntary out-migration from cities was increasingly enabled by the commuter boom, rural land came under threat. The 1947 Act gave local authorities jurisdiction over land use in their areas. Thus rural county authorities, often dominated by landowning and farming fraternities, were reluctant in many cases to release land and thereby appease the pressures on urban authorities. Central government had to find politically acceptable ways of land release. In these conditions land speculation was rife, and major developers bought up land banks at agricultural prices and then set about persuading the local authorities concerned to relax their restrictions.

The results were variegated. Land was released for development in many cases, but at an aggregate level the planning apparatus controlled the supply of land, thereby inducing increasing land and property prices in pressured rural areas and thereby polarizing opportunities to live in these areas towards those groups who could buy their way into these markets – a rural form of gentrification. Effectively, however, the land-use planning system was still in the business of accommodating the three main interests of agricultural land protection, house-building interests and landscape conservation.

The no-growth era was reflected by changing attitudes towards rural land use. With the rising influence of the conservation lobby, high-profile environmental policies were regarded as important, hence, for example, the expansion of green belt designations. However new conflicts emerged between agricultural land protection and provision of land for new development. In an atmosphere of fierce competition and rivalry local authorities have been very willing to set land aside for major commercial and industrial activity, particularly in prime locations such as greenfield sites adjoining motorways. The imperative of agricultural protection is being surreptitiously removed in these circumstances. It is argued that the restructuring of rural land use is necessary and that anyway there is currently no threat from a level of agricultural land-take (8000 hectares per annum) which is acceptable compared with postwar averages of around 15 000 hectares per annum. But, as Blunden and Curry point out, this breakdown of concern over agricultural land-take will be crucial if development rates were to boom again, especially as local authorities look to develop the least costly land which is often equated with the highest quality agricultural land.

Perhaps an even more perceptive and enlightening overview of this period of land-use planning is advanced by Reade (1987). He suggests that the 1947 Act, had it not been effectively repealed by the incoming Conservative government in 1953, would have contributed towards a significant redistribution of wealth and power in society. As it was policies for *planning* and policies for *land values* were carefully separated by both Conservative and Labour governments. Policies for land values were highly *politicized*, with see-saw policies emanating from party political viewpoints in government. Planning policies were *depoliticized*, and promoted as technical and neutral instruments of conflict resolution. Reade (p. 67) hypothesizes that the separation of planning and land value policies has served a fundamentally political purpose:

> So long as 'planning' is *not* discussed and understood as an integral part of this highly political matter of property speculation and land values, it is possible to maintain the illusion that this 'planning' succeeds in curbing any possible anti-social excesses on the part of the less scrupulous operators . . . In reality . . . the existence and nature of planning controls is a very important part of the explanation both of the level of property values, and of the way in which the property developers make their profits. To bring together land-values policy with land-use policy (or 'planning') therefore . . . would be to destroy the credibility and the legitimacy of this planning.

In other words, at the broad scale the postwar planning system in Britain has served to maintain the legitimacy of the development industry and its associated financial agencies. The interests of agricultural capital were being served by state subsidies and some land protection; the interests of development capital (despite their initial fears over the collectivization of the development decision) were broadly being served through land and property values promoted by planning policy. Could this be done without sacrificing rural land and landscape interests? It is to this matter that we turn next.

Conservation by designation

The principal plank of planning policies for countryside protection has been to designate elite areas of countryside as being of conservation value and therefore worthy of whatever special protection can be mustered from development control legislation. It was indeed the threat of development rather than that of the impacts of changing agricultural practices which provided the impetus for initial designation. Following strong pressure in the 1920s and 1930s from conservation and amenity groups and the inevitable wartime government committee deliberations over the future of rural land, the 1949 National Parks and Access to the Countryside

Act instigated a deluge of designation which was eventually to cover large tracts of the countryside of England and Wales (see Mather 1986 for a discussion of the Scottish case). It established the machinery for designating *National Parks* (NPs) and by 1957, ten such parks were defined in England and Wales covering 9% of the land area (MacEwen & MacEwen 1982a). It also gave the newly formed Nature Conservancy powers to acquire land by purchase, lease, or agreement, for management as *National Nature Reserves* (NNRs). Adams (1986) has commented that scientific nature conservation and landscape conservation were fundamentally divided at this point – a divide which has persisted throughout the period. Thus although the designation of NNRs has dealt with some pressing problems of threatened flora and fauna, other fundamental conservation issues remain problematic within the broader countryside.

The philosophy of the 1949 Act was clearly that of protecting elite landscapes against the prospect development. This philosophy of negative control was taken further with the designation of second-class and third-class NPs, *Areas of Outstanding Natural Beauty* (AONBs) and *Areas of Great Landscape Value* (AGLVs) respectively, and *Sites of Special Scientific Interest* (SSSIs) which might effectively be regarded as second-class NNRs. In the latter case the Nature Conservancy was to notify the planning authority of sites which were of ecological interest in the expectation that planning decisions on these sites would be influenced by their designation.

Add to these designations the burgeoning green belts around metropolitan areas (discussed above) and the subsequent promotion of *Conservation Areas*, where strict development control may be exerted, and *Environmentally Sensitive Areas* (see below), and the impression may be gained of a countryside awash with environmental designations. Yet the strategy of designation may well represent a major illusion of the genre commented on by Robin Best (1981) and discussed in the introduction of this chapter. It might be argued that at little effective cost, a great deal of political capital and kudos is to be gained by high-profile flag-waving in the form of drawing lines on maps and giving the enclosed areas an appealing title. This may be an over-harsh dismissal in the British case, but it does indicate weaknesses and flaws in the available implementation of policy connected with designated areas. Crucially, apart from the purchase of NNRs and very small super-elite sites in NPs, all land designated is in private ownership. In each case of designation, although to varying degrees, existing powers of development control planning as laid down in the 1947

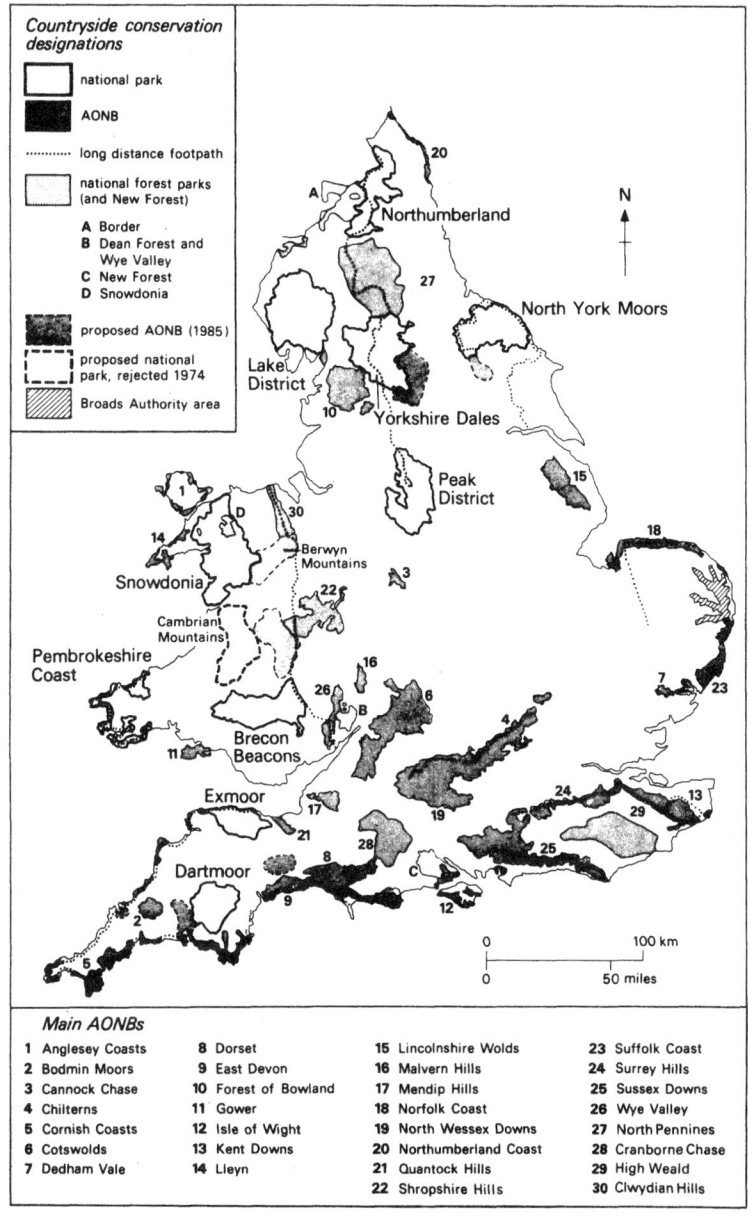

Figure 2.1 National parks, Areas of Outstanding Natural Beauty and the area of the Broads Authority (Crown copyright reserved).

Act were to be implemented more stringently. The belief was that development control could achieve 'a harmonious, well-ordered and well-designed countryside without interfering unduly with the rights of property owners' (MacEwen & MacEwen 1987 p. 7) thereby neatly achieving the juggling act of agricultural interests. Furthermore, it was believed that farming and forestry practices need not be subject to control as they had 'inherent' regard for the preservation of the rural landscape. Newby (1980) suggests that by dealing with the threat of unwanted development, the planning system was able to sustain a 'powerful alliance between agricultural and environmental interests' which 'remains largely undisturbed over strategic planning issues' (p. 243). Once again the legitimacy of a major sector of capital, in this case the agricultural industry, has been maintained to an extent by planning machinery which separates agricultural land uses and other forms of development.

In most cases, then, countryside conservation by designation was restricted to rather negative development control procedures which excluded the major productive rural land uses. Even so, NP status was transgressed by such major developments as the Trawsfynydd nuclear power station in Snowdonia and the Fylingdales early warning system on the North York Moors, and elsewhere incidents such as the flooding of Cow Green for a reservoir even though it enjoyed NNR and SSSI status demonstrates that even within development control decisions conservation objectives were often overruled.

Beefing up existing development control powers over elite stretches of designated private land was as far as government was prepared to be pushed in the early postwar period. As Blunden and Curry (1985 p. 124) suggest:

> In the long term, legislation and 'education' were seen as the only certain ways of fostering more environmentally-caring attitudes. Immediate threats to the heritage had to be met with direct action. Voluntary bodies had meagre resources, so it was inevitable that they would concentrate their efforts on highly valued landscapes.

The acceptance that conservation activities should be related to the meagre resources of voluntary bodies betrays the 'negative control plus self-help' approach. To persuade farmers of environmentally sensitive practices would entail compensation payments, and they were already receiving the support of what amounted to betterment proceeds from government subsidy of production.

During the 1960s there came a slow but growing recognition of the environmental damage caused by agricultural improvement (see Shoard 1980, Green 1981, Pye-Smith & Rose 1984). The tale of hedgerow removal, loss of moorland, chalk grassland and heathland, and replacement of deciduous with coniferous woodland is by now well known as is the assertion that such destruction was directly fuelled by grant-aided agricultural improvement. So while major countryside designations gave the impression that conservation planning was alive and kicking, the major impacts on that countryside suggested that designation alone was an insufficient policy response. The increasing popular interest in countryside environments tended to agree.

The growing strength of the conservation lobby reaped its initial reward in the 1968 Countryside Act which established the Countryside Commission to deal with the problems which were existing outside of the designated areas. Moreover, it began to give some teeth, although fairly immature milk-teeth, to the implied objectives of designation. It instructed the Ministry of Agriculture to take account of conservation issues in issuing improvement grants to farmers; it permitted the Nature Conservancy Council to pay compensation to farmers to maintain practices compatible with certain SSSIs, and it required farmers in NPs to notify their intention to plough moorland, in the expectation that a management agreement could be reached. These reforms did little to decelerate landscape change but they enshrined important directional indicators in the changing balance of power of countryside interests. In particular the introduction of compensation payments for the loss of state-subsidy 'betterment' was a crucial concession to the farming industry in order to win small gains for conservation interests. Neither interest was to be satisfied by this initial move, and the 1970s saw a strongly argued review of rural land-use policy options with which to remedy the growing conflict between agriculture and conservation. Given political neutrality, this might have been seen as a potential opportunity for reform of rural land-use planning. As it was, political ideology, prompted by entrenched structural interests meant that the search for new countryside management policies became something of a damage-limitation exercise.

The Thatcher Era I: voluntary management

The late 1970s and early 1980s witnessed a stream of graphic illustrations of a countryside threatened by the destructive force of mechanized and technological agriculture. Particularly telling were the highly publicized data on the postwar loss of specific habitat types (itemized in Table 2.1), which were later dubbed '36 years of failure' (Rose 1986 p. 73). Regional reports of loss (Table 2.2) added coals to the fire such that by the late 1970s first the Labour administration and then the new Thatcher government were obliged to act.

A range of academic alternatives had emerged from the ongoing debate, although to suggest that these were realistic policy options would be politically artificial if not naive. For example, one such

Table 2.1 Rural habitat loss

Lowland neutral grasslands including herb-rich (i.e. flower-filled) hay meadows: '95 per cent now lacking significant wildlife interest and only 3 per cent left undamaged by agricultural intensification'.

Lowland grasslands of sheep walks on chalk and Jurassic limestone: '80 per cent loss or significant damage, largely by conversion to arable or improved grassland (mainly since 1940)'. By 'improvement' the NCC refers to the fertilization, draining and reseeding, which converts semi-natural species-rich grassland into an artificial ley or pasture that can be highly productive (responsive to nitrogen inputs) but supports very few species.

Lowland heaths on acidic soils: '40 per cent loss, largely by conversion to arable or improved grassland, afforestation and building'.

Limestone pavement in northern England (flower-rich areas of bare rock with humid fissures in its surface): '45 per cent damaged or destroyed, largely by removal of weathered surfaces for sale as rockery stone, and only 3 per cent left undamaged'.

Ancient lowland woods of native broad-leaved trees: '30–50 per cent loss by conversion to conifer plantation or grubbing out to provide more farmland'.

Lowland fens, valley and basin mires: '50 per cent loss or significant damage through drainage operations, reclamation for agriculture and chemical enrichment of drainage water'.

Lowland 'raised mires' (mosses): '60 per cent loss or significant damage through afforestation, peat winning, reclamation for agriculture or repeated burning'.

Upland grasslands, heaths and blanket bog: '30 per cent loss or significant damage through coniferous afforestation, hill land reclamation and improvement . . . '.

After Rose 1986.

Paul Cloke

alternative was for conservation agencies to accelerate the rate of purchasing land as nature reserves. Although ideally, the ownership of land ensures appropriate management practices, in practice conservation organizations have hopelessly inadequate funds for the purchase of problem sites. Not only would such a strategy restrict their attentions to a few elite locations, but also there would be no guarantee of securing any particular site in the face of opposition on the open market from the larger-scale fractions of agricultural capital.

Table 2.2 Habitat loss in selected areas.

County	Habitat or area	Dates	Loss (%)
Avon	Meadows	1970–80	50
Bedfordshire	Wetlands	25 years	70
Cambridgeshire	Woodland	35 years	17
Cheshire	SSSIs	In 1980	7 damaged
Cumbria	Limestone pavement		
Devon	Woodlands	1952–72	20
	Grass and heaths (outside Nat. Parks)	This century	67
Dorset	Heathland	50 years	75
	SSSIs	In 1980	32 damaged
Essex	SSSIs	In 1980	9 damaged
Hampshire	Chalk grassland	Since 1966	20
Hertfordshire	Ancient woodland	Since 1850	56
Huntingdonshire	Hedges	30 years	88
Isle of Wight	Chalk grassland	14 years	18
Kent	SSSIs	Since 1951	40 damaged or lost
Lancashire	Lowland bogs	This century	99
Lincolnshire	Ancient grassland	30 years	50
Northumberland	SSSIs	15 years	33 damaged or lost
Nottinghamshire	Ponds	25 years	90
Oxfordshire	Floodplain meadows	3 years, 1978–81	20
Powys	Moorland	6 years	7
Shropshire	Prime sites	18 months	3
Staffordshire	SSSIs	10 years	25 damaged
Sussex	SSSIs	15 years	25 damaged or lost
Worcestershire	Ponds	55 years	35
	SSSIs	25 years	17 damaged

After Rose 1986.

If the extension of suitable ownership was impracticable, the next best thing was to suggest an extension of planning controls to cover changes in agricultural land use. Shoard (1980 p. 205), for example, has argued:

> Now that agriculture has become a major threat to our environment, however, the most logical way to deal with it within our existing system would be to extend the definition of *'development'* to include agricultural activity. The destruction of an ancient wood, a stretch of down or the remains of an Iron Age village matter at least as much to the community as the erection of a new porch on a house.

Aside from practical matters concerning the increases in bureaucracy necessary to implement and monitor the extension of planning controls, such a policy would inevitably draw fierce resistance from farmers and landowners in defence of private property interests. Although the Labour government was contemplating a form of planning control in threatened moorland areas, the incoming Conservative administration could not contemplate such an obvious attack on a significant part of their constituent political power-base. Similarly fundamental political objections were raised against any ideas of land reform. George's (1976) proposals for land taxation (as an alternative to land nationalization) received some popular support in the late 1970s, and her notion that 'it is not necessary to confiscate land, it is only necessary to confiscate rent' might artificially be seen as a policy 'option' which nevertheless was anathema to the major countryside interests outside of left-wing agencies in the conservation movement.

One further possibility for land-use policy reform was to press for a reduction in the levels of agricultural support emanating from the Common Agricultural Policy. Such a strategy, as described amongst others by Bowers and Cheshire (1983), would involve a fall in farm prices (and hence incomes) with a knock-on effect on lower land prices and as a consequence the intensity of land exploitation would decrease. Central to this idea is that it is the intensity of agricultural exploitation which is a focal cause of countryside damage.

In the event, government continued both to defend the ideology of land ownership and to respond to the interests of the farming lobby. Rather than invoking planning powers or land policy reform, there was an attempt to appease the conservation movement by establishing a system of voluntary agreements with farmers over conservation-sensitive sites. The Wildlife and Countryside

Act of 1981 permitted relevant authorities to enter into management agreements with landowners for the purpose of conserving or enhancing the natural beauty or amenity of land in the countryside. The Act has been widely criticized on a number of grounds. MacEwen and MacEwen (1982b p. 71) have called it 'unprincipled':

> It is a dead end from which another government will have to retreat before it can advance by a different route. It leaves agriculture and conservation on a collision course, but provides no way of regulating the conflict except by pouring small amounts of money into a bottomless pit.

More specifically the Act embraces the seeming paradox of *compulsory* agreement. The most productive use of management agreements has been in cultures of goodwill and co-operation between participants. By compelling landowners to give prior notification of particular intended land-use changes and then buying their goodwill through monetary compensation, the Act moves away from co-operative husbandry towards business tactics. Once again, land-use planning in Britain has encountered the central themes of betterment and co-operation, and the interests of landowning capital continue to be served under the new arrangement. Furthermore, as Blowers (1987) notes, the Act transgresses two previously well-established principles in this respect: that compensation should not be paid for the refusal of development; and that pollutors should bear the cost of avoiding environmental damage.

The principal criticism of the Act, however, relates to its scale and funding provisions. Its arena of action is restricted to small elite areas of countryside, including National Parks, SSSIs and other 'special' areas such as the Norfolk Broads. Not only is the bulk of the 'ordinary' British countryside thereby ignored, but the financial underwriting by government of compensation payments by conservation agencies is not guaranteed, and in practice significant shortfalls of compensation funds have been the norm. Conservation agencies have therefore had to prioritize endangered sites (a case of elitism within elitism – Cloke & Park 1985).

The implementation of the Act has not been straightforward. One of the major test cases concerned the threat by landowners to drain the Halvergate Marshes in Norfolk which represented the last remaining extensive piece of open grazing marsh in Eastern England. The story of Halvergate is told in detail elsewhere (Lowe *et al.* 1986, O'Riordan 1986) but in essence it provides a clear example of the inability of the Wildlife and Countryside Act to cope with a major confrontation between agriculture and conservation. The result of the confrontation was a cobbled-together arrangement under which the Broads Authority received government backing to establish an experimental Broads Grazing Marshes Conservation Scheme under which farmers could be compensated for agreeing to special land-management conditions. This compromise has been variously seen as 'just possibly a path-breaking approach to a new attitude to farming the landscape' (Lowe et al. 1986 p. 300) and as 'symbolic of the basic failure of government policy, which simply could not and would not protect the countryside' (Rose 1986 p. 77). Perhaps the most telling conclusion comes from Cox et al. (1986 pp. 68–9) who suggest that:

> The spectacle of an *ad hoc* arrangement . . . being formulated to resolve a conflict which could not be contained within the bounds of the Wildlife and Countryside Act not only exposed the Act's limitations but re-enacted the pragmatic and incrementalist policy sequence which had earlier, on Exmoor, given rise to its philosophy and mechanism . . . the process by which successive crises prompt new policy departures, or decisions with potentially major policy implications, suggests an inadequate strategy and a need to examine the social construction of power within a broader context to explain that inadequacy.

One outcome of the Halvergate issue has been the development of a new countryside designation – Environmentally Sensitive Areas (ESAs) where financial assistance is available for farmers who enter into voluntary agreements to ensure farming practices that maintain or improve the rural landscape. The initial six ESAs provide a small foundation on which the principle of management can be extended. It should be stressed, however, that the outcome of this particular round of countryside policy has been a clear and pragmatic decision to focus on a small number of elite areas, at the potential expense of the remaining rural landscape.

The Thatcher Era II: the politics and policies of ALURE

In February 1987 the Thatcher administration issued two sets of proposals which emanated from a government policy group charged with developing policy initiatives for issues of Alternative Land Use and Rural Economy (hence tagged the *ALURE* proposals).[2] ALURE came about because of the long-term political worries about the Common Agricultural Policy (CAP) and much more expedient concerns relating to the 1987 general election in Britain. The former centred on the increasingly untenable divide between national government strategies of economic efficiency and the seemingly ludicrous levels of over-production caused by the CAP, especially with the escalating costs of storing unwanted food. This situation looked even worse when various researchers publicized figures which suggested that under the EEC regime in Britain some 1.6 million hectares of dairying land, 2.0 million hectares of cereals land and 2.0 million hectares of land used for beef and sheep could be regarded as surplus to requirements by the year 2015. Public acknowledgement of such figures demanded a rethink of the rural land-use policy which had been founded in postwar years on the perceived need to retain as much land as possible for agricultural use because of a potential land shortage. The shorter-term worry was the danger of losing middle-class political support in rural areas over 'green' issues, and so the imperative was established for a 'greening' of policy, twinned with new initiatives for an increasingly troubled rural economy.

Two sets of proposals came from the ALURE discussions. The Ministry of Agriculture, Fisheries and Food (MAFF) established a £25 million per annum package on farm diversification:

(a) £10 million to encourage the development of farm woodlands.
(b) £3 million to expand the traditional forestry programme of the private sector.
(c) £7 million to double the number of ESA designations, and
(d) £5 million to grant-aid the diversification of farm enterprises.

At the same time, the Department of the Environment (DoE) removed the presumption that agricultural use of rural land should be paramount for planning purposes, and replaced it with a tripartite system of planning concerns relating to agriculture, environment and rural economic revival:

The agricultural quality of the land and the need to control the rate at which land is taken for development are among the factors to be included in that assessment. At the same time, full regard must be had *both* to the need to promote economic activity that provides jobs, including the contribution of small firms, and to the need to protect Green Belts, National Parks, Areas of Outstanding Natural Beauty, and other areas of good countryside.
(DoE 1987 para. 3)

The idea of ALURE was, out of these Agriculture and Environment proposals, to present a coherent and integrated package appealing to farmers, conservationists, middle-class rural residents and maybe even the house-building interests.

The problem with this task of integration lay in the implementation of the changes to land-use planning regulations. Although grades 1 and 2 of agricultural land would be exempt from the change (where 50 or more acres was involved), as was land in elite areas such as National Parks, AONBs, SSSIs and green belts, there were bound to be concerns over the potential reduction in planning protection of other areas of the countryside. These fears were further fuelled by interdepartmental rivalries within government which soured the announcement of the ALURE package. The Agriculture Minister (Michael Jopling), facing an unprecedented vote of censure from the National Farmers' Union, was linked with a series of unofficial press leaks which gave the impression that the Environment proposals would allow farmers a wide scope for diversification, even in the sphere of selling off land for housing development. Such suggestions were hardly likely to appeal to middle-class voters in the Conservative Party's rural heartland of the south-east of England, and these events served to scuttle the smoothing over of inherent contradictions in the ALURE proposals. The displeasure of Environment ministers was evident in *The Times* report of 10 February 1987:

> Mr Jopling's colleagues openly accused him of promoting his initiative by allowing it to appear that protected land would now be under threat from the housebuilders ... One ministerial source said: 'All this has done is gratuitously upset the *policy picture* (author's emphasis) we have successfully put across, which is to restrict housebuilding in the south-east and not build on the green belt and greenfield sites. Now he has come out and put his great size 12 gumboots all over our policy and we are now involved in a damage limitation exercise.' It was said that Mr Jopling's 'politically inept performance' amounted to mishandling on a big scale, involving one of the most sensitive political areas in the south of England. 'He has sown needless doubt in the minds of electors,' the source said.

The notion of a *policy picture* is important here. It is certainly premature either to bless the package with the name of policy (as many of the ideas are potentially contradictory) or to assess what will become of rural land use when the measures are implemented. ALURE, as with the Wildlife and Countryside Act which preceded it, appears both pragmatic and incremental. This is perhaps inevitable given that so many different fractions of the government's constituency of power are directly involved in the countryside arena. However, it would seem that by attempting to walk a tightrope between agriculture, conservation and development interests, the government has only succeeded in stirring up a hornets' nest of countryside protest.

The MAFF £25 million diversification package has been welcomed as a start, but unless further aid is forthcoming it will be derided by farming groups as insufficient to meet the crises caused by declining support from the Common Agricultural Policy. It is, however, the DoE proposals to change the basis of planning decisions for agricultural land which have drawn most fire. Fears expressed by conservation groups include that:

- protection of agricultural land has been diminished with no concomitant strengthening of conservation measures.
- policies in structure plans and local plans which are based on the prior presumption of protecting agricultural land will now be rendered useless.
- the previous rationale for protecting the countryside has now been removed, and no replacement rationale has been put in its place.
- the wider context of the Thatcher government's strategy for reduced levels of planning and giving greater scope for market-place decision-making give grounds for concern for the future of planning to protect the countryside.

Two fundamental issues emerge from these fears. First, will the way now be left open for developers to mount increasingly successful attacks on previously protected areas of countryside? Secondly, are these proposals part of a wider ideological offensive by government on the planning process? After all, the rate at which planning appeals against local authority refusals have been upheld by government has risen from 29% in 1979 to 40% in 1985. In addition, the government's consultation paper on *The Future of Development Plans* (see Brown 1987, Byrne 1987, and Wright 1987) suggests that a weakening of the strategic planning system in Britain would be in line with the ideological motivations of the current government. Seen in this pessimistic light, the ALURE proposals may be part of a wider design which reduces rural land-use planning to a form of management which encompasses only high-quality sites in selected designated areas.

The Department of the Environment has sought to calm these fears by stressing that countryside protection is important for its own sake, not (as previously) for the sake of retaining land in agricultural use. Even so, the spectre of a two-tier countryside remains. Johnston (1987) points out two occurrences pertinent to this fear:

(a) the DoE recently extended the landscape areas special development order (LASDO) procedure to cover local authority representations over farm buildings and roads, but these new powers apply only in national parks.
(b) the DoE also recently proposed new 'last resort' powers for compulsory restraint through landscape conservation orders. These, too, were only to be relevant in elite areas of national parks.

As Cloke and McLaughlin (1989) suggest, the unresolved question is whether countryside protection 'for its own sake' refers to some countryside which is already recognized as elite, or to all countryside. In the former case, what happens to the remainder? In the latter, what measures are forthcoming to maintain protection in the ordinary areas?

Conclusion

Analysis of rural land planning in Britain cannot be divorced from the wider societal context in which planning takes place and the forms and functions of the state within which planning represents but a limited series of mechanisms. It is increasingly difficult to give credence to accounts of countryside planning in Britain which suggest that planning is some kind of neutral arbitration mechanism between competing land-use interests. The brief review of land-use planning in rural Britain presented here clearly suggests that the role of planning has been wrapped up in the wider role of the state. Thus longer-term structural state-based changes have to be viewed alongside the more ephemeral redirections inspired by ideology and introduced by specific governments in order to establish a rounded picture of policy objectives and policy changes.

Two major structural factors have underpinned postwar rural land-use planning in Britain. First, from somewhat idealist wartime beginnings there has been a fundamental movement for planning to be used to strengthen the position of particular interests in society. As a major example, almost regardless of which government has been in power, land-use planning has been used to strengthen the economic and political power of development interests. Reade (1987 p. 65) goes so far as to suggest that:

> Government may in fact be using the DoE and the planning system to do for the property industry what political scientists have long seen the Ministry of Agriculture as doing for the farming interest – that is to strengthen its hand, to provide the conditions in which it can operate profitably. Indeed, the new present-day consensus seems to suggest that the purpose and scope of planning ought to be defined very much in these terms.

In these terms, any thought that land-use planning might be used to strengthen the economic or political position of other societal fractions – the consumer, the landless, or the environmentalist, for example – seems to be spurious.

The second structural underpinning of land-use planning in Britain is a basic enduring commitment to long-term conservation. This in some arenas conflicts with the use of planning to promote developer and producer interests and the interplay of these two factors has perhaps curbed the excesses which might be envisaged from an unfettered pro-developer or pro-farmer planning system. Conservation of highly valued rural environments and of heritage has remained as a fundamental structural component of rural land-use planning in the postwar period, and it seems unlikely that this position will alter even with the worst fears of ALURE.

There is a body of opinion, however, which would suggest that the mere tempering of support for capital interests by a fundamental regard for conservation is insufficient given the accelerating crisis of agriculture and rural land use. For example, Rose (1986 p. 77) clearly argues for fundamental reform:

> The whole basis of agriculture and land use must be overhauled. The present system cannot be sustained. But waiting for the wasteful polluting, resource hungry, ecologically unbalanced

British agricultural system to bleed itself to death is like waiting for a bull to do the same in a china shop. In its death throes and despite its lacerations, it will do vast and irreparable damage. First, therefore, we need immediate controls. Then we need fundamental reforms.

The sub-structural and more ephemeral policies of Thatcherism, however, appear to be taking us in the opposite direction. In favouring the private-sector developer and producer in the creation or adaptation of environmental surroundings in Britain, the policy initiatives of the Thatcher administration have continued to ensure that large-scale developers and fractions of agricultural capital have been the major beneficiaries of rural planning policy. Moreover, developers have been able to make use of their political power at local and national scales to promote the reformulation of the planning process so that their interests might be further served. The tendency for rural policies under Thatcher to be narrowly focused and partisan both socially and spatially does not engender too much hope that the reforms appealed for by Rose will come about in the foreseeable future.

The rural policies of the Thatcher government have been described by Blowers (1987) as 'the effort to balance conflicting interests in the Tory heartlands':

> The emphasis on private development in the outer city, combined with traditional support for farming interests, has provoked opposition from rural conservationists who also compose the Conservatives' constituency. This has been met by a rhetorical stress on the need to protect the most valued areas of landscape and green belts from development. Where agriculture and conservation are in conflict the Government has been anxious to accede to rural interests while simultaneously fearful of alienating farmers. As a result farmers have been compensated for not destroying areas or features of acknowledged environmental importance.
>
> (p. 291)

In this way, ideology is manipulated by pragmatic political necessity, as rural land-use policy as asked to serve various and often conflicting interests. Only when the conflicts between interests become so great that incremental policy practices are no longer sufficient to stave off political rebellion, will more radical changes occur to countryside management in Britain.

Notes

1 See page 24ff for discussion of betterment.
2 I am grateful to Brian McLaughlin for discussions on this issue. Our joint deliberations will be presented in Cloke & McLaughlin (forthcoming).

References

Adams, W. M. 1986. *Nature's place*. London: Allen & Unwin.
Ambrose, P. 1986. *Whatever happened to planning?* London: Methuen.
Ball, M. 1983. *Housing policy and economic power*. London: Methuen.
Barrett, S., M. Boddy & M. Stewart 1979. *Implementation of the Community Land Scheme*, Occasional Paper 3, School of Advanced Urban Studies, University of Bristol.
Best, R. H. 1981. *Land use and living space*. London: Methuen.
Best, R. H. & A. W. Rogers 1973. *The urban countryside*. London: Faber.
Blacksell, M. & A. Gilg 1981. *The countryside: planning and change*. London: Allen & Unwin.
Blowers, A. 1987. Transition or transformation? – environmental policy under Thatcher. *Public Administration* 65, 277–94.
Blunden, J. & N. Curry (eds) 1985. *The changing countryside*. Milton Keynes: Open University Press.
Bowers, J. K. & P. Cheshire 1983. *Agriculture, the countryside and land use*. London: Methuen.
Brown, C. R. B. 1987. The future of development plans – a reaction from the counties. *The Planner*, May, 15–16.
Byrne, S. 1987. The future of development plans – government proposals. *The Planner*, May, 11–13.
Cloke, P. J. 1979. *Key settlement in rural areas*. London: Methuen.
Cloke, P. J. 1983. *An introduction to rural settlement planning*. London: Methuen.
Cloke, P. J. & B. McLaughlin (forthcoming). Crossroads or blind alley? The politics of the ALURE proposals in the UK. *Land-use policy*.
Cloke, P. J. & C. C. Park 1985. *Rural resource management*. London: Croom Helm.
Countryside Commission 1987. *New opportunities for the countryside*. Cheltenham: Countryside Commission.
Cox, G., P. Lowe & M. Winter 1986. Landscape and nature conservation. In *Rural planning: policies into action?*, P. J. Cloke (ed.). London: Harper & Row.
Cullingworth, J. B. 1975. *Environmental planning: Vol. 1: Reconstruction and land use planning 1939–1947*. London: HMSO.
Davies, H. W. E. 1986. England and Wales. In *Handbook on land use planning*, N. N. Patricios (ed.), 295–332. New York: Greenwood.

Dawson, A. 1984. *The land problem in the developed economy*. London: Croom Helm.
Department of the Environment 1987. *Development involving agricultural land*, draft circular.
Flynn, A. 1986. Agricultural policy and party politics in post-war Britain. In *Agriculture, people and policies*, G. Cox, P. Lowe & M. Winter (eds), 216–36. London: Allen & Unwin.
George, S. 1976. *How the other half dies*. London: Penguin.
Green, B. 1981. *Countryside conservation*. London: Allen & Unwin.
Johnston, B. 1987. Countryside protected for its own sake. *Planning* **719**, 8–9.
Lowe, P. & J. Goyder 1983. *Environmental groups in politics*. London: Allen & Unwin.
Lowe, P., G. Cox, M. MacEwen, T. O'Riordan & M. Winter 1986. *Countryside conflicts*. London: Temple Smith/Gower.
MacEwen, A. & M. MacEwen 1982a. *National parks: conservation or cosmetics*, London: Allen & Unwin.
MacEwen, A. & M. MacEwen 1982b. An unprincipled Act? *The Planner* **68**, 71.
MacEwen, A. & M. MacEwen 1987. *Greenprints for the countryside?* London: Allen & Unwin.
McLaughlin, B. 1986. Rural policy in the 1980s: the revival of the rural idyll. *Journal of Rural Studies* **2**, 81–90.
Massey, D. & A. Catalano 1978. *Capital and land*. London: Edward Arnold.
Mather, A. S. 1986. *Land use*, London: Longman.
Newby, H. 1980. *Green and pleasant land?* London: Penguin.
Norton-Taylor, R. 1982. *Whose land is it anyway?* Wellingborough: Turnstone Press.
O'Riordan, T. 1986. Halvergate: anatomy of a decision. In *Geography, planning and policy making*, J. T. Coppock & P. Kivell (eds). Norwich: Geo Books, 189–228.
Pye-Smith, C. & C. Rose 1984. *Crisis and conservation*. London: Penguin.
Reade, E. 1987. *British town and country planning*. Milton Keynes: Open University Press.
Rose, C. 1986. The destruction of the countryside. In *Green Britain or industrial wasteland?* E. Goldsmith & N. Hildyard (eds). Cambridge: Polity Press: 66–78.
Shoard, M. 1980. *The theft of the countryside*. London: Temple Smith.
Wright, A. 1987. The future of development plans – a reaction from the districts. *The Planner*, May, 14–15.

3 Rural land-use planning in The Netherlands: integration or segregation of functions?

LEO M. VAN DEN BERG

Introduction

As one of the most densely populated countries in the world The Netherlands contains hardly any unused land. The impression one gets while travelling through (or over) the country is confirmed by a breakdown of the Dutch land-use statistics of 1983 (Centraal Bureau voor de Statistiek 1984). Of a total of 3.7 million hectares just over 150 000 ha (4.2%) are classified as natural terrain. If one adds to this the 335 000 ha of water, some of which is used intensively (for transport, recreation, consumption and irrigation), approximately 87% of the country (3.2 million ha) remains as land which is used in one way or another. About three-quarters of this land is farmland, 10% occupied by towns and villages, 9% by forests, while the remainder consists of roads, railways, recreational areas, and so on. Even in the more urbanized western part of the country (the provinces of Utrecht, North- and South-Holland) agriculture still occupies more than 60% of the land.

From the above it can easily be understood that for a long time rural planning in The Netherlands has been primarily agricultural planning: reclaiming farmland from water, swamps and other natural environments, and improving the working conditions of farmers by consolidation of agricultural holdings, road construction and control of water quantity and quality. Even the planning of settlements in newly reclaimed land has primarily been in terms of hierarchies of service centres for the farming population.

Of course, there have always been exceptions to this mainstream of rural planning. For instance, in the more feudal eastern and southern parts of the country the maintenance of a park-like landscape between the tenant-farms has all along been of great concern to the landowners. Likewise, the most unproductive sandy soils in the centre and north-east of the country were turned into forest plantations, mainly during the 19th century. But not until the 1960s was the gradual restructuring of the countryside of much concern to the urban population, who had found sufficient scope for recreation in forests and remaining areas of natural terrain as well as on the farms themselves. It was only then that the continuous enlargement of agricultural fields as well as the straightening of their edges, of roads and of watercourses started to worry larger numbers of people who saw the breakdown of the differentiation within the rural landscape. From then on, agricultural modernization met increasing opposition from the non-farming world.

One decade later it became apparent that the increasing intensification of agricultural (especially animal) production resulted in disturbing quantities of manure which polluted both surface and ground water. And when, in the 1980s, the markets for the traditional products of Dutch farming (dairy, meat, grains, potatoes and sugarbeet) became saturated and the EEC started to demand a reduction of the production of these commodities, the stage was set for a reformulation of the aims and scope of rural planning.

In order to make clear how rural land-use planning takes place it is necessary to summarize the main trends affecting agriculture, forestry, recreation, nature conservation and urban growth in The Netherlands. This will be followed by an overview of the institutional framework of land-use planning concerning rural areas. And lastly, through a number of examples, the present efforts to strengthen non-agricultural functions are shown. These efforts are discussed under two headings: functional integration or multiple use of land, and functional segregation or compartmentalization of rural space. The first heading implies a less intensive use of land by individual sectors, while the second allows for the intensification of land use per function and therefore an increasing specialization of space.

Land-use trends in the countryside

Farming

The total area of farmland in The Netherlands covers about 2 million hectares. This area has been decreasing at a moderate rate of 0.3% per annum between 1975 and 1984 (see Fig. 3.1). The decrease would have been more pronounced if substantial areas in the new polders in the IJsselmeer had not been taken into agricultural use during this period.

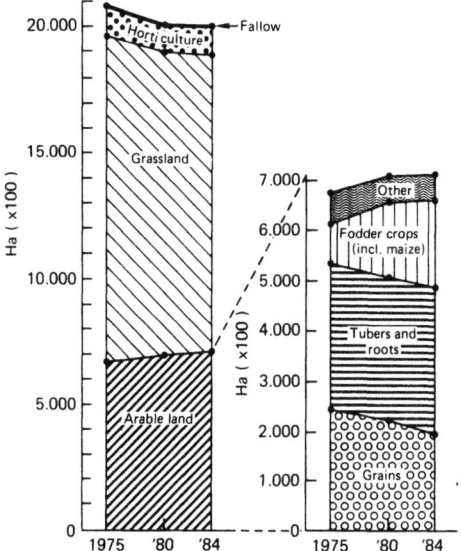

Figure 3.1 Shifts in hectarage of agricultural land in The Netherlands, 1975 to 1984.
Source: Centraal Bureau voor de Statistiek (CBS) 1986.

A central issue of rural land-use planning is the further reduction in agricultural hectarage. In the light of the present problem of overproduction of agricultural commodities within the EEC one might expect the total hectarage of farmland to decrease faster than before. Already, no new polders are being created, so that the supply of new farmland will slow down. However, the Dutch answer to agricultural overproduction in Europe would be a limited price reduction for the surplus commodities in combination with adjustments to crop rotation including longer periods of fallow, and the selective application of less intensive production techniques (Wossink & Renkema 1987). As far as this would lead to marginal land being taken out of production, very little of such land is expected to be situated within The Netherlands. On the basis of considerations of this nature the total area of farmland in The Netherlands is not expected to decrease below the figure of 1.8 million ha by the year 2000 (van Bruchem 1987).

So far, most loss of farmland has taken place as a result of urban growth and expected urban growth. This is illustrated in Table 3.1, where between 1981 and 1983 more than half of the

Table 3.1 Loss and gain of farmland in The Netherlands, 1981–3.

Other land-use category	Agricultural land use (ha) Replaced by other category	Replacing other category	Net loss
Traffic	723	98	625
Recreation	1743	61	1672
Built-up area	2292	166	2126
Building sites	2623	106	2517
Forest	461	45	416
Natural terrain	176	21	155
'Other' land	576	183	393
Water	270	16	254
Total	8864	696	8168

Sources: Statistiek van de Land- en Tuinbouw 1984, CBS 1986.

loss of agricultural land is shown to be replaced by built-up areas and building sites. Also recreational facilities have taken up a substantial amount of agricultural land. The losses to traffic and water are equally related to urbanization, the latter because of the excavation of sand for building and construction. As the resulting lakes are within easy reach of the urban population, they in turn become used intensively for recreational purposes: note the spectacular upswing of windsurfing over the last decade!

Most farmland is under grass. The relative decline of grassland since 1975 (see Fig. 3.1) is linked to the increasing popularity of maize as a fodder crop. Of the other crops the various grains are steadily on the decrease. Fruit- and ornamental trees are slightly on the increase, whereas the area of bulb flowers is stable, despite losses to urban growth. The latter are offset by conversion of grassland into new bulbfields, sometimes through the spectacular method of bringing sand to the surface from a depth of several metres. Over the same period, the number of cattle has increased by 11% to a figure of 5.5 million in 1984. The density of dairy cows per hectare increased likewise, from 1.6 in 1975 to 1.9 in 1984. A small though increasing proportion of them remains indoors throughout the year.

Of great concern has been the rapid increase of beef and pork production. While the number of farmers engaged in this field decreased slightly (see Fig. 3.2), the average number of animals per farm increased dramatically: fattening-calves from

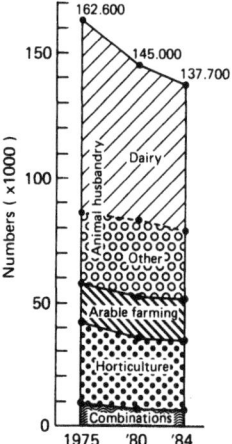

Figure 3.2 Trends in the numbers of registered farms in The Netherlands, 1975 to 1984.
Source: Centraal Bureau voor de Statistiek (CBS) 1986.

125 in 1975 to 231 in 1984, and pigs from 132 in 1975 to 306 in 1984. A similar trend is found in the poultry industry. Although these forms of intensification have occurred all over The Netherlands there are certain regions where piggeries and poultry farms are more concentrated. The province of North-Brabant and the western margins of the central plateau of the Veluwe experience the resulting problems of pollution most severely. These areas are known for their traditionally small agricultural holdings with a high rural population density on rather poor (sandy) soils. The surplus of manure produced by calves, pigs and poultry used to be most welcome on the nearby infertile fields and during the 20th century a system of land-independent livestock farming developed out of this. During the 1970s the introduction of new varieties of maize made it possible to use this on a large scale in The Netherlands, replacing grassland (cf. Fig. 3.1). This crop has the additional advantage that larger quantities of slurry from the piggeries and calf-fattening units could be spread over the fields than was possible on grassland. It soon became clear, from chemical analyses of ground water and drainage water, that too much of it was applied compared to what the plants could use. This necessitated interim legislation in 1985, which aimed at stopping the increase of land-independent livestock farming and also involved elaborate organizational and legislative efforts regarding the disposure of

manure. Today farmers are obliged to maintain records of the amount of manure produced and to contribute financially towards the transport of surpluses over distances of between 50 and 150 km to regions that can still use it. For the time being, these and other methods of handling regional surpluses of muck are subsidized by the state. Some progress is presently being made towards an economically and environmentally acceptable solution to this serious problem.

As a comparison between Figures 3.1 and 3.2 shows, the total number of farms in The Netherlands has decreased faster than the amount of land used by them. Most farming was and still is undertaken on holdings which can be operated by a single farmer with limited assistance from members of the household (approximately 3% of the farm businesses in The Netherlands are headed by a woman). Non-family labour has become relatively unimportant on Dutch farms. Most observers agree, however, that in the official agricultural statistics the labour inputs of wives and children are underestimated. Table 3.2 shows the degree of reliance on regular non-family labour in agricultural enterprises according to these statistics.

The average size of these holdings has increased from 17 ha in 1975 to 19.6 ha in 1984 for arable farming and animal husbandry, while for horticultural undertakings the increase was from 3.2 ha to 3.9 ha. The share of very small farms (with less than 2 ha), excluding horticulture, increased from 4.9% to 6.3% over the

Table 3.2 Reliance on regular labour (family and non-family) of farms in different regions of The Netherlands, 1984.

Major agricultural region	Number of farms employing a regular labour force	Average family labour force per farm (incl. farmer himself)	Average non-family labour force per farm
Marine clay regions	20 418	1.52	0.47
River-clay and loess	13 527	1.71	0.17
Peaty meadow regions	23 508	1.73	0.35
Sandy regions	65 730	1.79	0.17
Depeated moorlands	2929	1.53	0.21
Horticultural regions	7929	1.75	0.96
Total	134 041	1.72	0.29

Sources: Statistiek van de Land- en Tuinbouw 1984, CBS 1986.

same period. This illustrates the importance of intensive animal husbandry, which is largely land-independent and relies to a great extent on purchased feed. But also the share of large farms (in the Dutch context: farms of over 20 ha) increased: from 29.4% to 38.7%. More than half of the farms still consist of between 2 and 20 ha compared to almost two-thirds in 1975.

The total number of farms in The Netherlands has been on a steady decrease. While shortly after the Second World War over 240 000 agricultural enterprises were counted, this number had dwindled to less than 160 000 in 1975 and to 137 000 in 1984.

Part-time farming (requiring less than half of a farmer's working time) has in the past been common in certain regions only. For the country as a whole, the share of part-time farming has been increasing slowly since the Second World War. In 1950 10% of the farmers were counted as part-timers, while this figure was around 17% in the 1970s and just over 19% in 1985. Agricultural policy in The Netherlands strongly supports the full-time, professional farmer. Although agricultural extension work services are equally available to full-time and part-time farmers, credit facilities and the acquisition of farmland are much more difficult for a part-time farmer.

In order to survive economically in the farming business one not only has to work hard but also needs to be a real professional, to be willing to run considerable financial risks, and to apply the latest techniques. Many children of farmers opt for a different career which makes it possible to identify farms where a natural successor is missing. But also on farms with a potential successor the combination of legacy duties and the present limitations to the production per farm are making it increasingly difficult for someone to become a partner in, and eventually take over, somebody else's farm. The main mechanism for the rapid reduction of the agricultural population is through (early) retirement of farmers over the age of 50 who do not have a successor. Special funds have been set aside to make it attractive for these farmers to sell out. Some may actually stay in the old farmhouse and keep a few hectares as a hobby farm, but many leave the land altogether and settle in a nearby village or town. Surprisingly few data are collected about these approximately 2500 people who disappear from the agricultural statistics each year.

One specialized field of agriculture in which a group of rapidly professionalizing farmers co-operates intensely with research stations, agricultural extension workers, financial institutions and marketing organizations is that of greenhouse horticulture. In a very competitive world some 11 000 growers, over 3000 of whom are concentrated in an area of approximately 140 km^2 in the triangle between The Hague, Rotterdam and Hook of Holland, supply the markets of West Germany, France and Great Britain with fresh vegetables, fruit, flowers and pot plants. This achievement has been possible because of the joint application of new energy- and labour-saving devices, the optimization of growing conditions for plants, innovations in the fields of marketing and crop handling, and so on. Though presently highly competitive, the emanating system has remained fragile and in need of continuous adjustments to unexpected technical, economic and environmental developments.

Forestry

Virtually nothing remains of the natural woodland that must have covered the whole country in the Middle Ages. Most of the 33 000 ha of forests and woodlots, which altogether occupy less than 10% of the land surface, date from the 19th and 20th centuries and were planted either to offset the effects of overgrazing or to turn waste land into something productive. Many forests were established in periods of economic crisis by both private and state agencies, using labour which otherwise would be unemployed. During the First and Second World Wars these forests proved their value as a strategic fuel reserve. At present about 20% of the forests is owned by the State Forestry Service which increased its planted property from 51 000 ha in 1976 to 60 000 ha in 1985. The largest forests planted during recent decades are found in the new polders of the IJsselmeer.

Under present economic circumstances forestry is not considered viable as a private venture in The Netherlands unless it is heavily subsidized. At the same time approximately 80% of the Dutch wood requirements need to be imported. Local production covers a mere 7%, and 14% is made available through recycling. In this time of over-production in many agricultural commodities the search for fast-maturing fibre crops is therefore most urgent. So far, farmers have hardly responded to the call for tree planting. One reason for this has been the obligation to plant new trees wherever old ones are felled – a measure taken many decades ago to arrest the dwindling of forest resources in the country. For farmers and investors who are willing to plant fast-growing varieties of poplar and willow on agricultural land the government has now withdrawn this obligation. Even so, the various incentives are not yet considered sufficient.

Apart from wood production, forests act as a natural environment and perform an important recreational function in The Netherlands. Most forests are open to the public and recreational facilities like campsites, playing fields, footpaths, bridleways and cycle tracks are provided on a large scale.

In 1984 a national long-term Forestry Plan was formulated. This plan aims at 35 000 ha of additional forests by the year 2000, one-third to be situated close to the main cities. At present, regional forestry plans are produced which specify the prime and subordinate functions of public and private forests and natural areas.

Outdoor recreation

Many features of the Dutch rural landscape lend themselves to forms of outdoor recreation. Some have been specially created for that purpose (be it recently or long ago) whereas many more only required some minor adjustments to become suitable for 'recreational co-use'. These adjustments could be physical, such as minor bridges, footpaths, or parking facilities; or institutional, such as change of ownership or access rights. In this way, outdoor recreation combines reasonably well with forestry, the management of natural terrain and, last but not least, military training grounds. Although the army wishes to use its land more intensively, the consequent destruction of more of the scarce natural vegetation will not meet parliamentary approval. The prevailing coexistence with nature conservation and outdoor recreation is therefore likely to remain.

It was mainly during the 1960s and 1970s that a large number of areas were established as *elementen van formaat* (elements of stature): lakes created by excavation of sand, clay and gravel were used as nuclei for regional parks, with facilities for swimming, windsurfing, sunbathing, camping, allotment gardens, horseriding centres and the like. Several farms around these lakes had to be acquired by the public authorities involved. Although the location of these artificial lakes was determined by technical and economic factors associated with the excavations rather than by accessibility for large numbers of people, there is often a fortunate coincidence between the two, especially where sand was extracted to prepare building sites. Most of the gravel and clay pits along the rivers Maas and Rhine are quite far from the cities, however. Their edges have been developed more as holiday villages, often by private investment.

According to all policy documents the inhabitants of the 'Randstad' (the string of cities in the western part of the country) are most deprived of facilities for outdoor recreation, even after the *elementen van formaat* are completed. According to a 1985 outline plan for a 'Randstad Green Structure' some 6400 ha in this region will be developed into forests and recreational areas during the next 15 years. Under this programme, for which 420 million florins (over £100 million sterling) has been set aside, mainly strips along existing lakes and canals are proposed for development. The creation of large parks and forests as such is of lower priority than some twenty years ago.

Nature and landscape conservation

The gradual disappearance of natural and traditional farming landscapes started to draw public attention in The Netherlands at the turn of the century. In 1906 the first 'natural monument', the Naardermeer, a lake with surrounding marshlands south-east of Amsterdam, was bought by the Society for the Preservation of Natural Monuments that had been founded one year before. Almost one-third of the 150 000 ha of natural terrain in the country is now owned by this society. Other institutions owning such land with the objective of conservation include the State Forestry Service and several provincial and local foundations. The most valued, more or less natural landscapes include salt- and freshwater marshes, peat moors, sand dunes, small areas of shifting sand and pockets of natural woodland. Apart from their scarcity these landscapes derive value from the flora and fauna found in them.

Both scarcity and ecological considerations also make certain agricultural landscapes worth conserving. Since 1980 a number of 'National Landscapes' have been demarcated, areas of at least 10 000 ha each, consisting of coherent combinations of natural terrain, water, woodland, settlements and agricultural land. The purpose of the formation of National Landscapes is to maintain a minimum degree of differentiation between the various landscape types in the country, each with a unique history of colonization.

In these areas agricultural and other investments need to be in harmony with the characteristic relationships between elements of the landscape. For farmers this may well result in not making the kind of investments or carrying out the kind of activities that are recommended to their colleagues elsewhere. These farmers are now encouraged to enter into management agreements with the relevant authorities.

Urbanization

Dutch towns and villages have just completed an episode of rapid expansion. As most local councils had prepared themselves (and in many cases their land as well!) for this episode to last much longer, many farmers in the urban fringe who were bought out a couple of years ago have since been able to continue cultivating the land with annual leases. Several local councils have a hard time balancing their books now that they are unable to sell plots to companies who would have developed them for industry, offices, or houses. Along with a declining rate of investment in the building industry a new slogan has emerged in the national spatial policy documents during the early 1980s: the 'Compact City'. The policy is now to use derelict land or other open space within the built-up areas before new building sites are sought on the outskirts of towns. New claims on agricultural, natural, or forest land for urban growth have therefore become less likely during the coming decades. This leaves room, however, for three other types of urbanization in the countryside:

- leisure villages such as allotment gardens near the cities and caravan sites and marinas elsewhere;
- new highways and other infrastructural works cutting through agricultural holdings and other rural landscape units;
- urban uses of vacated farm buildings of a more or less conspicuous nature: hidden urbanization and a waft of urban sprawl.

The combination of a fairly consistent implementation of zoning regulations and the high cost of turning most Dutch soils into stable building sites makes a widespread urban sprawl through small-scale, private development less likely than, for instance, in neighbouring Belgium. In this respect an interesting gradient can be observed from the compact urban growth in the peat and clay areas around Amsterdam, Rotterdam and The Hague to a looser development around cities like Eindhoven on the southern sand plateau. A not too unlikely shift of the economic gravity of The Netherlands from the Randstad to the South-East would probably lead to less compact forms of suburbanization.

Agencies, guidelines and interest groups for rural planning

As elsewhere, rural planning in The Netherlands is organized at several territorial levels, both as 'integrated' planning and as sectoral planning. At the national level a State Physical Planning Agency (the Rijks Planologische Dienst: RPD) within the Ministry of Housing, Physical Planning and Environment tries to give a common sense of direction to all other agencies and individuals involved. By this Agency slogans like the 'Compact City', the 'Green Heart of Holland', 'Bufferzones' between towns in the Randstad, and most recently the 'Randstad Green Structure' are proclaimed, defined and presented for parliamentary endorsement. Naturally, the RPD needs to consult quite carefully with the sectoral interest groups, represented by the other ministries. For rural areas the Ministries of Agriculture and Fisheries (also responsible for forestry, nature and landscape conservation, and outdoor recreation), Transport, Waterways and Public Works, Economic Affairs and Defence are the most important partners in the ongoing debate of how to allocate limited space to competing activities.

The outcome of these discussions is laid down in a sequence of official planning documents: the First, Second, Third and Fourth Memoranda on Physical Planning of 1960, 1966, 1973–7 and 1988, respectively. The First Memorandum looks ahead to 1980, the Second and Third to around 2000. The Fourth Memorandum was not yet available at the time of writing but will probably cover a period up to 2015. The Third Memorandum is divided into one document on rural areas and one on urbanization. These two documents were soon followed by Structural Outline Sketches covering the first part of the planning period, up to approximately 1990, in greater detail.

Around 1980 a series of thematic (more sectoral) documents were produced by interdepartmental working groups, including the RPD. Five of these deal explicitly with rural areas. These are Structural Outline Plans for Land Development, Nature and Landscape Conservation, Outdoor Recreation, Military Areas and Civil Airports and Landing Grounds. A special 'Report on the Spatial Framework for the Randstad Green Structure' was produced by the RPD in 1985 to bring together the relevant ideas from the above Structural Outline Plans and important sectoral policy documents as far as these would be useful for the creation of green buffers within and between the major conurbations of the Randstad.

These documents are all fairly substantial, reflecting a great deal of work by teams of specialists, lengthy editorial debates and negotiations between the various sectoral ministries. For these negotiations the RPD acts both as platform and catalyst. Among other things the documents spell out general rules, and temporal and spatial priorities for planning activities at the lower administrative levels. In order for provincial or local councils as well as private or semi-governmental organizations to obtain the necessary planning permission and subsidies from higher authorities for the projects they want to undertake, satisfactory reference to these documents has to be made.

At the provincial level the same procedures are repeated, but at greater detail. Each of the twelve provinces is covered by one or more regional physical plans. These plans show where, for instance, farming can continue undisturbed or will be constrained by nature and landscape conservation measures, or where new landscapes are expected to be created. Like the national physical plans, these documents have no immediate consequences for individual landowners, but inform them on likely constraints 'in the public interest' if they should seek planning permission for something. These constraints may become far more serious if the regional physical plan is followed by local land-use zoning plans.

Provincial Regional Physical Plans are accompanied by a continuous outflow of background papers from the various sectoral agencies operating at a provincial level, which in turn reflect the shifts in their own priorities. Apart from the sectoral ministerial agencies that operate at the provincial level (like the army, agricultural extension workers, outdoor recreation, landscape and environmental protection officers) there are also private and public agencies very active here. Private agencies include farmers' associations, the Association for the Conservation of Natural Monuments (which has many years' experience of the acquisition and management of wildlife reserves), and the Dutch Automobile Association (ANWB) which looks after the interests of the tourist industry. Public agencies include the State Forest Service, the Government Service for Land and Water Management and the various water boards. In order to accommodate the frequent changes in perspective of the many agencies involved, the provincial regional physical plans are revised every 5 to 10 years.

At the local level the above agencies are again actively representing the interests of land users and developers. But the local councils are responsible for development control through the issuing of planning permission, building permits, permits emanating from the

Nuisance Act, and so on. By law these councils are also required to produce land-use (zoning) plans covering their whole territories, but for the truly rural parts of many Dutch municipalities such plans are either very dated and vague or missing altogether. The costs of having such detailed plans made or revised for large areas are considered prohibitive. And the benefits are slim because relatively little change in land use is expected in these areas.

Where more detailed land-use plans are made for rural areas, this is done in the context of land development projects or – more recently – 'management plans'. The latter have been prepared since 1977 for farming areas with valuable natural and landscape elements in them. These management plans are co-ordinated by the Bureau for Agricultural Land Management (Bureau Beheer Landbouwgronden – BBL), an agency within the Ministry of Agriculture and Fisheries which was already responsible for the acquisition of land from farmers, on a voluntary basis, in preparation of land development projects, nature reserves, urban growth, highway construction, and so on. Initially, 100 000 ha were to be demarcated in various parts of the country for the explicit reconciliation of the requirements of commercial farming with the objective of nature and landscape conservation. By the end of 1986 almost 70 management plans had been completed, covering one-quarter of the target area. Of these, less than 10 000 were proper management areas as the remainder were located in future nature reserves that had not yet been acquired by a nature conservation society. It is within such management areas that individual farmers can enter into management agreements with BBL. By the end of 1986 this had been done by 890 farmers and involved a total of 6334 ha (Annual Report BBL 1986).

Elsewhere in the countryside applications for planning permission tend to be considered one by one by the local council staff and many autonomous developments, which strictly speaking are illegal, are left unchecked. Action is taken only in the more controversial cases, where it is often the provincial planning authority overruling the silent or formal approval by local authorities. Examples are the construction of piggeries in areas where no building activity is expected to take place or where neighbouring residents resent the smell and traffic associated with such bio-industry. Another issue is that of farmers levelling the land or removing hedges in areas for which the regional physical plan stipulates the conservation of such characteristic landscape elements. Also the hiring out by a rural landowner of allotment gardens can cause planning problems. As such an area is likely to be zoned for farming a local council keeps quiet in the understanding that gardening in an allotment is just a special way of farming. But strictly speaking the latter has to be considered as outdoor recreation and as soon as the gardener puts up a cabin or storage shed he and the landowner may be in real trouble.

Special mention has to be made of the way in which the farmers have organized themselves and have their interests looked after. One of the reasons for the success of the Dutch farming industry has been its early organization into a number of associations along regional and denominational lines. Despite major cultural differences these associations have managed to co-operate effectively on issues affecting farming in The Netherlands as a whole. They are equally active at the national, provincial and local levels. Since 1954 all associations have worked together in one, very powerful corporation, the 'Landbouwschap', which not only has a strong influence on the Ministry of Agriculture and Fisheries, but is also represented on international, national, provincial and municipal planning committees dealing with rural land use and agricultural affairs. Through the Landbouwschap the government has the advantage of dealing with one sparring partner rather than a multitude of opponents and allies. In addition, the Landbouwschap acts as intermediary for government intervention and as legitimation of government policy. For the individual associations the Landbouwschap has the advantage of direct access to the state apparatus, to subsidies and, through its representation on important national committees, a share in the enacting and executive power. In order to maintain this somewhat privileged position the associations have to suppress internal differences and to accept a certain degree of authority from the Landbouwschap. The latter is facilitated by the technocratic, 'depoliticized' approach adopted by the Landbouwschap (Frouws 1987).

Land development

So far, rural planning in The Netherlands has been discussed in terms of grand ideas on zoning and development control. One may doubt whether under such a heavy load of regulations any major land-use change in rural areas could take place. In fact, the opinion is sometimes heard that these documents are all needed to check a number of strong, hardly controllable trends within a number of individual sectors, such as housing, industry and trade (urban sprawl), transport (a proliferation of highways and runways), and – last but not least – the modernization of the agricultural landscape. While urban and village growth is controlled quite successfully through physical planning it proves to be far more difficult to foresee and avoid the negative side-effects of a rapidly professionalizing and intensifying agriculture, mainly because they are far more diffuse and gradual.

The spatial aspects of the spectacular changes in productivity, capital-intensity and time- and labour-saving devices in farming are accompanied by a tradition of over 60 years of land development projects. These projects started off as relatively modest efforts at consolidating highly fragmented agricultural holdings. Very soon, however, these efforts became accompanied by the construction of new access roads and drainage works. The many projects thus carried out during the 1960s led to spectacular improvements of the working conditions of commercial farmers, but their effects on nature and landscape are generally considered less favourable (Volker 1986). Nowadays, many non-agricultural aims have become an integral part of land development projects. These include outdoor recreation, nature and landscape conservation, and the creation of a 'better' landscape.

Since 1935 the Government Service for Land and Water Use (Landinrichtingsdienst – LD) has provided the technical and organizational support for land development projects. While the LD began as a purely farmer-oriented agency it has gradually adopted a more comprehensive approach. This change of scope was endorsed in 1985, when the Land Consolidation Act of 1954 was replaced by the Land Development Act, which defines land development as 'improvement of rural areas in accordance with the functions attributed to them in the framework of physical planning'. This implies that through land development the functioning of a rural area as wildlife sanctuary, testimony of cultural history, recreation area, farmland and more is expected to be improved all in one go. The last section of this chapter will illustrate how this virtually impossible task is handled in a few concrete cases.

The new Act specifies four types of land development projects. Apart from the traditional land consolidation, in which the owners and users of agricultural land continue to have a final say over the decision to carry out a project along the lines set out by a preparatory committee, three new types are distinguished. One is the voluntary exchange of lots and usually affects only a few farmers at a time. The second covers the adjustments that have to be made to the parcelling of the land when farms are dissected by new highways, railroads, runways, and so on. The remaining type, which may best be translated into English as 'redevelopment', is reserved for the most complex areas. These are regions where non-agricultural functions are at least as important as farming. Here, the provincial authorities rather than the affected farmers decide whether the project will be executed or not.

The land development projects (which could just as well be described as rural reconstruction or rural renewal) that have been carried out in The Netherlands since 1924 cover more than 800 000 ha. Together with the 600 000 ha that are now in process this represents approximately 50% of all rural areas of the country (Steenhuis 1987). Between the moment a Local Land Development Committee is installed (consisting of representatives of the farming community, nature and landscape conservation bodies, municipalities and water boards) and the completion of a project, between 7 and 9 years may have passed in preparation and 10 to 15 years for execution. The LD provides the administrative and technical support for each project and makes sure the delicate procedures spelled out by the Land Development Act (see Steenhuis 1987) are followed. Briefing sessions and various forms of consultation with the local community constitute an important part of these procedures.

One of the duties of the LD is to make an impact assessment of the land development plans before their execution can start. This evaluation of the plans and of various alternative solutions for specific problems is very broad in scope and certainly more than a cost–benefit analysis (Bosma 1986). It considers economic, social and environmental effects of the measures proposed. The economic effects relate to agriculture from both the macro- and micro-economic perspectives, and to changes in the maintenance costs of canals, roads and other public facilities. Social effects include changes in the overall living conditions, possibilities for outdoor recreation, accessibility and road safety. Environmental effects relate to landscape and ecology but also to physical and chemical conditions of water, soil and atmosphere.

Only part of the effects can be formulated in monetary terms, but standardized criteria are also sought for the non-monetary aspects of the objectives. The results of this evaluation are very important for the decision whether or not to execute a land development plan.

The local land development committee, in close co-operation with designers, 'subsidiologists' and researchers within and outside the LD, has to find solutions at a reasonable cost for many technical problems. Many of these problems are related to the requirement of integrating agricultural with non-agricultural needs.

Much debate is taking place in The Netherlands as to how this integration is to be defined and implemented and as usual in such a geographical debate the central issue seems to be 'scale'. The most common dilemma for land development projects is how to combine improvement of the working conditions for the farmers (at as low a cost as possible) with the preservation of valuable landscape elements and wildlife habitats. The simple answer is zonation: to specify subregions in which optimal conditions for farming can be created and segregate these with buffer zones from other subregions where 'nature' can flourish. For a number of reasons this answer meets a fair amount of opposition:

- one aspect of landscape that makes it so valuable is the link between vegetation (meadow flowers, hedges, shade-trees, etc.) and farming practices: the landscape features are 'functional' and maintained automatically as part of the farming operations. When such features are no longer functional they will not be maintained or their maintenance would become too costly. To turn the least intensively used parts of a farming area into nature reserves without the continuation of some form of agriculture may well lead to the disappearance of characteristic landscape elements.
- because the optimal conditions for farming do not differ much between different parts of the country, segregation would lead to boring uniformity for those subregions all over the country that are earmarked for modern farming. Such uniformity can be reduced (but not avoided) if the scale at which these subregions are defined is one of individual fields instead of clusters of complete farms. More research needs to be done regarding the influence of the size and shape of agricultural fields on labour costs and edge losses under different economic circumstances.
- to turn the agriculturally least productive subregions (e.g. the wettest portions of a polder, or the most isolated fields) into nature reserves is not enough for the rarer species of fauna and flora to survive as long as such 'islands' are not connected by 'ecological infrastructure': corridors of wild or semi-wild habitats which allow these species to move from one area to another. This, in turn, may well be unacceptable to modern farming.

The remainder of this chapter illustrates what the outcome of such debates has been for two of the more complicated projects.

Leo M. van den Berg

A third example can be found in Naeff (1984). These examples are among the 101 projects, covering about 625 000 ha, that were in various stages of execution at the end of 1986 (Annual Report over 1986 of the LD). Meanwhile, the debates go on, and the outcome may well be very different for the 64 projects (288 000 ha) under preparation at that time (ibid.). For one thing, the present problems emanating from agricultural over-production seem to make farmers more willing to enter into management agreements and landscape maintenance contracts than they were until very recently. They are searching for supplementary income-generating activities to compensate for the loss of direct farming income as well as ways of reducing the costs of agricultural inputs, for instance through extensification where this is feasible. Such new developments will certainly influence the plans that start to be implemented within the next few years. In addition, more of the land development projects that are presently proposed are of the 'redevelopment' type, rather than that of 'consolidation': agriculture is likely to constitute a decreasing component of the multi-functionality that these projects seek to achieve.

Dilemmas and solutions in two complex land-development projects

Giethoorn–Wanneperveen

This 5000 ha project area forms part of a waterlogged region in the north-eastern part of the country. The picturesque village of Giethoorn and the adjacent lakes are very popular among tourists, about half a million of whom visit the area each year. The unique landscape was created by widespread, but small-scale peat-digging activities in earlier days. Dairy farming is the main agricultural activity but many fields are far from the farmhouses and only accessible by boat. This has been the main reason for the local applications for land consolidation ever since 1940, although it took until 1969 before a start could be made with preparations. In 1974 a local Preparatory Committee was installed and implementation of the land development plan could start in 1979, when 61% of the voting farmers and owners of agricultural land (representing 84% of this land) were in favour of it.

The plan produced by the Preparatory Committee is a delicate compromise between the interests of farming, nature and landscape conservation, and recreation. It consists of the following main components:

- 2600 ha (just over half) of the area is to be redeveloped for farming in such a way that the characteristic pattern of narrow drainage canals is maintained;
- the remaining 2400 ha is primarily a nature reserve. Here, only those works will be carried out that facilitate the management of such a reserve. Part of this (900 ha) consists of agricultural land, 250 ha is open water and 1000 ha is reedland or underwood.
- all improvement works have to be carried out in such a way that the various characteristic landscapes are maintained or reinforced. A landscape plan has been drawn to act as a guideline for this;
- certain canals will be improved for recreation, others closed altogether or closed for motorboats. This will enhance the natural value of some of the most vulnerable wildlife sanctuaries.

The improvements consist of the construction of a few kilometres of new roads and the widening and strengthening of most of the other roads. Even the fields in the reserves will be made accessible by roads, although these will not be open to the public. For modern farming a substantial improvement of the drainage system is considered essential. Therefore, five new pumping stations are to be built to lower the water table in the agricultural areas to about 1 m below the surface in winter and to about 70 cm in summer. In the reserves a much higher water level will be maintained. The new situation will enable farmes to harvest more grass or to keep more cows per hectare, to bring heavier machines on the land and cultivate it over longer parts of the growing season, and to reduce the risk of certain cattle diseases associated with wet grassland conditions.

Another delicate issue for improvement is the layout of farms. This is to be maintained as much as possible, but narrow fields several kilometres in length are highly impractical for farmers. Therefore, the plan provides for a maximum length of the lots of 1 km and a substantial lot for each farmer next to the main farm buildings. The plan provides for a voluntary relocation of seven farmhouses. As far as possible the new buildings will be made to fit in the natural landscape. In those areas where farming is given priority over the other functions the minimum width of the fields will be 50 m. This implies the filling in of a number of canals.

About 130 farmers have fields in the reserves-to-be, two of them also having their farmhouses there. At present, the Association for the Conservation of Natural Monuments owns over 1000 ha in this area. Until the remainder has also been acquired, on a voluntary basis, the farmers will be encouraged to enter into management

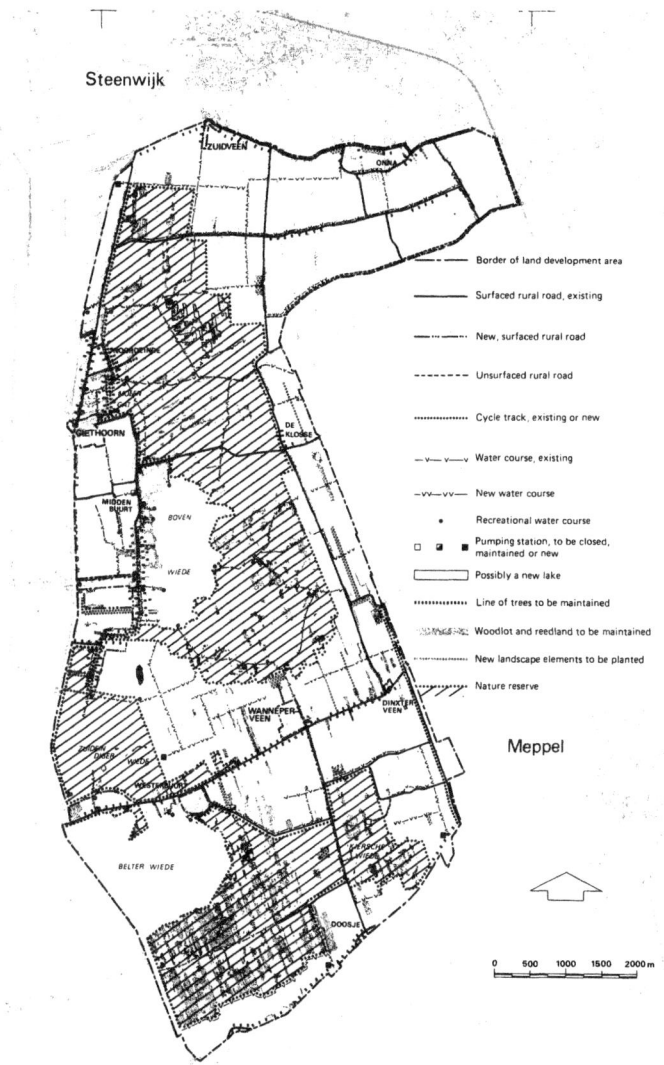

Figure 3.3 The Giethoorn-Wanneperveen land development project (Overijssel).
Source: Landinrichtingsdienst.

agreements with the Bureau for Agricultural Land Management. These agreements involve refraining from manuring and grazing or grass-cutting before a certain date so as to facilitate the hatching of meadow birds. After that date the mechanical cultivation of fields will be possible. The amount of compensation paid for this to the farmers is calculated carefully on the basis of comparison with income per hectare of nearby farmers without such limitations. In addition, farmers can receive payment for the maintenance of reedland and hedges. The management agreements in the reserves are meant to be of a temporary nature. In the long run the Association is expected to manage the reserves on its own.

A look at the maps accompanying the land development plan (see Fig. 3.3) gives an impression of the extent of segregation between areas set aside for farming, nature and recreation. Improved farmland is created in the north, east and centre of the area, while two reserves will emerge in which access for tourists will be limited to a few canals and agriculture will only marginally be involved. Intensive forms of recreation are to be largely confined to the two main lakes in the area and the adjacent villages. Farmers in the area seem to be hardly involved in the tourist industry, although their relatives may well be. This specialization is an indication of the high degree of professionalization in both industries.

Whereas most borders between the agricultural and natural areas are reasonably gradual, the natural drainage pattern in the north-west makes it difficult to lower the water table in the farming area without draining the natural area too much. An expensive, extra canal will be dug to reduce this problem. This canal will make it possible to let the drainage water from the agricultural area bypass the nature reserve. Likewise, when the agricultural area needs extra water during dry periods this can be obtained directly from outside rather than through the nature reserve.

In short, the result of this land development project is that in slightly less than half of the area reasonably good conditions are created for modern farming for a much smaller number of farmers than were in the area before. Elderly farmers without a successor are strongly encouraged to terminate their operations and sell the land to the state. The improved farming areas will be surrounded by buffer zones for which management agreements are applicable but where farmers are still allowed to use modern machinery. In the core areas of the nature reserves only those agricultural activities will be carried out (either by farmers or by voluntary labour and park staff) that are necessary to maintain the natural and landscape conditions that make these areas valuable.

When the plan was presented for voting in 1978 the total costs were estimated at about dfl. 36 million (£9 million sterling), which is dfl. 7200 per hectare. The landowners contribute less than a quarter of this, for which they can borrow money at a low interest rate of 3.5% per annum.

Rijnstreek-zuid

For this area of almost 4000 ha south of an old course of the Rhine east of the town of Leiden in the province of South-Holland a preparatory committee was installed in 1970 after several applications for land developments from the polder boards concerned had been endorsed by the provincial authorities in 1969. Execution of the land development plan could start in 1977.

Two types of farming are practised in the area: dairy farming covering approximately 3540 ha and 300 ha of tree nurseries. Farmers experienced serious problems of access to their fields, water management and farm layout. In addition, many farms are separated from their fields by the Leiden–Utrecht railway line which in many cases had to be crossed by the complete dairy herd four times a day. Parallel to the railway line a gas pipe is situated and a new motorway planned. The farm buildings are generally very old and many of them squeezed together along the old Rhine dyke on the northernmost edge of the area. At those locations there is insufficient space for enlargement of the buildings or construction of new ones as most non-agricultural land use is also concentrated in the same belt. When the land development plan was drafted in 1976 a 'natural' decrease of the number of dairy farms (due to the absence of successors) was expected, from 156 in 1975 to 123 in 1985.

The area of tree nurseries had expanded at a great rate during the 1960s and 1970s as it had proved to be a lucrative industry for which training, marketing and extension are available in the nearby centre of Boskoop. However, as these enterprises require much smaller lots than the dairy and arable farms from which the land is taken over, the existing road network was not sufficient. Appropriate space needed to be created for a substantial expansion of this specialized branch. Between 1970 and 1975 the number of tree nurseries in the area increased from 86 to 108 and this figure was expected to increase further to around 200 by 1985. The required space was found in the south-eastern corner of the area (see Fig. 3.4).

A further reason for the provincial and national authorities to support the applications for land development here was that

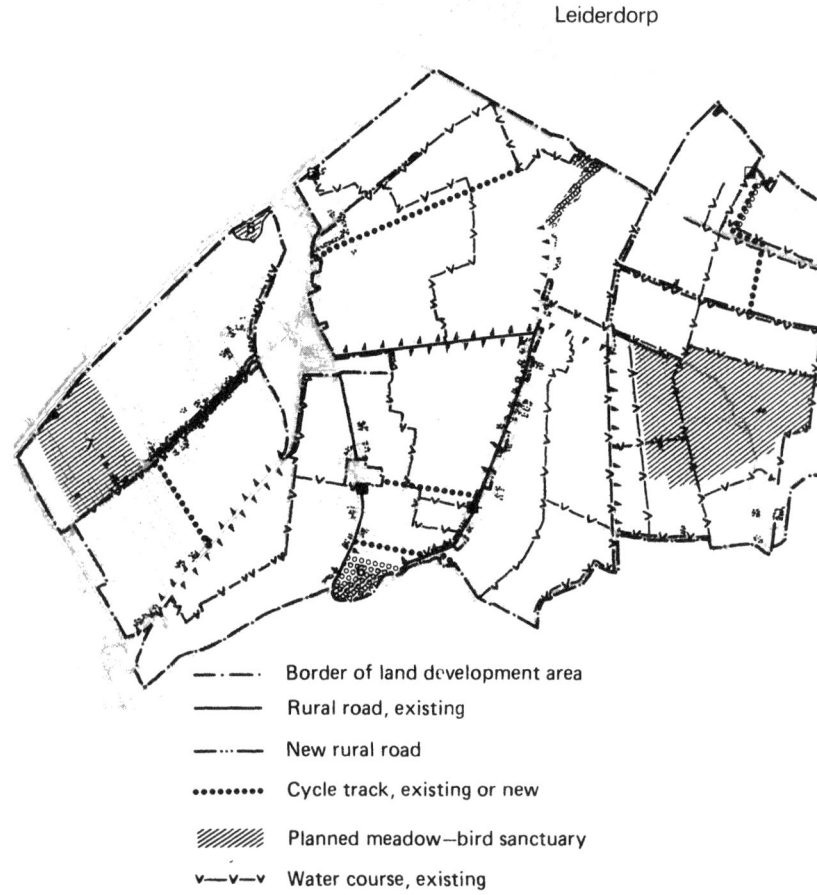

Figure 3.4 The Rijnstreek-Zuid land development project (South-Holland).
Source: Landinrichtingsdienst. nds, 1984

the autonomous developments in the area were likely to affect negatively the large-scale openness of the landscape, one of the assets of the 'Green Heart of Holland'. Facilities for outdoor recreation close to major population concentrations as well as conservation of some biologically interesting niches could also be brought about in the process.

The land development plan of 1977 which is presently being executed provides for the construction of 23 km of tarred, rural roads and 9 km of cycle tracks (for schoolchildren and tourists), and for the improvement of another 5 km of rural roads. In addition, the improvement of some private roads to remote farm buildings is eligible for a state subsidy of 50%. An important element of the plan is the removal of all (unguarded) private level crossings of the railway line. Some will no longer be needed after relocation of certain farms away from the northern belt. Others are being replaced by a smaller number of tunnels. The railway authorities are expected to make a substantial financial contribution to this exercise.

A delicate new pattern of water tables has been worked out in the plan. Depending on the soil conditions (clay, peat, or clay on peat) the polder level will be brought down to between 80 and 120 cm below soil surface. For the tree nurseries the prevailing level of 35–65 cm below the surface is acceptable. For the maintenance of these new water levels three pumping stations needed to be replaced and one added. Several canals had to be widened and a few new ones dug to facilitate a quick drainage in wet periods or an inflow of water during dry periods. The quality of the water in the southern part of the area, where the tree nurseries are concentrated, is not always good enough for this more vulnerable crop. Frequent circulation and inflow from the north will improve the situation.

In order to improve the layout for dairy farms a number of farm buildings had to be relocated from the crowded northern edge to the open middle zone. This takes place on a voluntary basis. To give access to these new farms two (dead-end) roads were constructed south of the railway line. These roads had to be made into dead-ends in order to facilitate the creation of a bird sanctuary in the central, most poorly drained part of the area. For the tree nurseries an intensive scheme of land consolidation and subdivision has been worked out.

Although the openness of the landscape has to be maintained as much as possible the concentration of tree nurseries in the southern polders will reduce this to a certain extent. The new farm buildings in the central part will have a similar effect, especially as the residents are encouraged to plant trees in their new gardens (subsidies of 80%). In addition, the plan provides for woodlots in the crowded belt between the Rhine and the railway line and for a few 'landscaping accents'. Other valuable elements of the landscape include a number of old windmills and interesting stretches of old canals. One of the windmills will be used to give one of the bird sanctuaries its own drainage at a higher water level than the remainder of the polder in which it is situated.

For the reallocation of land according to the plan 300 ha is needed: 105 ha for roads, watercourses and minor landscape elements, 95 ha for woodlots and a bird sanctuary, and 100 ha for enlargement of farms that will be relocated. When the project was launched in 1977, 133 ha had already been acquired by the state.

The costs of this project were estimated at almost dfl. 12 000 per hectare (1977 prices). About 30% of this is to be borne by the landowners, the remainder is covered by various state subsidies or the contributions of other interested parties (Dutch Railways, municipalities, the national gas company, and so on).

More than the Giethoorn–Wanneperveen project, the one for Rijnstreek-zuid involves an overall intensification of rural land use. Only in two relatively small areas are nature reserves to be established. However, in the course of execution the plan had to be revised on several occasions. For instance, in the original plan of 1977 (summarized in Fig. 3.4) the wildlife reserve was smaller than later on, while the new road connecting the relocated farmhouses in this area was not yet cut up into two dead-end roads. Also, the lowering of water tables had to be reduced locally under pressure from conservationists. In other words, in the course of plan implementation awareness of the biological value of the area has grown and could be accommodated to a certain extent.

Conclusion

The approach to the problem of marrying demands from the agricultural community for better working conditions with those of ecologists of maintaining or improving valuable natural habitats, is similar: for both projects create good conditions for modern farming at one place and the natural habitats at another. Management agreements could cover the buffer zones between the two, but as modern farming methods become more remote from those responsible for what have now become valuable 'natural' habitats, the farmers are less interested in entering into such agreements, unless the problems of agricultural over-production would force them. If not, a professional team of 'historical' farmers, contracted by the owners of these reserves, seems to be the only way of maintaining parks created by historic farming practices. The main dangers of the present solution are therefore the continued biological impoverishment of the farming areas along with a degeneration of the more 'natural' (nostalgic?) farming landscapes into unpredictable wilderness.

Nevertheless, the land development projects carried out in The Netherlands constitute the only way in this country for an integrated restructuring of rural areas, especially at the provincial level. While these projects still aim at improving the working conditions for those farmers who are expected to remain active in the area, they also act increasingly – though slowly – as a way of securing larger parcels and wider strips of land and marshes for non-agricultural functions, in full co-operation with the land users involved. In the process, the central agency responsible for land development projects, the Government Service for Land and Water Use, becomes increasingly a 'neutral' organization, operating between the Scylla of farmers' associations and the Charybdis of landscape and nature conservation groups.

In areas where the 'heavy' procedure of land development is not applied, a number of sectoral instruments are still available to strengthen the natural, recreational and landscape assets of agricultural and forest areas, including their ecological and recreational infrastructure, without restructuring. These instruments include the Landscape Plans and Management Plans for agricultural, natural and forest areas, which are presently being drafted under the responsibility of the State Forestry Service and the Bureau for Agricultural Land Management. Continuously, lessons are learned from earlier projects, and experiments are carried out with ways of integrating rather than segregating several of the functions of rural space. In many of the projects presently in preparation rather than execution the complexity has become even greater than in the two cases described. Here, the spatial claims of expanding cities are far more pronounced than in the projects carried out so far.

Acknowledgements

As most of the sources consulted for this chapter are written in Dutch referencing has been kept to a minimum. The reader is advised to consult directly with the Landinrichtingsdienst, Postbus

20021, 3502 LA Utrecht, for more information on land development projects. Copies of the Land Use Statistics and the Statistics on Agriculture, with short explanatory notes in English, can be obtained from the Netherlands Central Bureau of Statistics, CBS, Postbus 959, 2270 AZ Voorburg. The author further wishes to acknowledge the comments on draft versions of this chapter by Mrs E. G. M. Dessing, Mr J. M. L. Jansen and Mr J. A. Kester of the Institute of Land and Water Management Research in Wageningen and by Mrs G. Steenhuis of the Government Service for Land and Water Use (Landinrichtingsdienst).

References

Bosma, H. 1986. Evaluation in advance of the effects of land development projects in The Netherlands. Information Paper 6, Landinrichtingsdienst, Utrecht.
Bruchem, C. van 1987. Trendbreuk of continuiteit? Mogelijke gevolgen beleidswijzigingen voor enkele landbouwstructurele ontwikkelingen. *De Landeigenaar* 33, 11, 11-16.
Bureau Beheer Landbouwgronden 1987. Jaarverslag 1986, Utrecht.
Centraal Bureau voor de Statistiek 1984. Bodemstatistiek 1983, The Hague, Staatsuitgeverij.
Centraal Bureau voor de Statistick 1986. Statistiek van de Land-en Tuinbouw 1984, The Hague, Staatsuitgevery.
Dijk, G. van, A. T. J. Nooij & H. J. Silvis (eds) 1987. *Areaalbeheersing in de landbouwpolitiek*. Wageningse Economische Studien 8, Agricultural University Wageningen (contains English summaries).
Frouws, J. 1987. Areaalbeheersing in het landbouwpolitieke debat (in: van Dijk et al., op. cit.).
Held, R. B. & D. W. Visser 1984. Rural land uses and planning. A comparative study of The Netherlands and the United States. Amsterdam.
Landinrichtingsdienst 1987. Jaarverslag 1986, Utrecht.
Naeff, G. C. 1984. Land consolidation project in The Netherlands: the project from the Etten-Leur-Rucphen region. In Steiner, F. R. and H. N. van Lier (eds); *Developments in landscape management and urban planning*.
Steenhuis, G. (1987). Land development in The Netherlands. Contribution to the OECD project on Rural Public Management. Government Service for Land and Water Use, Utrecht.
Volker, C. M. 1986. The social impact of land consolidation, with particular reference to the Achterhoek area of The Netherlands. *Tijdschrift voor Sociaal-wetenschappelijk Onderzoek van de Landbouw* 1, 3, 1986, 241-57.
Wossink, G. A. A. & J. A. Renkema 1986. Bedrijfseconomische gevolgen en randvoorwaarden van areaalbeheersing (in: van Dijk et al., op. cit.).

4 Land-use planning in rural France

JOHN AITCHISON

Introduction

Over the past four decades successive French governments have established a complex (and often overlapping) array of institutions, organizations and agencies to deal with the planned development and management of land use in rural areas (Jung 1971, Monod 1974, Bontron *et al.* 1983, Laborie *et al.* 1985, Guichard 1986, Morand-Deviller 1987, Clout 1987). Some of these bodies, together with their differing policies and powers, have survived the test of time, some have been modified to accommodate changing economic and political circumstances, others have simply been jettisoned. It is not possible here to offer a full historical review of these varying shifts in attitude, approach and emphasis; the more limited intention is to examine a selection of the main legislative and regulatory measures that have been implemented both to control and orient patterns of land use, and to resolve particular conflicts of interest. In so doing, reference will be made to the executive role of the state, a hierarchy of administrative authorities (*régions*, *départements* and *communes*), and a host of other bodies, both public and private. Although the use and management of land constitutes the central focus of interest, it is to be appreciated that such matters need to be set in context, and cannot be divorced from a consideration of wider environmental, socio-economic and political issues.

The discussion begins with a brief summary of some of the main changes that have taken place in rural regions during recent years, and moves on to an examination of the increasingly important role played by communes in the shaping of land-use patterns at a local level. Since many of the policies relating to rural areas have tended in the past to be sector-directed (i.e. piecemeal rather than integrated) reference is then made to three important land-use activities – agriculture, forestry and nature conservation. Finally, to illustrate the emergence of more holistic approaches to the planned development of environments experiencing special difficulties, an assessment is made of policies and directives for two key zones – coastal margins and mountain massifs.

L'espace rural français

For purposes of statistical enumeration, the French population census draws a distinction between 'urban' and 'rural' communes. Although the basis of this distinction is rather crude, depending as it does on whether or not the size of population resident in the *chef lieu* of the commune is above or below 2000 inhabitants, it does enable a degree of discrimination in considering the demographic and socio-economic characteristics of two contrasting types of administrative environments. In the 1982 census 86.5% of the 36 500 or so communes were classed as 'rural'. Together, these areas claimed 85% of the national territory and 27% of the total population (14.5 million). Although for more than a century many rural communes have suffered the damaging consequences of massive depopulation (Schéma Général d'Aménagement de la France 1971), it is notable that over recent years a growing number have experienced a highly significant 'turn-around' (Bontron 1985b). Thus, between 1975 and 1982, rural communes as a whole recorded a 6.2% increase in population, as compared with a rise of just 2.2% for 'urban' communes. Such are the changes in the pace and direction of migration that *l'exode rural* has been replaced by *l'exode urbain* (Ogden 1985). These are aggregate statistics, of course, and it has to be recognized that during this period 44.5% of rural communes continued to record a decrease in population. In rural parts of the Massif Central (e.g. Cantal and Lozère) and Corsica the demographic situation is still a cause for concern (Béteille 1981, Estienne 1985). Population densities in rural France are generally of a very low order, with approximately 40% of communes in 1982 recording ratios of less than 20 persons per square kilometre – a threshold regarded by many as being particularly critical (Aitchison & Bontron 1981, Mathieu & Duboscq 1985). That said, however, around many small provincial towns, in selected coastal districts, and in other favoured localities, where population totals have been increasing rapidly, densities are much higher – in places exceeding 250 per square kilometre. Directing these trends are the profound changes that have taken place both in rural employment structures since the early 1970s, and in attitudes towards life in the provinces and life in the countryside (Ardagh 1984).

In 1954 French agriculture gave employment to just over 5 million people. By 1975 this figure had plummeted to 2 million as a result of a much-needed rationalization of holdings and systems of production (Girard et al. 1977, Bontron & Mathieu 1980, Pinchemel 1981). Since 1975 the fall in numbers employed has continued, albeit at a considerably reduced rate, and it is clear that rural France can no longer be regarded as dominantly agricultural in terms of its society and economy. Whereas in 1962 almost a half of all rural households were in some way connected with agriculture, by 1982 the percentage was less than a quarter. Only in Brittany, western Normandy, the Massif Central, le Grand Sud-Ouest and Corsica are there notable concentrations of *cantons* where farmers and farm workers account for more than a third of the active *rural* population. Be this as it may, agricultural activities still have a major influence on the landscape. In 1984, despite a steady decline since 1948, 57% of all land was under some form of agricultural use (Table 4.1)..

The impact of these trends within the agricultural sector has varied regionally, but by and large rural areas have managed to adjust to the changes through a diversification of economic activities (Calmès et al. 1978, Mathieu 1982, SEGESA 1983, Aitchison 1984a). The growth of the tertiary and quaternary sectors, and the establishment of small industries (Chavannes 1975, Bontron *et al.*

Table 4.1 Land use 1948–1984.

Land-use category	1948 Area (1000 km²)	%	1984 Area (1000 km²)	%	% Change
Arable land	189.5	34.4	178.0	32.4	−5.8
Permanent grass	123.0	22.3	123.8	22.5	0.7
Viticulture/horticulture	21.3	3.8	13.4	2.4	−37.1
Forest	111.0	20.1	146.0	26.6	31.5
Unimproved land	60.4	11.0	27.3	5.0	−55.0
Other land uses	45.9	8.3	60.5	11.0	31.8
Total	551.0		549.1		

Sources: L'Etat de l'Environnement 1985, p. 27.
1 Estimates – changes in definition.
2 Total areas based on different calibrations.

1979), has underpinned the rejuvenation of many problem rural regions, and is largely responsible for the move into the countryside of significant numbers of young, upwardly mobile families. In 1982, 16% of the heads of households in rural communes were classified as professionals or white-collar workers (cf. 5% in 1962). Changing attitudes in regards to housing (e.g. *maisons individuelles* in preference to *appartements*), and to the quality of living and working environments in general, are further reasons for the flow of people back into rural areas. In the period 1962–8, 40 000 new dwellings per year were constructed in rural communes (12% of the national total); between 1975 and 1982 the equivalent figures were 125 000 and 30% (Bontron 1985a).

These various trends are clearly of major import when it comes to considering contemporary patterns of land use in rural France. Not only do they complicate existing problems and pressures, they also give rise to new ones. As Bontron (1985b p. 20) has noted 'la tendance à la diversification de la société rurale est une tendance lourde, qui multiplie les enjeux contradictoires sur les formes d'usage de l'espace'. Before considering the ways in which these competing claims on rural land resources are reconciled, it is worth noting that in France, as in other parts of Western Europe, examples can be cited of rural areas that have either been abandoned (*espaces délaissés*) or are still struggling to revitalize shattered economies and societies (*espaces marginaux*), and more dynamic areas where the problem is one of controlling the process of rapid change and development (*espaces convoités* – Etudes rurales 1978). These sharply contrasting situations are responsible for the emergence of an intricate web of policies, legislative codes and regulatory measures which, collectively, have a major impact on the use and look of the land in rural France.

Plans d'occupation des sols and chartes intercommunales

Since 1983, with the major law on decentralization, individual communes and groups of communes have had a much greater control over patterns of land utilization within local areas. As far as individual communes are concerned, this expresses itself most forcibly through the compilation of *documents d'urbanisme – schémas directeurs* and *plans d'occupation des sols* (POS). These documents detail local land-use priorities, both long and short term, and normally seek to harmonize both developmental and conservation objectives. In the context of rural land-use planning POS are of

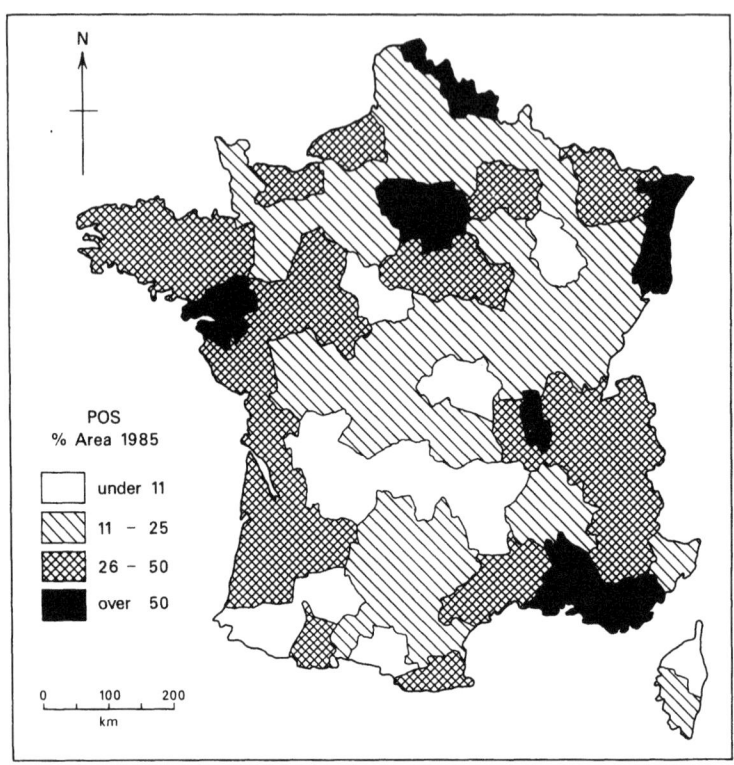

Figure 4.1 *Plans d'occupation des sols*, percentage of area, 1985.

key significance. However, it is not obligatory for communes to draw up such documents and there are notable regional variations in their incidence (Fig. 4.1). Not surprisingly they are most frequently encountered in those *départements* where there is considerable pressure on land resources (e.g. coastal regions and on the fringes of urban–industrial areas). Thus, the percentages of land affected by POS are at their greatest (in excess of 50) in the regions of Ile de France and Alsace, and in the *départements* of Nord, Rhône, Bouches du Rhône, Vaucluse, Var and Loire Atlantique. Less than 10% of the land is subject to such plans in a number of interior *départements* of the Massif Central (Corrèze, Cantal, Haute Loire and Lozère), in Corsica, and in parts of Aquitaine (Dordogne, Pyrénées Atlantiques) and Midi-Pyrénées (Gers, Ariège). Throughout the

Alpine region percentages range between 25 and 50. Although POS may apply to only 26% of the national area (144 000 km^2 in 1984), the areas concerned do have a resident population of 39 million (Ministère de l'Environment 1985).

POS impose limitations on the use that can be made of land within communes, and a broad distinction is initially drawn between 'urban' (U) zones and 'natural' (N) zones. The N zones are further subdivided into NA areas where urban developments will eventually take place, once the necessary infrastructural facilities have been made available; NB zones where some forms of diffuse urbanization are permissible; NC zones where the needs of agricultural or other economic activities (e.g. quarrying, mining) are of paramount importance, and where there is a strong presumption against unrelated forms of construction and development; and ND zones where the emphasis is on protecting sites, habitats and landscapes of great historical, ecological, or scenic interest. In terms of their respective areas, the U zones account for 9% of the total, NA for 4.1%, NB for 3.4%, NC for 51.4% and ND for 32.1%. Since 1983 the *conseils municipaux* and mayors of communes have had important powers in terms of prospective patterns of land use, and it is they who control the system through the vetting of development applications. Individual POS vary in sophistication and detail, however, and for many small rural communes they are often simply zonation maps accompanied by general land-use provisions.

Though the compilation of POS are the responsibility of individual communes, it is evident that the promotion of broader development initiatives at a micro-regional level requires a degree of co-operation between groups of communes. It was this realization that underpinned the system of *Plans d'Aménagement Rural* (PAR), established by decree in 1970 (MacKenzie 1983). Relating specifically to rural areas, these plans were drawn up by collections of communes – on average 36 communes – with similar problems and aspirations. Although the plans themselves have been criticized for being mere 'orientation' or discussion documents, their preparation did much to promote local interest and participation in the development process. Between 1971 and 1982 a total of 260 PAR were formally constituted. Following the 1983 decentralization law, however, the system of PAR has been replaced by that of *chartes intercommunales*. Whereas PAR were imposed from above, with projects for specified areas being launched by agencies of the state, intercommunal charters are meant to emerge spontaneously from local initiatives (Association

Nationale pour le Développement Local et les Pays 1986). Relating to all areas – not solely rural – charters can identify a variety of different management structures and systems of finance. More broadly based, constitutionally, they can also involve outside agencies and associations (e.g. professional bodies). Once formally structured, intercommunal units can establish contracts with their *départements*, their *régions*, or the state, to finance particular projects. As planning documents, charters also detail medium-term development priorities, as well as specific programmes for action. Should particular groups of communes forming charters feel the need to accord a high priority to the protection of vulnerable landscapes and habitats they can, if they so wish, seek official recognition as *parcs naturels régionaux* (see below). This latter option has not yet been exercised, but a number of communes in parts of three existing parks (Forêt d'Orient, Volcans d'Auvergne, and Pilat) have implemented charters.

Four years after its initiation the system of intercommunal charters has attracted considerable interest, and by August 1986 nearly 7000 communes had formed themselves into 263 planning units. Of these units, the majority (60%) are located in just six *régions* – Languedoc-Roussillon (37), Midi-Pyrénées (33), Rhône-Alpes (30), Bourgogne (29), Poitou-Charentes (18) and Alsace (11). To explain this pattern of concentration it can be noted that in a number of these areas administrations have vigorously sought to promote the notion of intercommunal charters, sometimes to the extent of giving financial support to communes wishing to engage in preliminary feasibility studies. In addition, it has been suggested that positive attitudes on the part of local political leaders have reinforced '*une pratique déjà ancienne de la solidarité intercommunale*' (Ministère de l'Agriculture 1987). The fact that many of the commune concerned had previously associated together in PAR underlines the significance of this latter point. The number of communes within individual charters varies greatly, ranging from 3 (e.g. Vallée de la Castellane, Pyrénées Orientales, with a population of 518) to 131 (Erve et Vegre, Mayenne and Sarthe, 90 000 inhabitants). As far as the specific goals of the various local planning units are concerned, considerable reference is made to such long-standing rural issues as the continuing need to improve landholding structures (e.g. *remembrement*) and land productivity (e.g. drainage and irrigation), to take full advantage of forestry (e.g. downstream wood-processing industries), to establish workshops and small industrial estates for local craftsmen and artisans, to stem the decline in the quality and range of social services, and to encourage environmentally sensitive forms of tourism. More recently, the problem of overproduction in agriculture and its implications for the farming community at large (*la déprise agricole*) has caused many charters to reappraise the whole question of diversification and alternative land-use strategies. It is too early to offer an overall assessment of the effectiveness of the charter system, but in November 1986 the *Comité Interministériel de Développement et d'Aménagement Rural* strongly reasserted its belief in this form of integrated local planning, as did a recent ministerial discussion document on *l'aménagement du territoire* (Guichard 1986).

Agriculture, forestry and the landscape

Although farmers and farm workers account for just 8% of the total active population, they are responsible for the management of nearly 60% of the nation's land. Since the 1950s, agricultural landscapes in many parts of France have been totally transformed as farmers, supported by a galaxy of subsidies, grants and loans, have sought to modernize and to improve profit margins and incomes (Wright 1964, Gervais *et al.* 1965, Houée 1972, Girard *et al.* 1977). In less-favoured mountain areas concern has focused on the deteriorating quality of grazing lands and the need to encourage younger farmers to take up abandoned holdings, if necessary on a part-time basis. Elsewhere efforts have been made to rationalize field systems, to increase the sizes of farms, and to stimulate innovation through the adoption of new technologies and progressive marketing systems. These various initiatives have been remarkably successful, for in just a few decades a traditional, largely peasant, economy has been radically restructured into a dynamic, highly capitalized and productive industry.

During the 1950s and 1960s agriculture was accorded an overwhelmingly high priority in planning and political circles and underpinned development strategies for most rural areas. Between 1949 and 1959, 1.5 million hectares of wasteland were recuperated and brought into agricultural production, and the area of fallow fell by two-thirds. Changes were especially dramatic in those areas where *sociétés d'aménagement régionaux* had been established. The eight mixed economy companies set up between 1955 and 1962 helped to create new agricultural landscapes in Aquitaine, the Massif Central, Languedoc-Roussillon, Provence, Corsica and in the Champagne region of north-eastern France. Forests were planted, scrublands were cleared and reclaimed for arable and grassland farming, vast irrigation networks were constructed and great tracts of land were drained. At the same time, landholding systems were rationalized, and new farms created. As more and more land came on to the market, partly as a result of high retirement rates in the farming community (stimulated further by a special retirement allowance – *indemnité viagère de départ*) and the continuing rural exodus, there was clearly a need to regulate the whole process of land transfers. The *loi d'orientation agricole* of 1960 was particularly important in this regard, for among other things it resulted in the formation of land procurement and distribution agencies (SAFER), and in efforts to avoid the emergence of holdings that were too small to provide a living for young aspiring farmers. In addition, ceilings on the sizes of holdings were instituted at departmental level to avoid the concentration of land in the hands of fewer and fewer farmers. In both cases the social goal has been to establish and sustain a nation of viable family farms. Not surprisingly, as in other areas of the world, these attempts to exert controls on patterns of land ownership have generated some tensions and conflicts (Rey 1982).

Between 1960 and 1975 state intervention in the development process was principally expressed through the delimitation of zones experiencing particular problems and warranting special attention. These included *zones spéciales d'action rurale* (1960), *zones d'économie montagnarde* (1961), *zones de rénovation rurales* (1967), and *zones agricoles défavorisées hors montagne* (1975). Although concerned with rural development in general, the structure and viability of farming systems continued to be a key issue within these various programmes. Although the needs of agriculture are still recognized in more recent rural planning policies there has been a notable change of emphasis. Of fundamental importance at the present time is the role that agriculture plays as a guardian of the 'natural' landscape. This expresses itself in two contrasting ways. First, it is recognized that agricultural land is under threat from various forms of development – urban encroachment, the expansion of infrastructure, and the demands of industry and the tourist trade being the most obvious examples. Accordingly, more and more reference is now made to the controls that communes and regional administrations can exert on the pattern and pace of land-use change, particularly in pressurized areas (e.g. coastal and peri-urban zones). In 1954 urban areas and infrastructures claimed 7% of the national territory, by 1975 the figure was 14%. The annual loss of agricultural land currently averages 50 000 ha. Between 1978 and 1983 the area of agricultural land in many *départements* to the west of Paris and along the Mediterranean coast fell by more than 2.5% – the greatest reduction being returned by Var (-15.2%). Other areas recording high losses, but in this case largely because of the abandonment of land, were Corsica and Alpes-de-Haute-Provence.

A second aspect of the landscape debate is the impact that changing agricultural practices can have on fragile habitats and ecosystems. The polemic has not been as vigorously pursued as it has in Britain, but none the less attention has been drawn to such matters as the loss of wetlands as a result of drainage schemes (e.g. Marais Poitevin – FPNF 1984), to the increased use of chemical compounds, and to the loss of fauna and flora that occurs with the removal of hedges, earth banks (*talus*), watercourses and trees in programmes of *remembrement*. Criticisms of this latter activity were well founded up until 1975. Brittany alone had lost 60 000 km of banked hedges and 5 million trees in ten years of *débocagisation* (Flatrès 1986). However, a modification to the Rural Code in 1975, and a growing awareness of dangers to the environment (including soil erosion), led to a reorientation of the whole process of *remembrement*, with emphasis being placed not only on its role in improving the efficiency of agricultural operations (through the creation of larger field units), but also its obligations in regard to nature conservation. Now, all land consolidation projects are obliged to carry out an impact evaluation, and it is the responsibility of the local organization controlling the exercise – *la commission communale d'aménagement foncier* – to ensure that adequate consideration is given to environmental and ecological implications. Thus, constraints may be placed on which trees or hedgerows have to be preserved. At the same time new plantings may also be encouraged (Mills 1983; Luginbuhl & Mortain 1986). In certain cases a *remembrement* may also form part of a more integrated rural land-use plan, including a POS. Such an approach is referred to as *remembrement-aménagement* (Ministère de l'Agriculture 1986). To date, the process of *remembrement* has affected nearly 40% of all agricultural land (12.5 million hectares). In addition to Brittany, particularly large numbers of operations have been undertaken in the regions of Centre, Champagne-Ardenne and Picardie. Of course, in these latter, largely open-field, regions the ecological impact of *remembrement* has been less controversial.

Part of the agricultural modernization process has been a general intensification of systems of production. This expresses itself most pointedly in the increased use that is made of inorganic fertilizers and pest control chemicals. Needless to say, inputs of these compounds are at their highest in the rich cereal-growing districts of the Paris Basin. Here each hectare of cultivated land on average receives over 300 kg of artificial fertilizers (N,P,K), and the pollution of rivers by nitrates is recognized as a serious and growing problem. In 1978 the agricultural industry used 2 million tonnes of nitrates, by 1984 the figure was 2.32 million tonnes. During the same period dramatic increases were also recorded in the application of fungicides, herbicides and pesticides.

Whereas the process of agricultural intensification in general is a matter of some concern to the environmental and conservation movement in France, it is of interest to note that the loss of moorland habitats through reclamation or overgrazing has not been a major issue. Indeed the main problem in mountain and upland regions has been the abandonment and neglect of grazing areas, and not their conversion to improved pasture lands. Unlike in the UK where agricultural subsidies and grants for farmers in less-favoured regions – especially large farmers – have been blamed for the destruction of moorlands, in France the various support measures are seen as being of vital significance in maintaining existing systems of production. In this regard it has to be said that the French Ministry of Agriculture has implemented a much more sophisticated policy which favours small farmers, and which is also sensitive to differences in physical environments. Thus, compensatory allowances for livestock are graded, with differential rates for 'high mountain', 'middle mountain' and 'piedmont' zones (Smith 1985); the special attributes of the Mediterranean mountain zone – *'montagne sèche'* – are also recognized and catered for.

Not surprisingly, an issue that has given rise to heated debate within French farming circles during recent years stems from the need on the part of EEC member states to cut levels of production in a range of agricultural commodities. As far as patterns of land use are concerned various scenarios have been proffered, some more dramatic than others. Over the next ten years, some foresee the abandonment of 5 million hectares of agricultural land, for others scrub vegetation is predicted to take over a further 7 million hectares. At present areas of this type (*friches, landes, macquis, garrigues*, etc.) claim between 3 and 5 million hectares (depending on which data source is used). In view of the uncertainties of the situation (i.e. the precise nature of future EEC policy) and the conflicting character of available information on the matter, it is not possible at this stage to offer really meaningful predictions on the likely outcome. It is certain, however, that virtually all sections of French agriculture will be affected – the recent collapse of land prices is but one manifestation of the problem – and that substantial adjustments will have to be made in land-use practices. Alternative land-use strategies are now being earnestly explored (Plassard 1985, GREP 1985).

The forests of France constitute a major element in the landscape. They extend over 14.8 million hectares, and account for some 27% of the total surface area. In certain *départements* the percentage cover exceeds 45 – Landes (63%), Vosges (48%), Gironde (47%), Var (46%) and Jura (46%). Proportions are at their lowest – under 15% – in the bocage regions of Brittany and Normandy (Fig. 4.2). Forests vary greatly in composition from one part of the country to another, but nationally deciduous species (*feuillus*) predominate (8.5 million hectares). The area under conifers (*résineux*) is 4 million hectares.

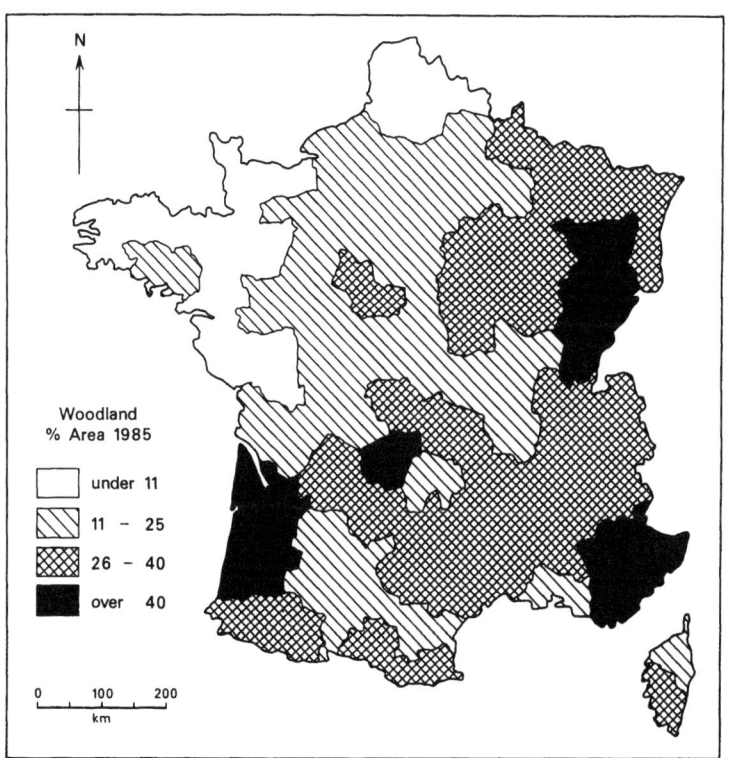

Figure 4.2 Woodland, percentage of area, 1985.

Given their economic, ecological and scenic importance, the many pressures to which they are subjected, and the ease with which they can be so easily destroyed, a number of regulatory codes have been enacted to ensure a high degree of protection to woods and forests. In the *Code Forestier* a distinction is drawn between those forests that belong to the state (*forêts domaniales de l'Etat*), public bodies and local authorities (mainly communes), and those that are operated privately. Approximately 27% of all forests fall into the first of these categories, and since 1964 the state forests have been managed by the Office National des Forêts (ONF). This body can also take on responsibility for woodlands owned by communes, but where this does not apply groups of communes are encouraged to form management syndicates. Overall supervision and control of planting and cutting operations, however, lies with the Ministry of Agriculture. Apart from its concern with commercial issues, the Ministry is charged with the important task of assessing the impact of these operations on local environments (e.g. the scenic implications of afforestation, the loss of amenity woodlands in the neighbourhood of large towns, the dangers of erosion in mountain areas following deforestation). Nearly three-quarters of all forests and woods in France are privately owned. Following a 1963 law, it is the 1.6 million proprietors of these forests who are held responsible for their careful management. A third of all private forests have had management plans formally approved by regional administrations, and a large number of operators have joined together to form *groupements forestiers*. To co-ordinate a more rational integration of agriculture and forestry certain *départements* have, following a special law in 1971, identified *périmètres d'actions forestières*. This procedure complements one established in 1922, which offers a high degree of protection to certain forests of great environmental or amenity significance (*forêts de protection*). All cutting operations in forests have to be formally approved either by the Ministry of Agriculture or by *commissaires de la République*, and each application must be accompanied by an environmental impact study. If accepted, the programme is subject to a special tax.

Each year vast areas of forest are lost as a result of fires and storms. In 1976, 88 000 ha were destroyed by fire, and in 1983 the Mediterranean regions of France alone saw 49 000 ha disappear. Apart from their cost to the nation, these catastrophes rob communities of valuable amenity areas, and conservationists of scientifically important habitats. Though climatic conditions are clearly of overriding importance (Wrathall 1985), it is evident that the ravages of fire have been facilitated in certain localities by a general deterioration in the level and quality of woodland management (e.g. the non-clearance of undergrowth). To add to this depressing state of affairs, over recent years the condition of forests, particularly in the north-east of France, has been seriously affected by atmospheric pollution. In Alsace-Lorraine and Franche-Comté nearly 20% of public forests have been badly affected by acid rain.

Coniferous plantations have come in for some criticism from certain sections of society; the claim being that such species are alien and basically unattractive. This criticism needs, however, to be set against the fact that conifers account for less than a third of all woodland and dominate the landscape in only a few areas (e.g. Landes). To this should be added the further argument that France has to import large quantities of timber to satisfy the demands of the paper, construction, furniture and other industries.

Landscape and nature conservation

A fundamental feature of many of the policies and codes of practice that have thus far been considered is an underlying concern with the quality of the environment. Although the central objective of many of these policies is to promote economic growth, this is not to be achieved without due regard to the impact of proposed developments on sites of great scenic, historical, or scientific interest. Apart from those already described, there are other laws and land management systems that focus specifically on the increasingly important issue of landscape and habitat protection (Chicoye & Derkenne 1983).

In France the first major law to be concerned with the protection of particular sites was passed in 1930. This piece of legislation defines a procedure whereby communes may accord a degree of protection to areas by designating them as either *sites classés* or *sites inscrits*. The first of these designations imposes extremely strict controls on the use that is made of such sites, and only in exceptional circumstances will ministerial approval be given for any changes in existing practices. By 1984 the total number of *sites classés* had reached 2337 (Fig. 4.3). The second of the designations gives a reduced form of protection and has been applied to nearly 5000 sites. Conscious of the fact that the unique attributes of certain landscapes of major national significance (e.g. Baie du Mont-St-Michel, Massif des Alpilles, Gorges du Verdon) needed to be more effectively safeguarded,

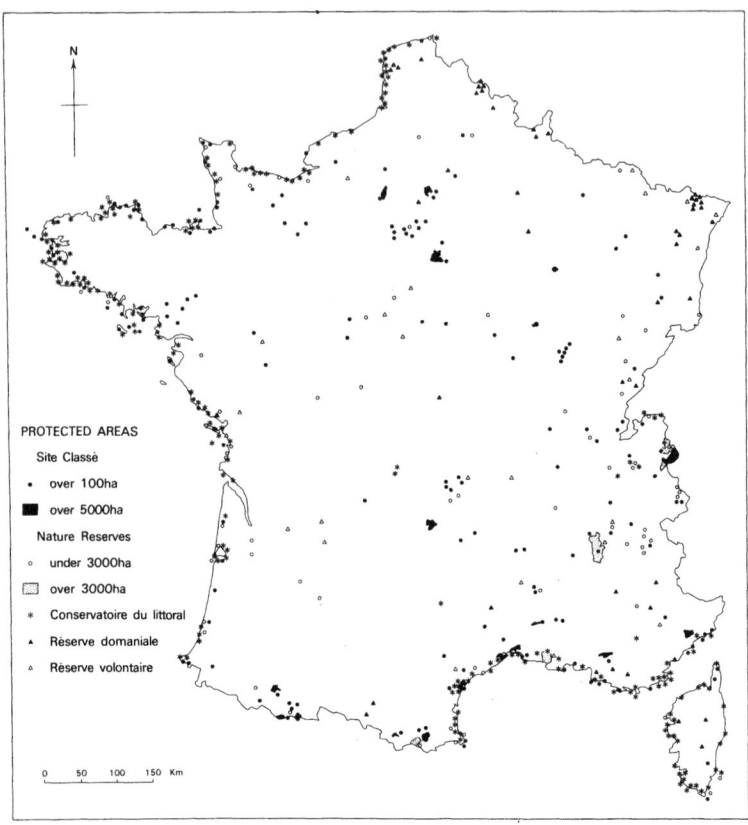

Figure 4.3 Protected areas.

the state, in 1982, embarked upon conservation and management programmes relating to *les grands sites d'intérêt national*. Strangely, it was not until 1961 that the law of 1930 was actually used for the designation of nature reserves. For thirty years interest centred solely on 'natural' monuments, picturesque landscapes, and sites with certain historical or artistic associations. Although 38 *réserves naturelles* were eventually established in the years that followed, it was only with the enactment of a new law in 1976 – *La Loi sur la Protection de la Nature* – that the process of designation gathered momentum. By the end of 1987 it is hoped that the number of nature reserves will have reached 100; at the beginning of the year there were 83.

These reserves cover an area of some 1000 km^2 (cf. 17 000 km^2 for the 5130 SSSI and NNRs of the UK) and vary greatly in size. Just over 70% are less than 500 ha in extent, whereas 13 exceed 2000 ha (Brochot & Bontron 1986). The main concentrations of sites are to be found in the Alpine *départements* of Savoie and Haute Savoie – around Mont Blanc and within the national parks of La Vanoise and Ecrins (Fig. 4.3). Needless to say, it is the dramatic glaciers, cirques, ridges, ravines and caves, together with a rich array of rare alpine flora and fauna (e.g. chamois and bouquetin), that make the reserves in these regions of such major importance. As to the largest of all the French nature reserves, this extends across the high limestone plateau of the Vercors overlooking the great Alpine trough to the south of Grenoble. The reserve, which was designated in 1985, actually lies within a regional nature park of the same name (see below) and covers some 17 000 ha. There are a number of reserves in the Pyrénées and the Jura, but in the whole of the Massif Central there are just three (including the limestone gorges of the Ardèche).

Of the 27 reserves dotted along the French coastline the most extensive is the Camargue (13 000 ha). Also set within a regional nature park, this wetland site of international repute only just avoided a major drainage and reclamation programme in the 1930s. With its halophytic vegetation and the watercourses of the Rhône delta the Camargue is a breeding sanctuary for large populations of migratory wildfowl. Elsewhere the coastal reserves include small islands off Brittany and Corsica, as well as lagoons, saltmarshes, estuaries, cliffs and sand-dune systems (e.g. the Landes of Aquitaine). To add to the variety, inland a range of sites have been designated, including broad-leaved woodlands, chalk meadows, marshlands, and areas of rich moorland vegetation.

In drawing attention to the rather slow pace at which nature reserves have been established in France, it is worth noting that the process of designation can be long and complex. After proposals concerning the possible creation of a reserve have been received (normally from within the administrative system or from local nature protection groups), *commissaires de la République* have to organize public inquiries, seek advice from the *Conseil National de la Protection de la Nature*, and then, possibly in the face of strong opposition from landowners and others, seek approval from the very highest level (the *Conseil d'Etat*) to pass an order officially recognizing the reserve. As with SSSIs in the UK, lists of prohibited activities are prepared with a view to maintaining the special character of designated sites. For rural communes experiencing economic difficulties constraints on the use that may be made of certain tracts of land can be frustrating – particularly if, as has been the case in numerous mountain and coastal areas, opportunities have been lost to develop tourist facilities. In total contrast to this type of situation, however, there are localities where nature reserves have been designated not so much to protect unique habitats but rather to prevent other changes from taking place. Thus, in the Pyrénées it is known that communes have established reserves simply to prevent outsiders (would-be builders of holiday homes) from settling in the area. Given this contentious state of affairs it is perhaps not surprising that only 20% of the land classed as nature reserves is under private ownership. Nearly 38% lies in the public domain (especially the inland marine reserves), and 42% belongs to communes. As far as private property is concerned the 1976 law does allow groups of landowners to take the initiative in establishing their own '*réserves volontaires*'. To date, however, less than 20 schemes of this type have been promoted. Finally, within the forests managed by the ONF, there are now some 60 reserves (*réserves biologiques domaniales*), covering an area of 4300 ha (Fig. 4.3).

One reason for the small number of designated nature reserves is the limited amount of information that has been available on the location and character of different ecosystems. Thus, it was only in 1982 the *Direction de la Protection de la Nature* commissioned a national inventory of *Zones Naturelles d'Intérêt Ecologique, Faunistique et Floristique*. When complete, this data base will be used to launch a new conservation initiative.

France was late in establishing a system of national parks, the first – La Vanoise – being formally designated in 1963, and the last of six as recently as 1979 (Aitchison 1984 – Fig. 4.4). As far as land-use management is concerned the most distinctive feature is the delimitation within each park of a central area where conservation and research interests take full priority. In these zones, which *in toto* cover some 3500 km^2, all forms of development that might disturb the physical and biological character of the areas concerned are prohibited. This is not the case in those parts of the parks that lie around the core regions (referred to as *zones périphériques*), and which extend over 9000 km^2. Here the aim is to encourage a more broadly based and integrated approach, with emphasis being placed not only on conservation but also on measures that will increase employment opportunities and improve the quality of services for local communities and visitors. It is to be appreciated that the five largest parks all lie within the main mountain massifs, and have

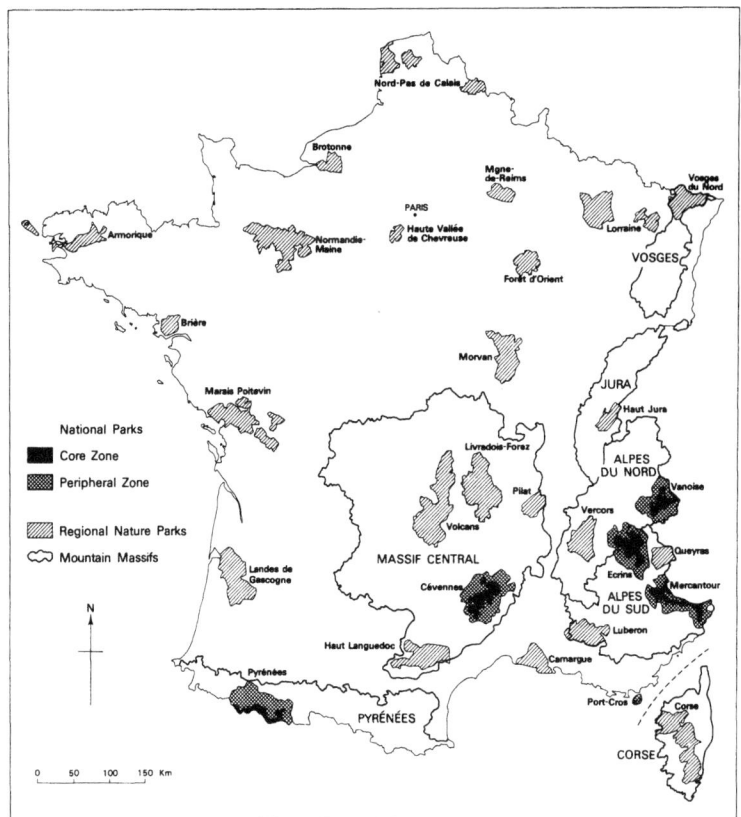

Figure 4.4 National and regional parks.

long been recognized as disadvantaged areas. That said, between 1975 and 1982 the resident population of the six parks has increased by 4% to a total figure of 153 000. Over recent years the system of parks has been subjected to severe criticism, partly because of the incoherence of policies for the peripheral zones, and partly because of problems at a local level (Besson 1983, Vadrot 1983, Leynaud 1985). The last park to be designated – Mercantour – encountered major difficulties with local communities (hence the tortuous nature of its boundaries), and a park proposed for the Ariège region of the Pyrénées has had to be abandoned.

Much more favourably received, and much more widely implemented, has been the system of regional nature parks (*parcs naturels régionaux* – Morineaux 1982, Aitchison 1984). At present there are 23 parks of this type. They are to be found in all parts of France (Fig. 4.4), cover approximately 32 000 km² (5% of the national territory), and have a resident population of nearly 1.5 million. Regional parks accord closely with current thinking on the appropriate model for micro-regional planning, and it is for this reason that the law on decentralization specifically allows groups of communes to draw up *chartes intercommunales* that lead to the establishment of local parks. Without entering into detailed discussion, it can be noted that parks are normally created in areas where there is a recognized need to protect unique landscapes and cultural traditions, whilst at the same time promoting economic growth and improving social services. Concern for the environment expresses itself in the establishment of nature reserves, in the rehabilitation of abandoned areas, in the provision of advice on the renovation of traditional buildings, and, more generally, in the careful scrutiny and monitoring of development plans and projects. Interestingly, in perhaps the most highly pressurized of all the rural areas of France – the countryside around Paris – there is just one nature park – the *Haute Vallée de Chevreuse*. However, a degree of protection to the landscape in this region (Ile de France) is accorded through the designation of *zones naturelles d'équilibre*. In the six zones that have been identified – Plaine de Versailles, Plaine de France, Plateaux de Brie, Plateaux du Sud, Hurepoix and Vexin – planners seek to control the nature and location of urban developments, to protect important sites (e.g. forests and lakes), and to promote opportunities for open-air recreational facilities.

Finally, by way of summary, it can be noted that in 1984 nearly 13% (69 300 km²) of all land in France was subject to very strict development controls. This figure is based on the areas of nature reserves, public forests, acquisitions of CELRL (see next section), the cores of national parks, ND zones of POS and *sites classés*. If other less heavily safeguarded areas are taken into account (e.g. NC agricultural zones of POS and other forests) then the total protected area increases to 169 600 km² – 31% of the national territory.

Le littoral

The French coastline extends for some 5500 km and constitutes a highly coveted and pressurized environment. In 1977 it was estimated that only 49% of this fringe zone remained essentially 'undeveloped'. Elsewhere, growth in tourism had led to the linear expansion of resort areas and to the creation of new pleasure complexes (e.g. La Grande Motte, Cap d'Agde and Port-Camargue in Languedoc–Roussillon). In addition, the attractions of coastal locations for those seeking holiday and retirement homes have contributed towards a general, and much criticized, increase in dispersed forms of settlement (e.g. in Brittany – Flatrès 1986). Likewise, the development of *'zones industrialo-portuaires'* and other sites (e.g. at Marseille-Fos, Le Havre, Calais-Dunkerque and La Basse Loire) for oil refineries, petrochemical, steel-making and engineering complexes, as well as nuclear power stations, has transformed significant stretches of coastline. Not surprisingly, given the intensity and diversity of activities that exist, population densities in many coastal regions are of a high order. Coastal communes have a total resident population in excess of 5 million (10% of the national figure on 3% of the area), with densities often above 250 persons per square kilometre. During the tourist season, however, this latter ratio can increase fourfold.

With the quickening pace of change, and in particular the need to protect the remaining sections of 'undeveloped' coast from insensitive and environmentally damaging forms of development, local authorities and the state have sought to exert rigorous controls over patterns of land use. Since the early 1960s a number of regulatory measures and management strategies have been adopted which relate specifically to coastal areas. The first major intervention was the creation of *missions interministérielles d'aménagement*. The remit of several of these organizations was to promote co-ordinated development programmes for specific coastal areas, in association with local authorities. The work of the *'mission'* for the Languedoc-Roussillon (established in 1963, and replaced in 1982 by a *'syndicat mixte'*) has been particularly vigorous (and contentious – Durrieu 1973), transforming in dramatic fashion the landscape, economy and society of this once neglected part of the Midi (Verlaque 1987). Similar *'missions'* were formed for coastal sites in Aquitaine, Corsica and Fos-Etang de Berre. Recognizing a need for a national policy, the government, in 1971, called for a report on coastal planning problems and priorities (Piquard 1974). Among its conclusions was the recognition that the planned development of the coast could not be left to individual local authorities through the operation of the system of POS. Besides being inadequately resourced, individual communes were only responsible for very small lengths of coast – on average 3 km. At this level of action and decision-making, integrated strategies relating not only to longer stretches of coast, but also embracing functionally associated hinterlands (*l'arrière pays*), could not be promoted. Subsequent responses to this criticism include the preparation of plans for coastal areas at regional level (*schémas régionaux du littoral*) and plans for more local areas which also take into consideration the use of coastal waters (*schémas d'aptitudes et d'utilisations de la mer*). The former include plans for the regions of Haute Normandie and Corsica, the latter for such areas as the Rade de Brest, Pertuis-Charentais and Baie de Saint-Brieuc.

A further direct result of the Piquard report was the creation in 1975 of the Conservatoire de l'Espace littoral et des Rivages lacustres (CELRL). This public body was specifically established to safeguard sites and habitats of great ecological value by purchasing land in coastal areas (and land bordering inland lakes). Such land can be acquired through normal market negotiations, but if necessary CELRL can expropriate areas or exercise a pre-emptive right of purchase. In theory, this land becomes inalienable and safe from damaging developments. Although CELRL delegates the management of its properties to local authorities, to other public bodies, or to specially constituted associations, it still defines the basic rules and regulations concerning the way in which they are to be looked after. By the end of 1984 CELRL had acquired (with finance from the state and private donations) 181 properties, covering 26 000 ha, and extending along some 324 km of coast (Fig. 4.3). The main areas are to be found in Corsica (8014 ha), and the *départements* of Bouches-du-Rhône (4814 ha), Hérault (2069 ha), Charente-Maritime (1292 ha), Pas-de-Calais (1104 ha) and Pyrénées-Orientales (1055 ha). Inland, purchases include a significant area around the lake of Sainte Croix de Verdon (Alpes-de-Haute-Provence).

Strict control over land management practices in coastal areas of high scenic or scientific interest can also be achieved through the delimitation by *départements* of *périmètres sensibles*. Although this system of regulation can be adopted for inland regions it is along coastal fringes that it has been most widely applied. Individual *départements* can acquire land within the delimited zones and to do so can impose a special tax (*taxe départementale d'espaces verts*). By January 1985, of the 26 coastal *départements*, all but three (Seine Maritime, Eure and Pyrénées Orientales) had delineated *périmètres sensibles*. The total area covered by this designation amounted to 94 500 km^2, with the largest expanses (over 6000 km^2) occurring in the *départements* of Pas de Calais, Somme, Ille et Villaine, Charentes Maritimes, Aude, Hérault, and Var. Within the protected perimeters it is possible for *départements* to identify *zones de préemption* – to which the public are normally given access – and 'protected zones' where land use is very strictly controlled. This latter regulation is applied most particularly in areas that are not already subject to POS or *schémas directeurs*. In summarizing statutory instruments for the protection of the 'undeveloped' coasts, it should be recalled that in many areas special nature reserves have been designated to help conserve a range of unique but vulnerable habitats, together with their associated fauna and flora (see above).

Given the range of pressures to which coastal areas are subjected, and the mixture of policies and regulatory systems that have emerged to control the rate and pattern of land-use change within such regions, a law was passed in January 1986 which seeks to co-ordinate and clarify planning aims and objectives. Taking account of the strengthened powers of local authorities, this initiative stresses the urgency of strong controls on urbanization (both concentrated and diffuse), extractive industries (e.g. gravel workings), land reclamation schemes (e.g. construction of marinas), and the disposal of waste products and pollutants; furthermore it emphasizes the need to improve the level of public access to beaches. As far as the process of urbanization is concerned a central proposal is that narrow, linear developments should be avoided and that every effort should be made to direct growth into the hinterland. In addition, where urban areas do expand along the coast, authorities are expected to ensure that these are sensitively interlaced with stretches of open space. The law on the development and protection of coasts complements a similar, integrating law relating to the equally problematic issues of land use and socio-economic change in mountain areas.

La montagne française

Whereas in coastal regions the essential problems stem from excessive and conflicting pressures on a confined resource, in the mountains the situation is much more varied and complex. Although conditions have changed over more recent years, many parts of the mountain zone are still suffering the consequences of a century of population decline and economic malaise (Béteille 1981, Aitchison & Bontron 1984, 1987). During this time the competitive weakness of pastoral farming systems, the demise of small-scale industries, the difficulties posed by a demanding physical environment, and the attractions of '*la région parisienne*' undermined confidence and resulted in a debilitating *'désertification'* of the mountain provinces. Not until the 1960s, however, was it accepted that *'la zone de montagne'* warranted separate and special attention (Barruet & Vaudois 1985, Knafou 1985). The zone itself was first delimited in 1961 on altitudinal and topographic criteria, but with shifts in policy these have since been widened to take into account other demographic and socio-economic factors. At the present time the mountain regions cover approximately 21% of the national area and have a permanent resident population of some 3.6 million. As far as comprehensive planning measures are concerned the key initial initiative was associated with the policy of 'rural renovation' in 1968. Thereafter a whole series of measures relating specifically to the support of farming communities were adopted (Rapport au Gouvernement 1974). These included compensatory allowances for livestock farmers (headage payments for cattle and sheep), grants to encourage the establishment of young farmers, and funds to promote landholding and stock management associations (*'associations pastorales fonciers'* and *'groupements pastoraux'*). With the coming of the EEC directive relating to farming in less-favoured areas in 1975 the appropriateness of these various measures was reaffirmed. In terms of agricultural land use the central aim is to halt the degeneration and abandonment of mountain grazings (e.g. *alpages*). Not only does this process have implications for the productivity of livestock farming systems, it is also of considerable environmental importance, particularly in terms of erosion, the hazards of landslips and avalanches, as well as of mountain ecology and scenery. In 1977 a national directive on the management and protection of *'la montagne française'* called for a more holistic approach to planning in these regions, and detailed a whole series of issues that needed to be taken into consideration. One particularly critical feature that was stressed concerned the land-use conflicts that can arise as a result of inadequately controlled tourist developments. In this regard the directive instituted a procedure relating to *'Unités Touristiques Nouvelles'*. This requires all large-scale projects (e.g. ski complexes) to be carefully scrutinized, with special reference being made in impact studies to the consequences for agriculture (e.g. the loss of more productive grazing lands in valley bottoms) and conservation interests. In practice, the procedure has succeeded in reducing conflicts between agriculturalists, local communities and developers, and in numerous instances has resulted in the reformulation of plans to accommodate particular grievances. Over the years various reports on mountain areas have drawn attention to the diversity of conditions that prevail, and the need to adopt developmental strategies that are sensitive to regional differences in the physical and human geographies of the areas concerned. This view was strongly emphasized in a very detailed and thoughtful report presented to the *Assemblée Nationale* in 1982 (Besson 1982). This report reviewed the situation in the mountain zone, re-emphasized its long-standing and continuing problems, and recommended that planned development and protection should be devolved to committees representing each of seven massifs – Alpes du Nord, Alpes du Sud, Corse, Jura, Massif Central, Pyrénées and Vosges (Fig. 4.4). The actual bounds of individual massifs enclose the mountains proper, together with surrounding areas; the aim being to identify planning zones that are functionally meaningful (i.e. in terms of social and economic interactions). In January 1985, after a critical consideration of a wide-ranging *projet de loi* (Ministère de l'Agriculture 1985), the government implemented a new law relating to the 'development and protection' of mountain areas. Because of its breadth and radical nature, this law was described as '*la première grande loi d'aménagement du territoire*'. As far as land-use patterns in montain areas are concerned the law confirms the need to harmonize conflicting interests regarding major developments, and stresses that decisions on such matters are to be taken by those living and working in the various massifs – and not, as so often in the past, by outsiders (Cognat 1973). Financial support for appropriate initiatives is drawn from general funds – *Fonds Interministériel de Développement et d'Aménagement Rural* (FIDAR) and *Fonds Interministériel d'Aménagement du Territoire* (FIAT) – and from a special fund relating solely to the massifs – *Fonds d'Intervention pour l'Autodéveloppement en Montagne* (FIAM). For the period of the ninth National Plan (1984–8), FIDAR, FIAT and various ministries have allocated FF 2.2 thousand million, and FIAM has an annual budget approaching FF 45 million. So far the Massif Central has been awarded by far the greatest share of this investment (FF 1.1 thousand million), followed by the Alpes du Sud (FF 346 million), Alpes du Nord (FF 262 million) and Pyrénées (FF 253 million). The law makes special reference to the problems facing farming communities (over a third of full-time holdings being classified as 'marginal') and again proposes measures to enhance the productivity of the pastoral farming economy through improvements to grazing lands. However, given more recent developments at EEC level, particularly in regard to systems of agricultural support, and the expectation that large areas of land will have to be withdrawn from production altogether (see page 85), the future for farmers in the *Haute Montagne* and *Montagne Sèche* does not look too promising. As in other upland areas of Western Europe it seems likely that farmers (many of whom are already multiple-job holders) will be encouraged (through special incentives) to see themselves more as guardians of the landscape, operating traditional low-input systems of stock management. In view of these changes, increasing emphasis could be placed on the role of forestry in mountain areas, both as a national resource and as a generator of extra income and employment. At the present time forests in the mountain zone cover 4.3 million hectares – almost a third of all French forests and a third of the mountain zone itself.

Conclusion

Given its territorial and political significance, it is perhaps surprising that there has never been a single ministry or agency responsible for the well-being of the French rural landscape (using the term landscape in its broadest sense). As the foregoing discussion has demonstrated, the use that is made of land is the concern of many different bodies. This proliferation of structures, together with the associated profusion of policies, laws and regulatory instruments, has created problems of overlapping and diverging interests; interests which mirror the equally diverse set of demands that are currently being placed on land resources in rural areas. That said, it has to be appreciated that significant efforts have been made to streamline the system and to open up opportunities for liaison and co-ordination. The establishment of DATAR (*Délégation à Aménagement du Territoire et à l'Action Régionale*) in 1963 was a notable step forward. Although not solely concerned with rural areas, this interministerial organization serves as an integrating and animating focus for a wide range of regional development programmes. DATAR has a particularly important role to play in the establishment of *contrats de plan Etat-regions*. These plans have been drawn up in the light of priorities identified within the ninth national plan, and are a means whereby state and regional goals are harmonized and funded. The plans themselves vary from region to region, but as far as rural areas are concerned special consideration is given to the seven mountain massifs, *zones rurale fragiles de plaine* (Aitchison & Bontron 1984), and problem coastal zones. Since 1983 political decentralization has also given a powerful impetus to integrated planning at a micro-regional level, with communes and groups of communes now having much more say in the way that local resources (particularly land) could and should be used.

Despite the economic crises of the 1970s and the difficulties that still have to be faced in reducing unemployment levels, there can be no doubt that conditions in much of rural France have improved considerably over the last ten years. This improvement is due, in no small measure, to the impressive array of support and control mechanisms that have been experimented with, and refined, in the never-ending struggle to develop and protect *l'espace rural français*.

References

Aitchison, J. W. 1984a. Coefficients of specialization and diversification: employment in rural France. *Area* **16** (2), 121–9.
Aitchison, J. W. 1984b. The National and Regional Parks of France. *Landscape Research* **9**, 2–9.
Aitchison, J. W. & J.-C. Bontron 1981. L'avenir des zones à faible densité. *La France rurale: images et perspectives*, Travaux et Recherches de Prospective **81**, 82–160. Paris: La Documentation Française.
Aitchison, J. W. & J.-C. Bontron 1984. Les zones rurales fragiles en France: une approche méthodologique, *Bulletin de la Société Neuchateloise de Géographie* **28**, 23–53.
Aitchison, J. W. & J.-C. Bontron 1987. The mountain zones of France: a review of attributes and policies. *Rural Systems* (in press).
Ardagh, J. 1984. *Rural France*. London: Guild Publishing.
Association Nationale pour le Développement Local et les Pays 1986. *Les chartes intercommunales de développement et d'aménagement: un bon outil*, ANDLP, Paris.
Barruet, J. & J. Vaudois 1985. La politique de la montagne. *Revue de Géographie Alpine* **72**, 329–46.
Besson, L. 1982. *La situation de l'agriculture et de l'économie rurale dans les zones de montagne et défavorisées*. No. 757, Assemblée Nationale, Paris.
Béteille, R. 1981. *La France du Vide*. Paris: Litec.
Bontron, J-C. 1985a. Evaluation et interprétation du mouvement récent de construction en milieu rural. *Association des Ruralistes Français*, Colloque National, Amiens.
Bontron, J-C. 1985b. Population et espace rural: vers une nouvelle dynamique. *Pour*, 10–23, Privat, Paris.
Bontron, J-C. & N. Mathieu 1980. Transformations agricoles et transformations rurales en France depuis 1950. *Economie Rurale* **137**, 3–10.
Bontron, J-C., J. Mengin & L. Velard 1979. Effets de l'industrialization en milieu rural. *Recherche Sociale* **69**, 1–63.
Bontron, J-C. *et al.* 1983. Eléments de réflexion sur l'aménagement et l'espace rural en France. *Geographia Polonica* **46**, 193–216.
Brochot, A. & J-C. Bontron 1986. *Les Reserves Naturelles Françaises*. Paris: SEGESA.
Calmès, R. *et al.* 1978. *L'espace rural français*. Paris: Masson.

Chavannes, G. 1975. *Des usines à la campagne. L'industrie en milieu rural. Etude de politique industrielle.* La Documentation Française. Paris.
Chicoye, C. & V. Derkenne 1983. Protection des sites ruraux et du patrimoine rural, 95–111, *Colloque Franco-Espagnol*, Madrid.
Clout, H. 1987. France. In *Rural policies and plans*, P. Cloke (ed.). London: Allen & Unwin.
Cognat, B. 1973. *La montagne colonisée*. Paris: Les Editions du Cerf.
Durrieu, Y. 1973. *L'impossible régionalization capitaliste; temoignages de Fos et du Languedoc*. Paris: Anthropos.
Estienne, P. 1985. Evolution des populations communales dans le Massif Central au cours du dernier quart de siecle (1954–1982). *La Revue d'Auvergne* **99**, 357–72.
Etudes rurales 1978. *Campagnes marginales, campagnes disputées*, Special edition, **71/72**, 1–315.
Flatrès, P. 1986. *La Bretagne*. Paris: Presses Universitaires de France.
FPNF 1984. *Développement alternatif et gestion des espaces naturels*. Nouvelles Breves, Fédération de Parcs Naturels de France, Paris.
Gervais, M. *et al.* 1965. *Une France sans paysans*. Paris: Seuil.
Girard, J. P. *et al.* 1977. *Les agriculteurs*, Vol. 1. Paris: Les Collections de l'INSEE.
Groupe de Recherche pour l'Education Permanante 1985. Trois scenarios pour l'agriculture française, *Pour*, 53–7, Privat, Paris.
Guichard, O. 1986. *Propositions pour l'aménagement du territoire*. Paris: Documentation Française.
Houée, P. 1972. *Les etapes du developpement rural*, Vol. 2. Paris: Ouvrières.
Jung, J. 1971. *L'aménagement de l'espace rural: une illusion économique*. Paris: Calmann-Levy.
Knafou, R. 1985. L'évolution de la politique de la montagne en France. *L'Information Géographique* **49**, 53–62.
Laborie, J-P. *et al.* 1985. *La politique française d'aménagement du territoire de 1950 à 1985*. Paris: La Documentation Française.
Leynaud, E. 1985. Les parcs nationaux: territoires des autres. *L'Espace Géographique* **14**, 127–38.
Luginbuhl, Y. & B. Mortain 1986. *Le paysage du Boischaut: une identité*. Paris: SEGESA-CNRS.
MacKenzie, J. 1983. *Rural planning in France: the evolution of subregional planning procedures*. Department of Town Planning, Polytechnic of the South Bank, Research Monograph.
Mathieu, N. 1982. Questions sur les types d'espace ruraux. *L'Espace Géographique* **2**, 95–110.
Mathieu, N. & P. Duboscq 1985. *Voyage en France par les pays de faible densité*. Paris: CNRS.
Mills, S. 1983. French farming: good for people, good for wildlife. *New Scientist*, November, 568–71.
Ministère de l'Agriculture 1985. *La montagne: une loi, une politique*. 1–78, Paris.
Ministère de l'Agriculture 1986. *Paysage et remembrement*. Paris:

ANDAFAR. Ministère de l'Agriculture 1987. *Où en sont les chartes intercommunales.* Direction de l'Espace Rural et de la Forêt, Paris.
Ministère de l'Environnement 1985. *L'etat de l'environnement.* Paris: La Documentation Française.
Monod, J. (1974). *Transformation d'un pays: pour une géographie de la liberté.* Paris: Fayard.
Morand-Deviller, J. 1987. *Le droit de l'environnement.* Paris: Presses Universitaires de France.
Morineaux, Y. 1982. *Les Parcs Naturels Régionaux,* Notes et Etudes Documentaires, 4439–40, La Documentation Française, Paris.
Ogden, P. E. 1985. Counterurbanization in France: the 1982 population census. *Geography* 70, 24–35.
Pinchemel, P. 1981. *La France,* Vol. 2. Paris: Armand Collin.
Piquard, M. 1974. *Le littoral français.* Paris: La Documentation Française.
Plassard, F. 1985. Agricultures: le defi téchnologique. *Pour,* 39–48, Privat, Paris.
Rapport au Gouvernement 1974. *La montagne: elements pour une politique.* Paris: La Documentation Française.
Rey, V. 1982. *Besoin de terre des agriculteurs.* Paris: Economica.
Schéma général d'aménagement de la France 1971. *La transformation du monde rural.* Paris: La Documentation Française.
Société d'Etudes Geographiques et Sociologiques Appliquées 1983. *Méchanismes et limites des processus de spécialization/diversification de l'espace rural.* Equipe Analyse des Espaces Ruraux L.A. 142, Rapport de Synthèse, Paris.
Smith, M. 1985. *Agriculture and nature conservation in conflict: the less-favoured areas of France and the United Kingdom.* Langholm: Arkleton Trust.
Vadrot, C. M. (ed.) 1983. *Faut-il supprimer les parcs nationaux?* Paris: Presse Universitaire de Vincennes.
Verlaque, C. 1987. *Le Languedoc-Roussillon.* Paris: Presses Universitaires de France.
Wrathall, J. E. 1985. The mistral and forest fires in Provence–Cote d'Azur. *Weather* 40, 119–24.
Wright, G. 1964. *Rural revolution in France: the peasantry in twentieth century France.* Stanford, Calif.: Stanford University Press.

5 Rural land-use planning in West Germany

BRIAN J. WOODRUFFE

Introduction

In common with other West European countries West Germany has experienced very substantial pressures for change in the fabric of its rural landscape over the last three decades. Extensions to the built-up areas of towns and villages, the intensification of the road network, and the development of new sites for modern land uses, such as energy generation and specialized recreational activities, have been the main sources for *Landschaftsverbrauch*, the consumption of the rural landscape, as the process has been described by Rach (1987). Proposals for meeting these land requirements have stimulated debate at local levels but more especially at national level where federal government policies have been questioned and, in some cases, tested severely (Hucke 1985). Media coverage of environmental issues has widened public awareness and interest but has also increased concern about the nature and impact of contemporary changes. This concern was manifested through the rapid emergence and political success of the Green Party (*die Grünen*) in the 1983 election when it captured 27 seats in the Bundestag and took 5.6% of the total vote (Capra & Spretnak 1984). Inevitably, and paralleling this environmental questioning, there has emerged a mix of conservation measures and planning restraints from both federal and state governments to guide land-use change and to soften the landscape impact of new developments.

In addition to these extrinsic demands and controls, the inherent rural scene has witnessed change from within – through the modernization of agriculture and farm structures, through the need for efficient systems of timber production and forest management, and through a reassessment of the place of wildlife and of the status of natural or semi-natural habitats. Although there has long been both a patriotic attachment to and a professional interest in Germany's landscape, it is only in recent years that care for this landscape (*Landschaftspflege*) has become formally incorporated into schemes and plans. But of greater significance is the point that, in many schemes, incorporation involves landscape care and treatment as an accountable item that has to be financed, and therefore it does appear now to be firmly embedded in West German rural planning practice.

Land-use trends

The current situation and recent trends are summarized in Table 5.1 under the nine broad land-use groupings used in government records and publications. Though agriculture is the dominant land user, the area occupied by agriculture has undergone a significant decrease over the last two decades: since 1960 almost 700 000 ha has been taken out of use, and the rate of reduction has increased from a mean of 116 ha per day in the 1960–70 period to 146 ha per day in the 1981–5 period. The present figure of 13.5 million hectares includes much farmland no longer in continuous usage and, according to the 1986 land-use census, the area of land in active production totalled only 12.0 million hectares, 48.2% of the land area of West

Table 5.1 Land use trends, 1981–5.

	1985		Change 1981–5		
	000 ha	%	000 ha	%	ha per day
Agricultural uses	13 547.5	54.5	−213.3	−1.6	−146.1
Woodland	7360.0	29.6	+32.0	+0.4	+21.9
Moor and heathland	171.0	0.7	−21.0	−10.9	−7.5
Semi-natural land	231.6	0.9	−10.9	−2.6	−7.5
Water areas	444.3	1.8	+14.5	+3.4	+9.9
Recreational land	146.1	0.6	+17.6	+13.7	+12.1
Built-up land	1540.2	6.2	+101.4	+7.0	+69.4
Other settlement uses	218.8	0.8	+17.4	+8.7	+11.9
Transport land uses	1210.5	4.9	+41.5	+3.6	+28.5
Total area	24 869.4	100.0	–	–	–

Sources: Statistisches Bundesamt 1987, Rach 1987.

Germany. Contractions in area also characterize natural and semi-natural lands which have been reclaimed and converted to other uses though their rates of reduction are now modest by comparison with previous periods. By contrast, the extent of woodland has been steadily expanding and now covers almost 30% of the country. Predictably the highest rates of land conversion have been to settlement uses, but noteworthy is the upward trend in land given over to recreational uses; the rate for this category has accelerated from 5.4 ha per day in 1960–70 to the present 12.1 ha per day.

These land-use changes apart, in essence the West German landscape has remained predominantly rural in appearance and the three main uses still account for almost 85% of the federal area (Table 5.2). Only the *Länder* of the Saarland and Nordrhein-Westfalen fall noticeably below this average; the latter contains much of the Rhine–Ruhr urban agglomeration yet has retained much open countryside and extensive wooded districts which have been defined as recreational parks (*Erholungsgebiete*) or protected landscapes (*Landschaftschutzgebiete*) (Bürger 1986). Moreover, 32% of the Saarland and over 29% of Nordrhein-Westfalen lie within designated Nature Parks (*Naturparke*) (Table 5.7). The most rural of all the *Länder* is Bavaria where at least 88% comprises farmland and forest, and where there are additional stretches of natural terrain in the Alps.

Table 5.2 Main rural land uses in the *Länder*, 1985.

Land	Agricultural land 000 ha	Moor and heath 000 ha	Woodland 000 ha	Rural land uses: Area	% Land
Schleswig-Holstein	1160.1	15.5	140.2	1315.8	83.7
Niedersachsen	2916.0	128.3	984.0	4028.3	84.9
Nordrhein-Westfalen	1851.8	5.6	838.1	2695.5	79.1
Hessen	956.0	0.1	835.8	1791.9	84.9
Rheinland-Pfalz	914.7	0.4	781.5	1696.6	85.5
Baden-Württemburg	1786.6	3.3	1305.5	3095.4	86.6
Bayern	3804.1	16.6	2378.2	6198.9	87.9
Saarland	120.0	0.2	85.1	205.3	79.9
Totals*	13547.5	171.0	7360.0	21078.6	84.7

*Includes Hamburg, Bremen and West Berlin.
Source: Statistisches Bundesamt 1987.

Brian J. Woodruffe

Land-use issues in the agricultural landscape

The two dominant issues concerning the West German agricultural landscape stand in contrast to each other. The intensification and modernization of farming together with planned improvements in basic infrastructure have brought substantial modifications to the traditional farmed landscape. Furthermore, these developments have impinged on other aspects of the rural scene, such as the status or diversity of ecological sites, the function of farm woodland, and the recreational use of the countryside (BmELF 1978a). At the other extreme, considerable tracts of land have been withdrawn from permanent agricultural use. This trend has had consequential effects on landscape quality and has raised searching questions about alternative land uses, about the role of the farmer as a landscape manager, and about the future socio-economic structure of the rural communities affected (Andreae 1984). By comparison to these two widespread problems, other land-use issues tend to be more localized and more readily resolved. Amongst these can be mentioned the ubiquitous competition for land on the fringes of the main urban agglomerations where protective policies are often severely tested by pressures for development (Lintner 1985). By contrast, the problems underlying the separation of forest grazings and woodland in parts of the Bavarian Alps have presented planners with intricate questions about future ownership, animal management, recreational usage, and landscape conservation (Ruppert 1982).

Reorganization of the agricultural landscape

Over the last three decades agriculture in West Germany has been open to wide-ranging influences, some originating from economically and socially motivated policies at both federal (*Bund*) and state (*Land*) levels, others filtering through from directives and financial prescriptions associated with the Common Agricultural Policy of the EEC. Influences outside agriculture have played a part: amongst these are changes in national demands and tastes for certain foods, urban dwellers' desires for open-air recreation and access to natural areas, and the wishes of farming families to grasp opportunities for additional income especially in tourist regions. One major influence on the location of planned improvements has been land ownership and inheritance patterns. Modern agricultural layouts based on large farms of 20 or more hectares have evolved more readily in the areas of undivided inheritance – in the lowlands of Schleswig-Holstein, Niedersachsen and in central regions of Bavaria. Where gavelkind or divided inheritance is found – in the Saarland, the Rhinelands and the central uplands of Hessen in particular – the small size of farms and the fragmentation of land have restricted economic change and abandoned farmland is more in evidence (Thieme & Laux 1982). It is areas characterized by these and similar constraints that have received most attention from government programmes of land reorganization and where the challenge to conserve scenically varied and ecologically diverse landscapes is most exigent.

Although the economic incentive of price support measures for cereal and cash crops have encouraged West German farmers in favoured regions to modernize and intensify their enterprises, modifications to the rural landscape have not been so marked as those in areas where reorganization programmes (*Zusammenlegung* and *Flurbereinigung*) have been completed. In the years following the Land Consolidation Act of 1953, the fundamental aim was to increase agricultural production and create viable farming units. In general, little attention was paid to the nature of landscape changes, to the aesthetic qualities of newly consolidated land, or to the effects on wildlife and habitats. Localized impacts depended on the scale of reorganization that was required and on the existing topographic characteristics (Hoisl 1986a). In some places, modifications retained many inherent features of the rural scene, and modest increases in field sizes did not materially affect landscape patterns. But elsewhere, substantial alterations were seen as very necessary. New settlements and road networks were developed, and many farms were relocated in open countryside, a process known as *Aussiedlung*. Wet areas were drained, semi-natural habitats were reclaimed and larger, regular-shaped fields were marked out. The advent of modern machinery and technological innovations have added to the scale of change through the need for better access roads to land, the removal of features hindering efficient field layouts, and the construction of larger buildings and spaces for processing and storage.

The loss of valued features in the cultural landscape, the reduction in diversity of natural and semi-natural habitats, the alleged effects of pesticides and fertilizers, together with the increase in environmental awareness and concern within West Germany in the early 1970s, all helped to bring about a reappraisal of the aims and procedures of land consolidation schemes. A revised law – the *Flurbereinigungsgesetz* of 1976 (amended in 1980) – introduced wider terms of references and a change in emphasis of the general aims.

Care for all aspects of the cultural landscape was promoted alongside increases in production and improvements in employment opportunities within agriculture and forestry. The countryside was to be considered in its entirety rather than an actual or potential zone of conflict between competing interests. To achieve this fundamental change in approach required a comprehensive system of land-use and landscape planning and an implementation mechanism. West Germany's long tradition of landscape research had ensured that landscape ecology had a higher profile than in many other European countries; the extension of this discipline to landscape planning and thence to land consolidation schemes was therefore relatively straightforward (Stiles 1983). Nevertheless, as Hoisl (1986a) has pointed out, the ecological and aesthetic objectives of any *Flurbereinigung* plan, very relevant as they may be, should not reduce the economic advantages of land consolidation.

Flurbereinigung schemes

The probability of conflicts and friction arising between uses and users is very high simply because of the scale of reorganization under *Flurbereinigung* procedures. Throughout West Germany between 4000 and 5000 schemes are currently in progress and these affect the reorganization of around 4 million hectares of farmland and about 2.5 million hectares of other land uses. Each year some 300 schemes are completed, that is, approximately 7% of all schemes, and the average time for completion is 15 years. These figures include not only the principal process of *Flurbereinigung* itself but other procedures such as accelerated amalgamation (*beschleunigte Zusammenlegung*), voluntary exchange of land (*freiwilliger Landtausch*) and long-term leasing of land (*langfristige Verpachtung*). The distribution of the main consolidation scheme and the financing for 1984 is shown in Table 5.3.

Any *Flurbereinigung* project normally consists of three distinct phases (BmELF 1980):

(a) An initial phase of 3 to 4 years involves the preliminary planning of the road and drainage networks together with the associated landscape conservation proposals. Evaluation of the land quality is also carried out at this stage.
(b) The second period, which may last up to 7 years, sees the construction of community and public projects, and the distribution of newly consolidated land to landowners.
(c) The final phase of 4 to 7 years covers the completion of other construction work, the finalizing of legal agreements,

Table 5.3 *Flurbereinigung* schemes, 1984.

Land	Schemes in progress number	Schemes in progress ha	% Agricultural area	Schemes completed	Expenditure million DM
Schleswig-Holstein	293	326 031	27.7	42	11 018
Niedersachsen	391	526 189	17.3	18	52 368
Nordrhein-Westfalen	308	612 593	32.9	18	60 248
Hessen	348	224 065	23.4	18	26 399
Rheinland-Pfalz	493	215 971	23.6	29	46 501
Baden-Württemburg	643	582 363	32.5	26	56 642
Bayern	1727	1 360 053	35.6	78	241 202
Saarland	54	38 416	31.9	3	4 851
Total 1984:	4257	3 885 681	28.3	232	499 228
1982:	4333	3 993 757	n/a	323	489 232
1980:	4681	4 242 172	n/a	343	528 244

Source: BmELF 1985, Statistisches Bundesamt 1986.

amending land records and maps, and dealing with outstanding community problems.

It is important to recognize that the reorganization process involves non-agricultural land uses; consequently, the overall integration of these differing uses requires careful planning and thoughtful implementation. Table 5.4 lists the areas and proportions of the main land uses in schemes under way in 1984. The high proportion of land under vehicular use reflects the deficiencies of the pre-consolidation situation and the need for access to landholdings. A measure of the attention now being paid to conservation and leisure uses – about 7.5% of all reorganized land – can also be gained from these figures.

The basic format of consolidation schemes remains the same in all *Länder* but the importance attached to restructuring methods can vary considerably between them. Although the federal Land Consolidation Act of 1953 set out the principal legal framework for the *Flurbereinigung* programme, further legal provision was required at *Land* level to cover the practical measures for implementing schemes at village level. In Bavaria land consolidation has been stressed as a significant component in rural development programmes and it has been heavily financed over the last 20 years.

The present 1900 schemes in progress cover almost 20% of the state, an area of 1.4 million hectares. Moreover, the consolidation of agricultural land is closely linked with other development objectives and particularly with village renewal plans (*Dorfemeuerung*). It has been estimated that some 5000 villages in Bavaria stand in need of some degree of renovation and modernization (Strössner 1986). In the Alpine zone measures to help retain the traditional grazing pastures are seen as particularly relevant because of the recreational use made of these landscapes and the value of tourism to the local economy (Ruppert 1982). Furthermore, it has been suggested by Strössner (1986) that the management of woods and forests has been neglected and that the fragmented ownerships of more than 400 000 ha are in urgent need of amalgamation. Those areas having priority for reorganization and renewal projects have been carefully defined and include:

(a) areas where farmland is highly fragmented,
(b) areas where farming settlements lack basic public utilities,
(c) areas affected by extensive land-using operations,
(d) areas where communities have undergone marked changes in economic or social structure,
(e) areas classed as unfavourable for economic agricultural production,
(f) areas where large-scale abandonment of farmland has occurred, and

Table 5.4 Land uses in *Flurbereinigung* schemes, 1984.

Land use	hectares	%
Vehicular land (outside villages)	1 342 024	21.2
Drainage and water related uses	405 469	6.4
Building developments	185 534	2.9
Environmental protection, waste disposal, etc.	53 205	0.8
Conservation of nature, landscape and monuments	223 860	3.5
Leisure and recreation uses	248 255	3.9
Total non-agricultural uses	2 458 347	38.8
Total agricultural area	3 885 361	61.2
Total *Flurbereinigung* area	6 344 028	100

Source: BmELF 1985.

Table 5.5 Financial support for *Flurbereinigung* projects in Bavaria, 1983 and 1984.

	1983	1984	%
	1000 DM		1984
Construction of roads and tracks	194 150	197 842	47.7
Protection and land improvement works	33 302	25 237	6.1
Water supply and drainage installation	25 630	20 522	5.0
Direct restructuring of land	30 999	35 711	8.6
Intermediate land acquisitions	56 323	77 413	18.6
Village or farm renovations	47 345	48 434	11.7
Landscape conservation	5896	8977	2.2
Leisure and recreation uses	1019	429	0.1
Total costs	394 664	414 565	100

Source: Hoisl 1986a.

(g) areas adjacent to the frontier with the German Democratic Republic where special economic development is required.

The financing of land consolidation has been shared between federal sources and funds from the individual *Länder*. The current budget on all types of *Flurbereinigung* scheme is running at over 500 million DM (Table 5.3). Differences occur between *Länder* in respect of how schemes are financed since each scheme will demand different inputs. Variations in terrain and poor initial access to fields, for example, can easily raise costs of surface drainage and field roads above expenditure levels on other aspects. Elsewhere, deficiencies in soil quality may necessitate elaborate improvements or basic protection against wind erosion or sheet wash. Details are shown in Table 5.5 of the distribution of financial support among the various sectors for schemes in progress in Bavaria in 1983 and 1984; immediately apparent are the high costs of roadways and, by comparison, the low proportions for conservation and leisure uses. This breakdown of expenditure into sectors serves to demonstrate both the complexity and comprehensiveness of *Flurbereinigung* planning and the intricate nature of landscape reconstruction (BmELF 1978b).

Marginal land and unused agricultural land

A second significant issue centring on agricultural land and the cultural landscape concerns two types of land which for one reason or another are removed from production. These two types of land are, first, tracts of land zoned as marginal or uneconomic (*Grenzertragsflächen*), and secondly, unused or abandoned farmland which has been traditionally termed 'fallow' or 'social fallow' (*Brachland, Sozialbrache*). Both types give rise to irregularly and poorly used land which may result in untidy and fragmented landscapes where the lack of sustained management can lead to soil erosion, drainage impediments, slope and terrace collapse, fire, and other physical hazards especially in hilly or mountain regions. Physical deterioration of the landscape is not the sole problem since the encroachment of these hazards on to nearby land opens up questions of legal liability and compensation for damage or loss of production. In addition, adjoining pastures and cultivated fields may be adversely affected by the spread of pests, plant diseases and weeds from unused plots. Neglect of these former agricultural tracts does not make them automatically valuable for wildlife because of the short-lived phases of succession to woodland, though they can serve temporarily as local refuges for both plants and animals (Surber 1979). The change in appearance of the landscape is often regarded as visually detrimental and consequently such areas tend to be avoided for leisure-time purposes although some do have potential recreational uses.

The marginal lands – *Grenzertragsflächen* – are areas specifically identified in conjunction with the land evaluation process in the early stages of *Flurbereinigung* and similar land restructuring schemes. Essentially, they comprise tracts of land which can neither be used economically in the long term because of unfavourable farm management opportunities, nor improved substantially in quality because of inherent natural deficiencies. The criteria used to define them can vary according to region and market circumstances but normally consist of measurements of yields (either crop or animal production), an index of the difficulty with which land may be worked (e.g. angle of slope), and an indication of the development and management costs required to regularly work the land. In the evaluation exercise prior to reorganization, *Grenzertragsflächen* may be defined within a broader scale of land suitabilities ranging from prime quality land, through land with lesser or greater limitations, to land that is particularly unsuitable. The scale may apply to arable land as well as to grazing or pasture land (BmELF 1980).

The areas that come under the heading of 'fallow lands' are not as readily defined as *Grenzertragsflächen* and are not confined to poor quality soils. In fact many hectares of *Brachland* occur on potentially very productive land. The reasons such land is not farmed may reflect an unfavourable landholding structure, better employment opportunities outside agriculture, or simply land speculation for development. *Brachland* is not a feature peculiar to West Germany: estimations in 1980 within EEC countries indicated that some 6.4 million ha of usable land were lying vacant in France (3.9 million ha), Italy (2 million ha), Belgium and Luxemburg (1 million ha), and West Germany (0.3 million ha). The current extent in West Germany is not known in detail since official recording ceased in 1978 and because it is not easily identifiable in the rural landscape. It has been the subject of considerable research in its own right (Hartke 1956, Dege 1973) and in association with land and landscape planning (Ruppert 1982). Though there was a very steep increase in the area of agriculturally unused land during the 1960s to a figure of 308 000 ha in 1974, the rise levelled off in the mid-1970s to reach 313 000 ha by 1978. It was suggested by Wild (1983) that government schemes of land restructuring together with economic controls, the lack of non-agricultural employment in rural areas, and the reuse of land were keeping increases in fallow land at modest levels. However, other observers have forecast that surplus production and lower prices in EEC countries combined with incentives to retire from farming would stimulate a significant rise in the total area of unused land by the mid-1980s, perhaps to a peak of 1.5 million ha, 12% of the agricultural area (Andreae 1984).

One characteristic of *Brachland* within the Federal Republic is that it has a very uneven distribution. This is very evident from the figures in Table 5.6 which show the situation in 1978, the last year in which data on 'unused agricultural land' (*nicht mehr genützte landwirtschaftliche Fläche*) were published. The Saarland had by far the highest proportion with around 12% of its farmland being out of use (Guth 1982), but there were also substantial extents in Rheinland-Pfalz and Hessen. Much of this unused land coincided with the dissected uplands of central Germany – the Spessart, Odenwald, Westerwald – but there were also concentrations in the Black Forest, along the Alpine fringe in southern Bavaria (Bayerische Staatsregierung 1972), and in districts adjacent to the main urban agglomerations such as the Siegerland. Some of these areas are characterized by the custom of partible inheritance (*Realerbteilung*) which has led to intense fragmentation of farms and complex division of fields. Today it is not worthwhile farming these lands and consequently they lie for the most part unused (Thieme 1983). At a local scale, therefore, proportions of unused land can rise substantially and it is not unusual to find *Gemeinde* with 20% or more of their lands in an unused state.

Table 5.6 Unused agricultural land, 1978.

Land	Agricultural area (000 ha)	Unused land (000 ha)	%
Schleswig-Holstein	1132.2	3.8	0.3
Niedersachsen	2779.1	13.7	0.5
Nordrhein-Westfalen	1830.7	38.7	2.1
Hessen	888.6	55.9	6.3
Rheinland-Pfalz	875.6	63.6	7.3
Baden-Württemberg	1716.2	41.2	2.4
Bayern	3669.4	62.6	1.7
Saarland	114.6	14.4	12.6
Total	13 006.4	312.7	2.4

Source: Statistisches Jarhbuch der BRD 1978.

The basic problem with both *Grenzertragsflächen* and *Brachland* is one of finding alternative uses. This is regarded not only as an economic problem for private and community landowners but also as a socio-political issue because of the public interest in conserving the cultural landscape. It has been suggested that there are five possible types of use, not all equally applicable to all rural areas with unused land. In some localities there may be no likelihood of other uses being found and an abandoned landscape may well prevail for the foreseeable future (Ort 1983). The five possibilities are:

- extensive agricultural or para-agricultural enterprises such as sheep grazing, cattle breeding, pony raising, or deer farming,
- keeping the landscape as open farmland by periodic grazing or mowing,
- afforestation,
- recreation and open-air activities,
- reversion to natural habitats.

The two agricultural options are dependent first on local conditions being suitable for continuous grass growth, secondly on creating an economic environment with low-level or secondary employments, and finally on relative costs of development and sustainment of the enterprises. Afforestation too is subject to economic considerations and it has also become a landscape issue. With almost 30% of the countryside under woodland, it is being argued that, in some parts of West Germany, additional planting will destroy the traditional balance of uses and valued landscape patterns. Although possibilities for leisure-time uses would appear to have great potential in both regional and local contexts, it is unlikely that conversions to recreational uses such as sports centres, picnic sites, or weekend-home settlements will absorb large areas of land.

Clearly, the solution sought in any particular community will centre on the opportunities represented by the restructuring of the land-use pattern as a whole and not on piecemeal decision-making about individual tracts of unused land. Any resolution of the question of alternative land uses would seem therefore to be most effective through schemes put into operation under the *Flurbereinigunggesetz* and in association with local land-use plans (*Flächennutzungspläne*).

Agriculture and landscape plans

Provisions for dealing with rural land reorganization are now embedded in a structured set of integrated plans which may involve state, regional, district and local community co-operation. At all these levels conservation of the natural and cultural environment has to be taken into account whether plans are directed towards the countryside or are concerned with the development of built-up zones. This requirement resulted from the Federal Nature Conservation Act of 1976 which stated as its objectives:

> Nature and landscape in built-up and uninhabited areas are to be protected, managed and developed so that the capability of natural systems, the effective use of natural resources, wildlife habitats, as well as the variety, special characteristics, and beauty of nature and landscape are safeguarded as the basis for human life and as prerequisites for man's relaxation in the natural environment.

These objectives and the regulations in later sections of the Act have been augmented by further legislation by each of the *Länder* (Wittkämper & Stuckhard 1984). In effect, each *Land* has been required to prepare landscape programmes (*Landschaftsprogrammen*) setting out their provisions to meet the aims of landscape and nature conservation (BmELF 1978b). In problematic or sensitive regions detailed landscape planning guidelines (*Landschaftsrahmenplan*) may have to be drawn up. Once these frameworks have been established, the preparation of local landscape plans can proceed in order to describe the existing landscape conditions, evaluate sites and features, define aims for landscape development and specify measures for their implementation (Stiles 1983). Land consolidation procedures have to accord with the objectives and guidelines for landscape planning, as do proposals for other land-use developments. Although West Germany has had a long history of landscape science, these recent requirements have stimulated fresh approaches to the mapping, evaluation and management of landscape components. Research into methods of evaluation (Hoisl *et al.* 1985, Hoisl 1986b), the preparation of planning guidelines (BmELF 1980), and discussion about restrictions on uses in protected zones (Deselaers 1986) all indicate the importance now attached to landscape issues and landscape quality.

Village renovation schemes (Dorferneuerung)

As mentioned earlier, many land restructuring projects incorporated plans to rationalize farm locations and layouts within settlements as well as improving farm dwellings and living conditions. At first sight these additional responsibilities would appear to enlarge and complicate the land reorganization processes but, as Strössner (1986) has stressed, renovation of villages in Bavaria was regarded as an essential adjunct to any land consolidation project. Since the aim of agricultural land consolidation was to aid its economic use, it was seen as only logical to accompany this objective with the reorganization, renewal and perhaps relocation of farm buildings and working spaces so that the farm as a total unit could function more efficiently (Herms 1984). Small-scale renewal had been progressing for almost two decades but in the mid-1970s the Federal government and some *Länder* governments went a stage further and took the opportunity to establish policies and comprehensive programmes to improve village structures and facilities for all village residents. Thus the schemes under the broad heading of *Dorferneuerung* are not merely concerned with reshaping land use but also with enhancing community life and with conserving the intrinsic and aesthetic character of rural settlements. The latter concern stems from the now widespread recognition of the village as an important contributor to the scenic quality of the cultural landscape. Despite the laudable aims and the benefits that have ensued, recent village renovation schemes have raised socio-political issues within communities largely because interests other than farming have become involved. As elsewhere in Europe, the in-movement of new people to villages has broadened opinions about the nature, location and scale of economic or residential development, about the ways in which the rural heritage should be conserved or altered, and about the appropriateness of new facilities. Planners too have been subject to critical comment and they have recognized the need for proposals to be cautiously advanced and for plans to be sensitively prepared (Darmer 1985).

Interest in planning villages is not a recent trend as much discussion over development sites and social changes has occurred in parallel with the preparation of land-use plans (*Flächennutzungsplan*) (Landeskulturverwaltung Hessen 1974). However, as a mainstream activity of rural land planning in West Germany today, village renovation and development has evolved from two other sources: first but less significantly, from the field of architectural conservation (*Denkmalschutz*) which has long encouraged care of the historic environment, and secondly from land consolidation procedures. Section 37 of the updated Land Consolidation Act of 1976 widened the responsibilities of the relevant authorities: 'Village renovation measures may be undertaken; building plans and similar plans shall not prevent the built-up area of a village from being included in a Land Consolidation Plan.' The items to be taken into account covered:

> orderly building development, the protection of the environment, the preservation of buildings of architectural or historic interest, recreational uses, the management of water resources, public transport, agricultural settlements, part-time farming and allotment gardens, and the form and appearance of the village and landscape.
>
> (ArgeFlurb 1980)

The real stimulus to getting schemes moving came in 1977 with an investment programme for improving agricultural structure and coastal protection (*Zukunftsinvestitionsprogramm zur Verbesserung der Agrarstruktur und des Küstenschutzes*). Over the period 1977–80, this programme made available some 267 million DM (160 million DM from Federal sources and 107 million DM from the *Länder*), and it gave support to 1325 renovation schemes (BmEFL n.d.). In turn this volume of financial aid triggered off yet more investment by community organizations and private individuals; but in doing so, it also opened up debate about methods of village renovation and village development and it gave rise to questions about the status and value of villages in German society (Henkel 1984).

Prior to 1977, renovation of farm dwellings and associated buildings had been carried out within land consolidation schemes but in a rather piecemeal fashion which frequently overlooked aesthetic considerations and landscape impacts. With the increased interest resulting from the 1977 programme, aims and methods were thought out and guidelines issued by the *Länder* planning authorities. In Hessen, for example, renovation projects were to

- preserve and develop the individual character of each village,
- set the village in its context with respect to the natural environment and the surrounding landscape,
- improve living and working conditions and environmental quality by making good any deficiencies in functions and buildings especially in the old village centre,
- preserve the regional identity of building materials and, where necessary, find new appropriate uses,
- conserve and improve buildings and facilities needed for community purposes and for public and private services,
- rearrange streets and paths but in such a way that the townscape is preserved, property surroundings are improved, and the diversity of uses is retained,
- improve working conditions for farming, local trades and other small businesses,
- interpret leisure and recreation provision in relation to the needs and circumstances of the village.

To put aims such as these into practice, model schemes and illustrative plans were prepared for different-sized villages, for villages with various plan forms and for villages in different locational contexts (Bayerisches Staatsministerium des Innern 1982). Many of these guideline documents are fully illustrated, thus emphasizing the design, style and appearance of buildings, the relevance of greenery, spaces and landscape setting, and the desirability of carefully examining the juxtapositioning of land uses within settlements.

The achievements of *Dorfemeuerung* schemes in combination with *Flurbereinigung* projects are quite impressive by European standards. Much has been done in a short period of time to keep farm or local families living in older, modernized properties in the village core, as well as to retain and refurbish the inherent village character and environment. Whereas some parts of villages have experienced selective street widening through the removal of constrictions, complementary pedestrianization and harmonious resurfacing has enhanced other parts. Rationalization of both public and private parking areas has taken place with a consequent improvement in aesthetic quality in many village centres. Spaces and greenery have received much attention: attractively laid-out squares with seats, tables and features to facilitate social contact, such as children's playgrounds and chessboards, have enriched village centres. Awkwardly shaped redundant sites have presented opportunities for planting trees, shrubs and flowers, and reorganization of property boundaries have in some cases permitted new footpaths to be created. Peripheral sites have accommodated new community functions such as sports fields, tennis courts, swimming pools, graveyards and camping sites. This reorganization of land uses and the range of infrastructural alterations has depended not simply on the characteristics of the villages selected for renovation but also on the emphasis placed on particular measures by the respective *Länder* governments (BmEFL n.d.). For example, in Baden-Württemburg financial aid has been concentrated on the renewal of farm property in villages throughout the state, whereas the Saarland centred its schemes on villages subject to marked changes in social structure. The focus of attention in Schleswig-Holstein has been on the conservation of the built environment in a very limited number of villages. By contrast, investment in the other states has been directed towards rural communities in regions identified as having weaknesses in their economic and social structure (*schwach struktierte Räume*). The significance of *Dorferneuerung* was emphasized when in 1984 the federal government renewed its commitment to support the *Länder* in their efforts by funding village renovation as a separate item in the overall rural development programme (BmELF 1985).

Issues in conserved landscapes

Over recent decades a diverse spectrum of protected and designated landscapes has been created throughout West Germany.

Prominent amongst these are four National Parks, 64 Nature Parks (*Naturparke*), 2380 Nature Reserves (*Naturschutzgebiete*), and 10 wetland reserves (*Feuchtgebiete*). The administrative background and the intrinsic character of these areas are well illustrated in Duffey (1982). Their distribution is rather uneven as can be appreciated from the percentage figures in Table 5.7. The four National Parks are all peripheral whereas Nature Parks tend to be concentrated in the central regions close to the major urban agglomerations (Fig. 5.1). Further variety is added at *Land* level where there are officially defined recreation areas (*Erholungsgebiete*), protected landscape zones (*Landschaftsschutzgebiete*), and protected natural and historical features (*Natur-* and *Kulturdenkmäler*). Forest and wooded areas are also recognized for their protective functions in addition to their more obvious ecological characteristics. In Bavaria a comprehensive classification has been applied to woods and forests (Bay.SLU 1974) according to the protection afforded to wildlife (*Naturwaldreservat*), against avalanches (*Lawinenschutzwald*), against noise especially along motorways (*Lärmschutzwald*), against air pollution (*Immissionsschutzwald*), and against soil erosion (*Bodenschutzwald*).

Given this diversity of designations, it is not surprising that conflicts and friction between land users have arisen or that the effectiveness of legislation relating to protective policies has

Table 5.7 Nature Parks and Nature Reserves, 1986–7.

Land	no.	Nature Parks (1987) km²	% area	no.	Nature Reserves (1986) km²	% area
Schleswig-Holstein	5	1867	11.9	115	170	1.1
Niedersachsen	12	7402	15.6	428	762	1.6
Nordrhein-Westfalen	14	9955	29.2	443	210	0.6
Hessen	9	6135	29.1	308	150	0.7
Rheinland-Pfalz	6	4557	23.0	234	150	0.7
Baden-Württemburg	5	3522	9.9	480	329	0.9
Bayern	17	20846	29.5	303	991	1.4
Saarland	1	825	32.1	29	4	0.2
Total*	64	55147	22.2	2380	2797	1.1

*Total includes sites in the city states of Hamburg and Bremen.
Source: Statistisches Bundesamt 1987.

Table 5.8 Damage to woodland and forests (*Waldschäden*), 1986.

Land	Woodland 000 ha	% damaged 1984	% damaged 1986	Level of damage: Slight	Level of damage: Medium	Level of damage: Severe
Schleswig-Holstein	140	27	40	26	12	1.1
Niedersachsen	962	36	37	26	9	1.9
Nordrhein-Westfalen	854	42	41	30	10	1.1
Hessen	829	42	48	29	18	1.2
Rheinland-Pfalz	770	42	46	38	8	0.5
Baden-Württemburg	1303	66	65	42	21	2.1
Bayern	2446	57	64	38	25	2.0
Saarland	74	31	42	31	10	1.2
West Germany	7389	50	54	35	17	1.6

Source: Bundesministerium für Ernährung, Landwirtschaft und Forsten.

been questioned. Such issues are most in evidence where high proportions of rural land are zoned and where protective functions overlap and appear opposed to one another. For example, in wooded reserves the objectives for the hunting of game animals differ from those of forestry interests or recreational pursuits (BmELF 1983). Lang (1986) identified four conflicts: a reluctance to plant tree species that are food sources for game; economic loss and forest degeneration through tree-bark damage by deer; the disturbance of game by recreation activities; and the lack of predators which may produce imbalances in numbers of game animals. Lang suggested broad-based training for forest managers as one means of resolving these conflicts. The fact that some 23.5 million hectares of countryside carry hunting rights indicates the potential size of this problem.

Many of the issues in protected areas come to notice through land-use conversions, the development of new functions, and the intensification of existing activities. Mineral extraction, flood-control works, power station construction and highway improvements have all been carried out in conserved areas. But a major threat from extraneous sources is air pollution and acid rain. Millions of trees in the Federal Republic have been damaged to such an extent that this damage (*Waldschäden*) is regularly assessed. The inherent attractiveness of some protected landscapes is endangered, timber production is threatened, and ecosystems are changing particularly those encompassing water areas and streams.

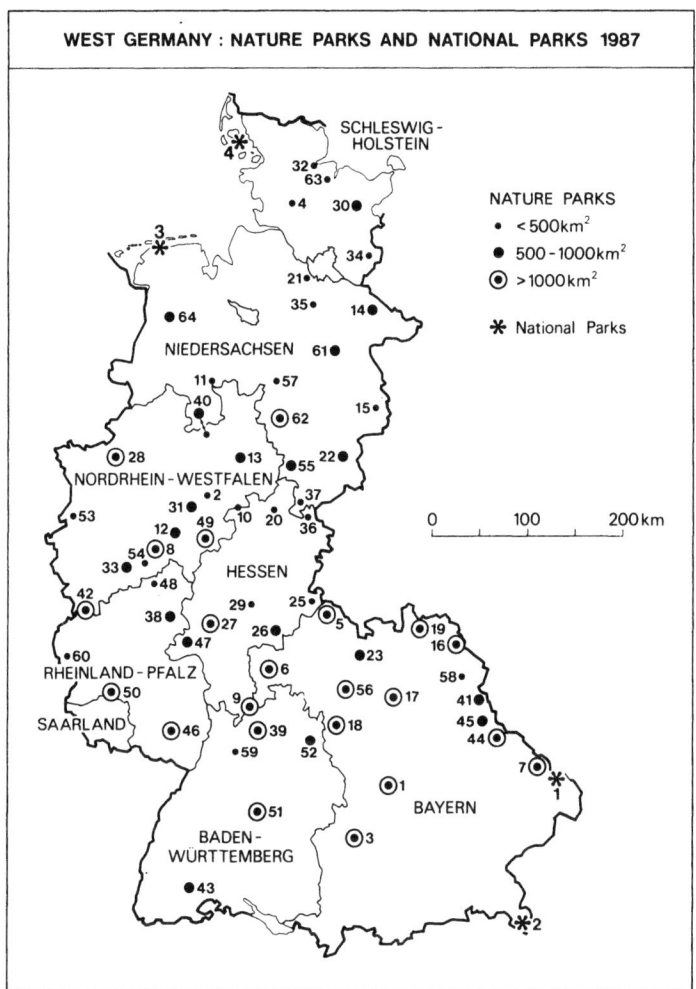

Figure 5.1 West Germany: Nature Parks and National Parks, 1987. See opposite for key

The scale and widespread nature of this problem is evident from the data on proportional damage in Table 5.8.

All forested parts of the country are affected but especially those with extensive stands of the most susceptible species – Norway spruce, white pine and Scots pine. Many of these forests are found

	Nature Parks	Land	Established		Nature Parks	Land	Established
1.	Altmühltal	B	1969	37.	Münden	NS	1959
2.	Arnsberger Wald	NW	1961	38.	Nassau	RP	1962
3.	Augsburg-			39.	Neckartal-Odenwald	BW	1980
	Westliche Wälder	B	1974	40.	Nördlicher Teutoberger		
4.	Aukrug	SH	1970		Wald-Wiehengebirge	NS,NW	1962
5.	Bayerische Rhön	B	1967	41.	Nördlicher		
6.	Bayerischer Spessart	B	1963		Oberpfälzer Wald	B	1971
7.	Bayerischer Wald	B	1967	42.	Nordeifel	NW,RP	1960
8.	Bergisches Land	NW	1973	43.	Obere Donau	BW	1980
9.	Bergstrasse-Odenwald	H,B	1960	44.	Oberer Bayerischer Wald	B	1965
10.	Diemelsee	NW,H	1965	45.	Oberpfälzer Wald	B	1971
11.	Dümmer	NS,NW	1972	46.	Pfälzerwald	RP	1958
12.	Ebbegebirge	NW	1964	47.	Rhein-Taunus	H	1968
13.	Eggegebirge-			48.	Rhein-Westerwald	RP	1962
	Teutoburger Wald	NW	1965	49.	Rothaargebirge	NW	1963
14.	Elbufer-Drawehn	NS	1968	50.	Saar-Hunsrück	RP,S	1980
15.	Elm-Lappwald	NS	1976	51.	Schönbuch	BW	1974
16.	Fichtelgebirge	B	1971	52.	Schwäbisch-		
17.	Frankische Schweiz/				Fränkischer Wald	BW	1979
	Veldensteiner Forst	B	1968	53.	Schwalm-Nette	NW	1965
18.	Frankenhöhe	B	1974	54.	Siebengebirge	NW	1959
19.	Frankenwald	B	1973	55.	Solling-Vogler	NS	1966
20.	Habichtswald	H	1962	56.	Steigerwald	B	1971
21.	Harburger Berge	HAM	1959	57.	Steinhuder Meer	NS	1974
22.	Harz	NS	1960	58.	Steinwald	B	1970
23.	Hassberge	B	1974	59.	Stromberg-Heuchelberg	BW	1980
24.	Hessenreuther/			60.	Südeifel	RP	1958
	Manteler Wald	B	1975	61.	Südheide	NS	1963
25.	Hessische Rhön	H	1963	62.	Weserbergland-		
26.	Hessischer Spessart	H	1962		Schaumburg-Hameln	NS	1975
27.	Hochtaunus	H	1962	63.	Westensee	SH	1969
28.	Hohe Mark	NW	1963	64.	Wildeshauser Geest	NS	1984
29.	Hoher Vogelsberg	H	1958				
30.	Holsteinische Schweiz	SH	1986				
31.	Homert	NW	1965		National Parks		
32.	Hüttener Berge-						
	Wittensee	SH	1970	1.	Bayerischer Wald	B	1970
33.	Kottenforst-Ville	NW	1959	2.	Berchtesgaden	B	1979
34.	Lauenburgische Seen	SH	1959	3.	Niedersächsisches		
35.	Lüneburger Heide	NS	1920		Wattenmeer	NS	1986
36.	Meissner-			4.	Schleswig-Holsteinisches		
	Kaufunger Wald	H	1962		Wattenmeer	SH	1985

in the Harz Mountains, the Fichtel-Gebirge, the Black Forest and the Bavarian Forest, all recognized as being of high scenic quality and embracing several of the protective categories noted above. In the Bayerischer Wald National Park the problem is acute and features in the park's education programme for visitors. The long-term effects will result in limited regeneration of trees, a lowering of the timber-line on mountains, and increased erosion and avalanche frequency (Bibelriether 1984). To help counteract these changes, the federal government in 1984 provided 33 million DM for reafforestation and nutrient application to forest soils (BmELF 1985). Management in damaged areas is already having to cope with changes in landscape character but changes in ecological qualities may undermine the essential reasons for designation and protective policies.

Issues and problems arising from the development of tourism and the intensification of outdoor recreational pursuits have necessitated continual amendment of management policies. With an increased public interest in wildlife and environmental conservation, management changes have been very noticeable in areas defined as important for scientific investigation and for monitoring natural processes. On the other hand it has been argued that existing protective policies are ineffective against recreational demands. A nation-wide survey by Fritz (1977) concluded that more than half the Nature Reserves (*Naturschutzgebiete*) had been encroached upon or partially damaged by recreational activities or visitor traffic. In 64 of the 905 areas surveyed, bathing and swimming was permitted, and in 34 reserves holiday homes had been sited. The degree of protection afforded depended largely on the emphasis given to nature conservation by the *Länder* authorities. Despite recent concern about environmental conservation, Brahms et al. (1986) noted that camping was a permitted activity in 42% of all Nature Reserves in Niedersachsen, and in only 9% was there complete exclusion of any form of leisure use.

The problem of accommodating increasing numbers of visitors is exemplified by the management changes made in the Lüneberg Heath *Naturschutzpark*. Originally bought in 1920 by the Nature Conservation Parks Association to protect the fragile, vulnerable low-lying heath- and marshlands, today most of the 7000 ha are open to public use (Toepfer 1981). Large car-parks have had to be provided and a network of paths, cycleways and riding routes has been laid out. Four visitor information centres have been established and several of the original medieval farms are now preserved as historical monuments. Two thousand litter bins have been distributed. Maintenance of this visitor infrastructure is now a major task of park management comparable with conservation of the primeval habitats.

Not everywhere is it accepted that provision for visitors is inevitable. In the Altmühltal Nature Park in middle Bavaria, litter bins, seats and shelters have been removed from sensitive sites. Proposals in the amenity plan of 1982 envisaged a widespread distribution of camping places and sites for water sports at a level of provision that would have conflicted with *Land* regulations on nature conservation. The Bavarian Nature Conservation Act 1973 stated that at least 75% of a Nature Park must have the status of a protected landscape essentially free of public uses. The aim of the Act was to raise standards of landscape conservation and ensure the survival of valued natural habitats. Though this has stimulated efforts towards more effective nature conservation, it has not made reconciliation with recreation interests any easier (Dümmler 1983).

Throughout the 250 km length of the Bavarian Alps a different approach for dealing with tourist developments has been tried since 1973. In this area the interests of farmers, forestry, conservation and visitors have to be integrated because all have a need to use this varied and scenic landscape. By virtue of the diversity and abundance of their alpine flora and fauna, large sections which adjoin reserves in Austria have been designated as *Naturschutzgebiete*; the eastern section in Berchtesgaden was declared a National Park in 1979. However, widespread proposals to extend access for tourists through cable-car systems, chair lifts and scenic roads, and develop ski routes and accommodation, threatened to reduce the wilderness character of this Alpine landscape. To channel development and meet conservation needs, a threefold zoning scheme was introduced through the 1972 Development Programme (Bay. SLU 1973).

Zone A covered the main settlement areas where new infrastructure was to be concentrated. Here special care was necessary to avoid intruding on the alpine grazing system which was particularly sensitive to change but which also functioned as a landscape gardener. In zone B, which included the lower mountain slopes and forests, limited-access installations were to be permitted as long as landscape and conservation regulations were complied with and the risk of erosion or avalanches was not increased. Zone C covered the remoter mountain tracts where the aim was to keep undamaged the scenic and natural qualities. Recreation access had to be passive in nature – ski-trails, walking and observing wildlife – and without vehicular intrusion. This zoning approach has not removed all conflict but it has reduced pressure on protected sites; equally importantly it has provided a framework within which additional facilities can be planned for a popular and highly valued part of the German countryside.

Conclusion

Over the last three decades the rural landscape of West Germany has undergone a fundamental reshaping through a wide-ranging series of planned programmes that have reached out to affect both major and minor uses. Some of the consequent changes have been in response to critical economic situations, some to meet new functions for rural space, and others to resolve issues and problems. Most impressive have been the efforts made to accommodate the needs of all users and to think of the countryside as an entity rather than a collection of diverging uses. The emphasis placed on the roles of the natural environment and the inherited landscape has been particularly noteworthy. These approaches have not always worked effectively and not all issues have been resolved.

Nevertheless, these ideas and experiences in West Germany have demonstrated that, by bringing rural interests together, substantial progress is possible in creating new landscapes for the future.

References

Andreae, B. 1984. Landbau oder Landschaftspflege? *Geographische Rundschau* 36, 187–94.
ArgeFlurb 1980. *Land Consolidation Act*, Schriftenreihe der ArgeFlurb 6, Munich.
Bayerisches Staatsministerium des Innern 1982. *Planen und Bauen im ländlichen Raum*, Munich.
Bay.SLU (Bayerisches Staatsministerium für Landesentwicklung und Umweltfragen) 1973. *Planung und Umwelt 2 – Erholungslandschaft Alpen*, Munich.
Bay.SLU 1974. *Raumordnungsbericht 2*, Munich.
Bayerische Staatsregierung 1972. *Raumordnungsbericht 1971*, Munich.
Bibelriether, H. 1984. Bayerischer Wald National Park threatened by air pollution. *Parks* 9 (2), 1–3.
BmELF (Bundesministerium fur Ernährung, Landwirtschaft und Forsten) 1978. *Landschaftspflege und Naturschutz*, Bonn.
BmELF 1978b. *Flurbereinigung zur Förderung der Landentwicklung im Raum der Stadt Ahaus, Westfalen*, Landesamt für Agrarordnung Nordrhein-Westfalen, Munster.
BmELF 1980. *Flurbereinigung – Naturschutz und Landschaftspflege*, Series B – Special Publication, Munster-Hiltrup.
BmELF 1983. *Flurbereinigung und Wild*, Series B – Special Publication, Bonn.
BmELF 1985. *Die Verbesserung der Agrarstruktur in der Bundesrepublik Deutschland 1983 und 1984*, Bonn.
BmELF n.d. *Die Verbesserung der Agrarstruktur in der Bundesrepublik Deutschland 1979 und 1980*. Mönchengladbach.
Brahms, M., C. von Haaren, H. Langer et al. 1986. *Naturschutzansprüche und ihre Durchsetzung*. Schriftenreihe des BmELF A-331, Bonn.
Bürger, K. 1986. Entwicklung von Natur und Landschaft. *Information zur Raumentwicklung* 1 (2), 45–55.
Capra, F. & C. Spretnak 1984. *Green politics*. London: Hutchinson.
Darmer, G. 1985. Das Dorf im Wandel: Gedanken zur Ökologie der Dorfentwicklung und Erneuerung in Niedersächsischer Landschaft. *Landschaft und Stadt* 17, 81–91.
Dege, E. 1973. Weinbau, Obstbau und Sozialbrache am oberen Mittelrhein. *Erdkunde* 27, 34–54.
Deselaers, D. 1986. Nutzungsbeschränkungen in Natur-, Landschafts- und Wasserschutzgebieten. *Agrar Recht* 16 (4), 97–104.
Duffey, E. 1982. *National parks and reserves of Western Europe*. London: Macdonald.

Dümmler, H. 1983. Altmühltal: Germany's largest Nature Park. *Parks* **8** (1), 11–13.
Fritz, G. 1977. Zur Inanspruchnahme von Naturschutzgebieten durch Freizeit und Erholung. *Natur und Landschaft* **7**.
Guth, R. 1982. Die Bedeutung der Sozialbrache und der Grenzertragsboden für den agrarstrukturellen Wandel in Saarland. *Berichte über Landwirtschaft* **60**, 221–9.
Hartke, W. 1956. Die Sozialbrache als Phänomen der geographischen Differenzierung der Landschaft. *Erdkunde* **34**, 257–69.
Henkel, G. 1984. Dorferneuerung in der Bundesrepublik Deutschland. *Geographische Rundschau* **36**, 170–6.
Herms, A. 1984. Dorfentwicklung, eine Existenzfrage für die Landwirtschaft. *Berichte über Landwirtschaft* **62**, 364–71.
Hoisl, R. 1986a. Landschaftsveränderung durch Flurbereinigung. *Vermessungswesen und Raumordnung* **48**, 268–76.
Hoisl, R. 1986b. Grundstückswertermittlung in der Flurbereinigung. *Zeitschrift für Kulturtechnik und Flurbereinigung* **27**, 303–12.
Hoisl, R. et al. 1985. Landschaftsästhetik in der Flurbereinigung – Skizze eines Forschungsprojekts. *Zeitschrift für Kulturtechnik und Flurbereinigung* **26**, 346–53.
Hucke, J. 1985. Environmental policy: the development of a new policy area. In *Policy and politics in the Federal Republic of Germany*, K. von Beyme & M. G. Schmidt (eds), 156–75. Aldershot: Gower.
Landeskulturverwaltung Hessen 1974. *Das Dorf*, Wiesbaden.
Lang, W. 1986. Knowing the forest. *Naturopa* **52**, 8–9.
Lintner, P. 1985. *Flächennutzung und Flächennutzungswandel in Bayern: Strukturen, Prozessabläufe, Erklärungsansätze*. Münchner Studien zur Sozial- und Wirtschaftsgeographie 29, Munich.
Ort, W. 1983. Regionale Auswirkungen der Agrarmarktpolitik. *Berichte über Landwirtschaft* **61**, 161–95.
Rach, D. 1987. Landschaftsverbrauch in der Bundesrepublik Deutschland. *Informationen zur Raumentwicklung* **1** (2), 27–43.
Ruppert, K. 1982. Die deutschen Alpen – Prozessabläufe spezieller Agrarstrukturen. *Erdkunde* **36**, 176–87.
Statistisches Bundesamt 1986. *Statistisches Jahrbuch 1986*, Wiesbaden.
Statistisches Bundesamt 1987. *Statistisches Jahrbuch 1987*, Wiesbaden.
Stiles, R. 1983. An outline of landscape planning in West Germany. *Landscape Research* **8** (3), 23–7.
Strössner, G. 1986. Land consolidation in Bavaria: support given to rural areas. *Irrigation Engineering and Rural Planning* **9**, 53–9.
Surber, E. 1979. Fallow lands. *Naturopa* **33**, 15–17.
Thieme, G. 1983. Agricultural change and its impact in rural areas. In *Urban and rural change in West Germany*, T. Wild (ed.), 220–47. London: Croom Helm.
Thieme, G. & H.-D. Laux 1982. Regional disparities in West German agriculture. In *Planen und Lebensqualität*, G. Aymans (ed.), 73–88. Bonn: Ferd. Dümmlers Verlag.

Toepfer, A. 1981. A priceless heritage. *Naturopa* **38**, 21–2.
Wild, T. 1983. Social fallow and its impact on the rural landscape. In *Urban and rural change in West Germany*, T. Wild (ed.), 200–19. London: Croom Helm.
Wittkämper, G. W. & P. Stuckhard 1984. *Landschaftspflege und Naturschutz in Nordrhein-Westfalen*. Schriftenreihe des BmELF A-300, Bonn.

6 Rural land-use planning in Japan

Michael Hebbert

Introduction

Japan is a country that stands out in any comparative context but especially so when the topic is land utilization and the comparison is with the older industrialized nations of Western Europe, North America and Australasia. The feature most marking it out from all other cases discussed in this book is the much greater intensity of land use in the Japanese archipelago. The total surface area of these precipitous, rocky islands is about one and a half times the size of West Germany. But since most of the land is too steep and harsh for use, a population of 120 million (equal to France and West Germany combined) and the production and consumption demands of the world's most buoyant economy must crowd into a habitable land area of 85 000 km² (a sixth the size of France). Japan is alone at the very top of the scale if we compare land utilization in terms of population per unit area (Table 6.1), and stands out just as strikingly at the bottom in terms of agricultural land per capital (Table 6.2).

How, then, does Japan fit into the larger pattern of this book? Other chapters reveal much underlying similarity in the conflicts

Table 6.1 Comparative population densities (persons/km²).

	USA	France	UK	FDR	Japan
Gross density (total land area)	23	97	229	250	301
Net density (habitable area)	34	132	249	349	925

Source: Rural Development Planning Commission 1981.

Table 6.2 Agricultural land area per capita (cropland and permanent pasture.

Country	Area (hectares)
Australia	31.0
Canada	3.0
USA	1.8
France	0.6
UK	0.3
Netherlands	0.3
Switzerland	0.3
West Germany	0.2
Japan	0.04

Source: FAO 1986, own compilation.

and policy dilemmas thrown up by rural land-use planning in countries of widely varying geography and culture: the tensions, for example, between modern technologies of food production and nature conservation, between preservation of wilder landscape and exploitation of resources under the soil, between urban development pressures and rural scenery and ways of life. All may be thought symptomatic of deeper and endemic tensions in advanced industrial society between man and nature, technology and the organic, transitory consumption and lasting values. The higher a country's population density and its rate of economic growth, the more strongly we might expect such tensions to dominate rural land-use policy.

Japan breaks the pattern. Although the country has, as we shall see, a system of land-use planning more elaborate than any fellow OECD member, its policy environment for rural land matters is fundamentally unlike all others. The reason is not far to seek. Japan, unlike other countries discussed here, is an oriental civilization. Geographers have always recognized a fundamental division between oriental and occidental approaches to land use. The East's space-intensive and highly 'artificial' cultivation of rice on paddy-fields, fertilized by water-borne bacteria, contrasts with Western styles of cultivation which rely more on the soil's 'natural' processes of replenishment through crop rotation, fallowing, and the grazing of large animals (Beardsley *et al.* 1959 ch. 6, Berque 1982). Japan, like other oriental countries, has historically sustained its growing populations by the highly laborious and costly process of constructing paddy-fields and linking them into irrigation systems. To this day the pattern of Japanese land use and cultivation much more resembles her impoverished or industrializing Far Eastern neighbours than her fellow OECD members, as may be seen from a comparison of current land–labour ratios in Table 6.3.

In the rice economy, the dichotomy between town and countryside has never been as strong as in Western civilization or acquired the same force as an analogy of man's relation to nature. Rice paddy is itself man-made and its irrigation channels require constant maintenance through collective human effort, just as the streets and canals of a town do. Being labour-demanding and productive in equal measure, a landscape of rice-fields supports a high density of human settlement quite unlike the depopulated rural landscapes of the occident. The real contrast, as Berque (1982) demonstrates with both geographical and linguistic erudition, is between forested wilderness and the inhabited area or oecumene of pastures, fields, paddy, and built-up land. 'The rural', as a category embracing cultivated and wild areas but excluding urbanized areas, is a concept foreign to Japanese thinking, and so are the connotations of rural naturalness and vulnerability, and the consequent need for protection, which have been such a common theme of my fellow authors.

In an attempt to echo the different nature of the issues in the Japanese context, this chapter will begin with a short survey

Table 6.3 Cropland area per agricultural worker.

Country	Area (hectares)
China	0.2
South Korea	0.4
Vietnam	0.4
Laos	0.6
Indonesia	0.6
India	0.8
Japan	1.0
Kampuchea	1.2
Far East	0.8
Western Europe	6.6
North America	56.4

Source: FAO 1986, own compilation.

of the nation's land resources, highlighting the contrasts between habitable and other areas, and showing the pervasiveness of human intervention in both. The pattern of land utilization is then described both in terms of the fixed stock and of flows between use categories. Lastly, the chapter summarizes current law and policy, with some words of explanation about the politics of rural land.

The land of Japan

The Japanese islands (there are 3922 in all) are flung far across the western Pacific from 20° to 46° N and from 122° to 154° E. Even the four main islands of Hokkaido, Honshu, Kyushu and Shikoku, which have over 98% of the total land area and on which we shall be concentrating, have a climatic range from the subarctic to the warmly temperate. In the rugged landform of the islands north–south contrasts combine with the effects of Siberian and subtropical air masses and a strong windward–leeward contrast in precipitation patterns to produce a kaleidoscope of local variation. As Trewartha puts it (1965, p. 9) 'the country is composed of numerous small isolated units which almost defy generalized synthesis'. However, in the context of the present chapter, generalize we must.

The most important generalization about the land of Japan is that it is narrow and rocky. Pushed up by the collision between the Asian and Pacific tectonic plates, Japan has the highest earthquake rate in the world and over 60 active volcanoes. There are 25 mountains over 3000 m high (the tallest being Mount Fuji at 3776 m), but their ubiquity matters more than their height. Of the surface area 61% is officially classified as 'mountain', 23% as 'hill' or 'upland' and only 14% as 'lowland' (see Fig. 6.1). A complex geology has scattered the precipitous metamorphic and tertiary rocks, and the somewhat gentler sloping granites and volcanics in fair measure through the four main islands, giving a broadly comparable landform and distribution of gradients in each. All over Japan we find the same basic pattern of fast-flowing rubble-filled mountain streams falling rapidly through deeply incised valleys to debouch into a shallow silted sea. The coastal plains between the rocky headlands are not large, being made by the accumulation of river-borne mud and rubble on deeply sloping geological strata (Trewartha 1965 ch. 1). A children's song about a train ride captures the essence of the resulting landscape:

Rural land-use planning in Japan

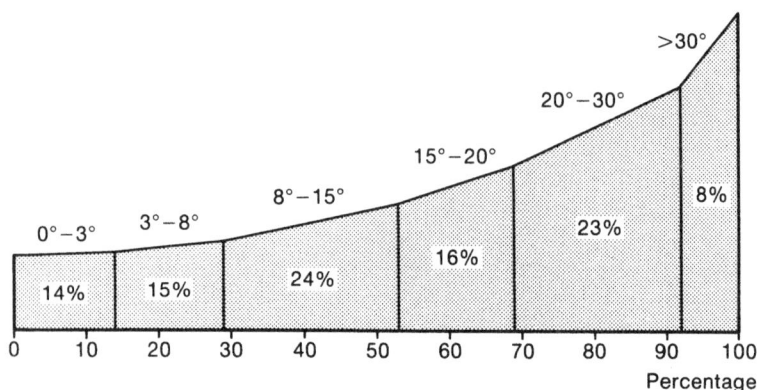

Figure 6.1 Classification of land in Japan by gradient.
Source: *Japan Statistical Yearbook* 1986 Table I-8.

> Now in the mountains
> Now by the beach
> Out across the iron bridge
> Back into the tunnel
> Out of the darkness and on to the plains.

Early cultivators in Japan faced a far less hospitable environment than their counterparts on the wide, fertile plains of Europe. The land of the sea-plains was marshy and liable to annual flooding by waters cascading out from the hills whereas inland areas of habitable land, such as the Kanto plain – Japan's largest at 13 000 square kilometres – were often droughty, with a deep water table, and their soil a coarse volcanic ash leached of nutrients by the abundant rain. The struggle to create a fertile agricultural landscape began in prehistoric times and continues today. The land of Japan is man-made, not naturally given.

There have been four great periods of advance. The first was the *Johri* system of land reclamation, from AD 645, whereby extensive areas of coastal land were diked, irrigated and subdivided into meticulously numbered square plots (many fields keep their number to this day). Stable feudal conditions during the Edo era (1603–1867) permitted more ambitious schemes such as the building of *Waju* settlements behind polder-style embankments on delta land, the construction of major canals to bring the dry volcanic soils of the Kanto plain into cultivation, and much terracing of steep hillsides. In the Meiji era (1868–1912), when Japan was opened up for the first time to the West, marshes were reclaimed and lagoons drained with Dutch technology while German legal techniques of land readjustment were used to rationalize scattered peasant holdings. Lastly, the land area of Japan has been fundamentally modified by modern civil engineering intervention in postwar years, as we shall see below. Over the past 2000 years an essentially artificial landscape has been created, its plains recovered from the estuarine swamps, its rivers corseted in concrete and masonry, its natural tree cover replaced by afforestation in all but the most inaccessible mountain areas (Beardsley *et al.* 1959, Trewartha 1965, Yoshikawa *et al.* 1981). We shall review the resulting pattern of land utilization (Fig. 6.2) under three broad

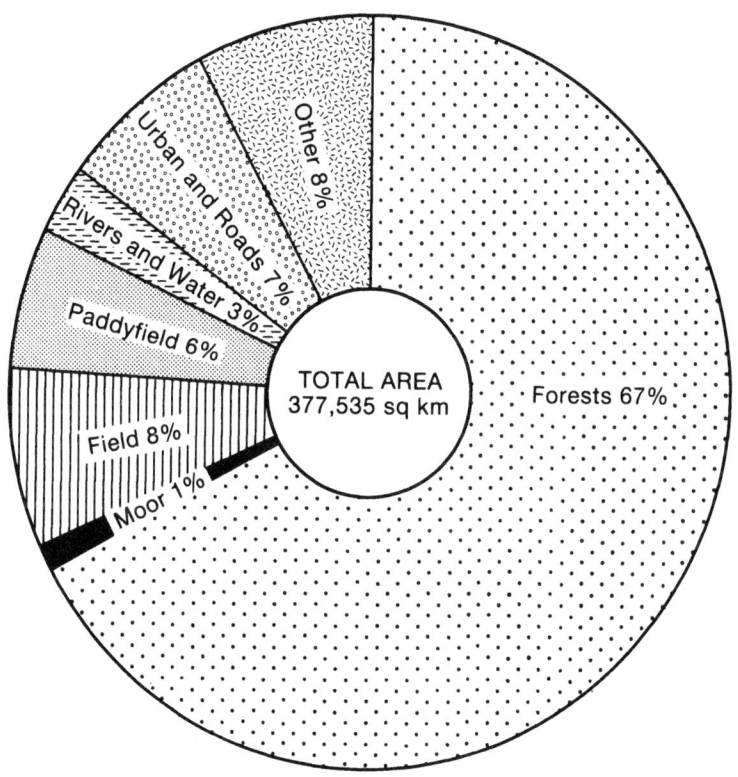

Figure 6.2 Classification of land in Japan by use.
Source: *Japan Statistical Yearbook* 1986 Table I-6

heads, looking first at the forest area, next at agricultural land, and last at urban-related land uses.

The forest

Japan has over 25 million hectares of forest (see Fig. 6.3). It occupies over 60% of the area of each of the four main islands, and Scandinavian proportions of 70% and more in 20 of the 47 prefectures. About a fifth of forest is true wilderness, being either unusable *genya* (wild scrubland) or inaccessible to man. The remainder serves a variety of public and private purposes.

Historically, the forests were owned by feudal landlords, villagers having common rights to gather timber, coppice trees and make charcoal from their local woods. The 1946 land reform, which redistributed farmland to the cultivators, left forest ownership

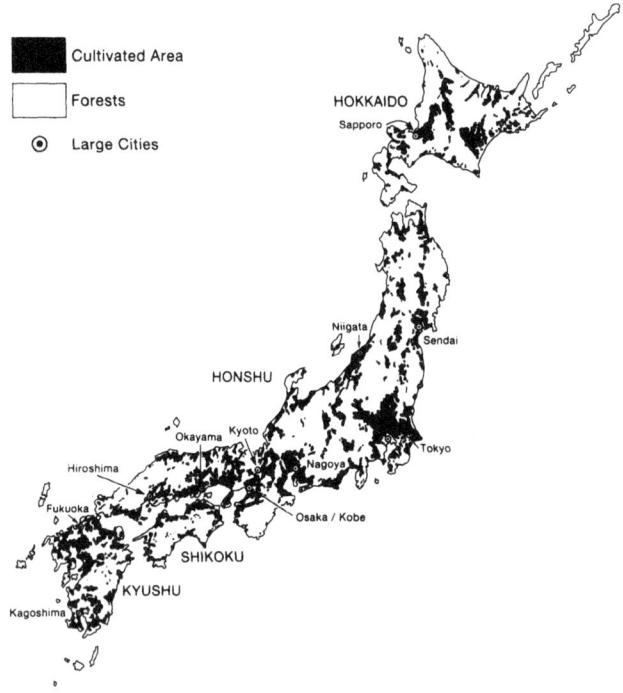

Figure 6.3 Forests and cultivated land in Japan.

untouched. Much forest therefore continues to be held privately in medium-to-small blocks. The state also has extensive holdings. Lastly, almost half the rural settlements retain their commons – averaging 28 ha – though the availability of artificial fertilizers and bottled propane fuel means that they are little used for their original purposes (Fukutake 1980). Other hamlets relinquished communal woodlands to the government or divided them among farmers. Altogether there are more than 5 million individual owners of forest land.

The most important forest product is of course timber and the history of its exploitation in Japan is not altogether happy. Throughout the great flowering of urban civilization in the Edo period, landlords devastated the natural forest cover of broad-leaved oaks and beeches, selling the timber to fire the pottery kilns, iron smelters and salt driers of the coastal cities. Planned reforestation in the Meiji era covered the hills with quick-growing species of pine, but these stands were again over-exploited during the Second World War, while bad husbandry reduced most of the broad-leaf forest to small trees of coppice dimensions valuable only for firewood. During the past 40 years the government has promoted a programme of clear-felling and replanting which now covers almost 10 million hectares or 40% of the total area. But these artificial forests are still young, and as they mature, domestic output of timber continues a steady decline, falling from 50 million cubic metres in 1961 to 42 million cubic metres in the early 1980s.

Besides the economic exploitation of timber the forest area also acts in various ways as a public good. It protects the headwaters of reservoirs that serve the great centres of population and industry with water and hydroelectric power; forestry prevents gravel and boulders being swept by the short, torrential mountain streams to block up dams and irrigation canals and discharge on to cropped fields; the forest provides a wind-break for settlements in the steep valleys; and last (and perhaps also least) it offers scenic beauty and recreation for humans and a habitat for wild animals.

To secure these various social ends the Japanese government has designated almost 8 million hectares as 'Protection Forest Area', within which exploitation is regulated and the state has preferential purchase rights. Three-quarters is protected to ensure the conservation of headwaters and a further quarter to prevent soil erosion. Overlapping with this designation are the 3.3 million hectares of 'National Parks' and 'Quasi-National Parks' shown in Figure 6.4 (and a further 2 million hectares designated at a local level as 'Prefectural Natural Parks'), most of them located

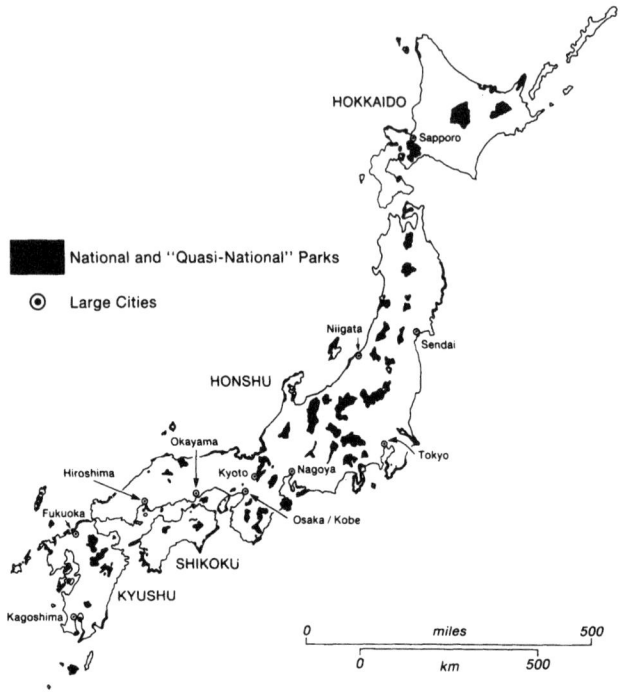

Figure 6.4 National parks in Japan.

in forest land. Again, park designation brings additional controls on development, and certain rights of subsidized public purchase which have not, however, been widely exercised.

Outdoor recreation in mountain areas continues to grow modestly rather than spectacularly. Though the strongest Japanese leisure preferences are for more urban and commercially oriented sports such as golf or baseball, the out-of-town parks attract visitors by the hundred million (see Table 6.4). The Japanese enjoy their mountains in a gregarious urban way, with advertisements and souvenir kiosks much in evidence and loudspeakers and fairy lights strung along the tree trunks at the more popular beauty spots. Some 1000 hot springs, located in the widely distributed young volcanic rocks, have been developed as spas and are a major attraction for visitors. Excursions of all kinds are often organized by employers, who, for example, own more than half of the country's currently registered mountaineers' huts. Upland walking in the difficult terrain has been

Table 6.4 Natural parks, 1984.

	No. of parks	Total area (million ha)	Visitors per year (millions)
National Parks	27	2	342.5
Quasi-National Parks	54	1.3	286.9
Prefectural Parks	298	2	243.3

Source: Japan Statistical Yearbook 1986 Tables 20–1.

made possible through the provision, mainly by local authorities, of well-defined and brightly signposted 'Hiking Tracks', which have increased rapidly in number in recent years to almost 1500. Second-home developments in mountain areas still seem to occur only on a modest scale, though data are hard to obtain. The 1983 Housing Census listed only 216 000 second homes in the whole of Japan, with significant concentrations in mountainous prefectures such as Nagano (25 200) and Shizuoka (23 000).

Taking an overall view of land-use issues in Japan's mountainous forest spine, what is perhaps most noticeable to Western eyes is the absence of that demand for an artificially preserved sense of remoteness, and facilities for private communion with nature which create so many policy problems for planners in Western Europe and North America. Japanese eyes see no more incongruity in the red-and-white striped radio pylons which now crown many peaks than in the familiar coastal lighthouse.

Agriculture

The United Nations' Food and Agriculture Organization (FAO) seems in a quandary when classifying Japan for comparative statistical purposes. Though clearly, as we saw at the outset, a typical Far Eastern rice economy in terms of farm size and structure, its productivity is vastly superior to any other. (In fact Japan is grouped with Israel and South Africa as one of the only three 'Class 1 Developed Market Economies' outside North America, Western Europe and Oceania.)

Viewed from the air, the cultivated land area has a timeless appearance. Of a total 5.5 million hectares, 57% are farmed as rice paddy (*suiden*) and 23% as unirrigated upland fields (*hata*) (Noh &

Kimura 1983 p. 41). Rural hamlets lie at intervals of only a few hundred metres in the irrigated area and not much further apart in the uplands. Except in Hokkaido, which has been colonized by the Japanese government in the present century, both fields and holdings are minuscule, two-thirds of the latter being smaller than 1 ha, and only a handful exceeding 6 ha. The land reform carried out in 1946 was, as Fukutake stresses, a reform and not a revolution. It transferred farm ownership but did not consolidate holdings, which were if anything fragmented still further in the late 1940s by the return of soldiers (1980 p. 10). Since then, although every other aspect of rural life has been turned upside-down, the size distribution of farm holdings has remained remarkably steady.

Meanwhile, population movement and growth have decisively favoured the towns. Farming, which occupied more than a quarter of the workforce as recently as 1965, now occupies fewer than 5 million persons (10 million household members), a smaller proportion than in Western Europe as a whole and quite unique in South-East Asia (see Table 6.5). But these small farmers, declining in number and advancing in average age, are no marginal class left in the wake of economic progress. Quite the contrary. For political reasons discussed below, postwar governments have favoured the agricultural sector with a rice price which has kept farm household incomes on a parity with urban wage-earners. And nine out of ten farming families do in fact draw additional incomes from non-agricultural occupations, incomes which in 68% of households exceed their farm earnings. (The complex regional variations in income patterns are analysed by Ishii 1980.)

The pattern of agricultural land use in contemporary Japan has to be seen in the light of the four factors just mentioned: peasant

Table 6.5 Percentage of economically active population in agriculture, 1985.

Sweden	4.7
Netherlands	5.0
France	6.7
Japan	8.3
North America	3.2
Western Europe	8.6
Far East	62.5

Source: FAO 1986, original compilation.

proprietorship, rural depopulation, political clout, and a high degree of involvement of farm families in the urban economy. Put simply, the result has been a powerful stimulus to mechanization, and a strong disincentive to sell land.

The push for modernization began immediately after the war with the establishment of the Agricultural Extension Service, working with study groups of farmers to whom land reform had given a new economic stimulus to improve yields. The political weight of the farmers' co-operatives sustained the momentum of rural infrastructure programmes while their growing prosperity enabled them to buy ever more sophisticated capital equipment, most of it devised by Japanese manufacturers especially for the small-scale cultivator. Where a prewar farm population of 14 million relied almost entirely on animal and human power, their 10 million heirs are nowadays mechanized on a substantial scale, as the examples in Table 6.6 show. With mechanized planters, monorail or cable conveyors, lightweight sprinklers, vinyl greenhouses and artificial fertilizers, crops have increased as effort has diminished. The productivity of Japanese farming per unit area is now the highest in the world, with especially striking increases in the market gardening crops such as cucumbers, lettuces and tomatoes which are grown under glass or vinyl. The only aspect of productivity to fall in postwar years was in the traditional practice of double-cropping of rice paddy, probably because the insertion of a second crop – barley, rape seed, or soy beans – between the rows of growing rice is still very labour-intensive, too much so for today's part-time farmers. However, the percentage utilization rate of rice paddy (planted area divided by cultivated area, expressed as a percentage) which was as high as 134% in 1960, has levelled off at 103% since 1975, and is of course still very high when viewed comparatively.

Lastly, farmers are landowners. The land reform of 1946 transformed a class of lowly peasants whom townsfolk regarded as the 'unfortunates' into proprietors of one of Japan's scarcest resources – land! They have used their windfall with great canniness. Land values have appreciated better than any other asset in postwar Japan. Even in the deeper rural areas, its value has been buoyed up by the demand for housing and local industry. Near major urban settlements the appreciation has been astronomical. As the unchanging farm structure shows, owners have reacted primarily by hanging on to their holdings, as a matter of straight economic rationality compounded by the cultural factors of ancestor worship and peasant attachment to family land. The stickiness of the

Table 6.6 Ownership of agricultural machinery (millions)

	Combines and threshers	Rice-planting machines	Tractors and cultivators	Total number of farms
1971	0.08	0.046	3.5	5.3
1981	0.9	1.9	4.2	4.6
1986	1.1	2.1	4.4	4.3

Source: *Japan Statistical Yearbook* 1987, original compilation.

farmland market means that the few large-scale commercial farmers have had the greatest difficulty expanding and can only do so through leasing, not purchase. And what has really moulded the pattern of urban development has not been planning policy (of which more below) but the strong speculative involvement of farmers determined to hold and maximize the value of their land portfolios over the long run.

Urban land

No account of rural land use would be complete without reference to the urban dimension. It goes without saying that Japan's postwar resurgence from the devastation of the Second World War to global industrial leadership has been accompanied by a massive urbanization (see OECD 1986).

From the very extensive literature on the modern Japanese city we need just draw out one paradox of great importance for land utilization – the combination of very high urban population density with low building coverage. The urban population densities stand out clearly when compared against those of OECD members at comparable levels of economic well-being. They rise to a peak in the cities of Tokyo and Osaka, with residential densities of 8600 and 6600 persons per square kilometre (Statistical Indicators on Social Life 1984). But in contrast to, say, Hong Kong, Japanese cities are not densely built up. The predominant building height is between one and three storeys with higher residential flats accounting for only a minuscule proportion of the dwelling stock. Dwellings are small because they are built on small plots, which is due in turn to the piecemeal manner in which small-scale landowners, the farmers, release portions of their holdings for development. The most striking land-use characteristic of the areas of postwar urban growth is the continuing presence of small cultivators, clinging tenaciously to the residual parcel of land which is their best investment asset and tax privilege. In metropolitan Tokyo almost 7400 ha of farmland were still under cultivation in 1982, and the amount being released for development each year was minimal (150 ha in all) and diminishing (NLA 1987). Sasaki (1981) studied a typical commuting town, Koganei, with a mushrooming population of over 100 000, some 25 km west of Tokyo. In a fully urbanized municipality with a high density of over 9000 persons per square kilometre, he found that 40% of the original 1950 farm households continued in agriculture, with an average holding of less than 0.6 ha apiece. Only 8 of the 295 households worked full-time in agriculture. The favourite crop of these suburban agriculturalists is garden shrubs.

Land conversion between uses

Japanese bureaucracy prepares outstandingly detailed data on land utilization giving precise information on both the land stock and on flows between categories. The current balance of the main land uses, summarized in pie-chart form in Figure 6.4, is given in detail in Table 6.7. Note the amount of forest land within the boundaries of the Major Metropolitan Areas (defined administratively by the Tokyo, Osaka and Nagoya prefectures and those adjacent), and also farmland's 16% share of the metropolitan land area.

The relative growth and decline of different categories of use can be traced from year to year in the annual reports of the National Land Agency. The rate of change has closely followed the growth rate of the national economy, peaking in the late 1960s and early 1970s. In the present decade both the number and area of land transactions has stabilized or declined. Table 6.8 shows the steep decline in the rate of land-use conversion. It also reveals the complexity of the transfer pattern. To appreciate it, we need to step outside the conventional rural planning ideology which sees the total stock of land as fixed, and urban development as a zero-sum game in which urban gain equals rural loss. The Japanese case proves surprisingly different.

First, in defiance of the old real-estate aphorism that 'land ain't being made nowadays', Japan has continued to manufacture it from the sea and the mountains. Sea reclamation has been a highly significant source of land, especially for the heavy industrial areas or *Kombinahts* built near to the main port areas of Tokyo,

Table 6.7 Land use in Japan, 1983 ('000 square km).

	Cultivated	Farmland Meadow & pasture	Forest	Grassland	Water area	Roads	Residential	Urban Industry	Offices & shops	Other
Total land area										
377.8	54.1	1.4	252.6	3.0	11.6	10.8	11.1	1.5	2.0	29.7
100%	14.3	0.4	66.9	0.8	3.1	2.8	2.9	0.4	0.5	7.9
Land use within the 3 major metropolitan areas – Tokyo, Osaka, Nagoya										
39.3	6.3	0.0	20.6	0.0	1.4	1.9	3.4	0.5	0.6	4.6
100%	16.0	0.0	52.4	0.0	3.6	4.8	8.7	1.3	1.5	11.7

Source: *Japan Statistical Yearbook 1986* Table I-6.

Table 6.8 Trends in land conversion (hectares).

	Mean 1970–2	1982
Farm to urban	44 600	24 200
Forest to urban	21 800	7900
Forest to farm	31 300	12 100
Farm to forest	19 900	3700

Source: National Land Agency 1983.

Nagoya, Osaka–Kobe and the Inland Sea Industrial Region, where raw materials could be unloaded directly from deep-water quays into a complex of petrochemical or iron and steel plants, linked on a flow-line system. The prodigious appetite for land of such developments could not be met from rice paddy. Between 1965 and 1975, 60 000 ha of sea were reclaimed for industry. Not all the coastal sites were shallow – some required landfill to a depth of 50 m (Dawson 1984 p. 92). In the early 1970s, 3500 ha of new industrial land were being created each year. In the 1980s the rate has fallen to between 500 and 1000 ha, still a significant contribution to industry's new floor-space requirement.

The sea and the marshes have also yielded much new farmland. In the late 1960s, when losses to housing and industry were highest, agricultural reclamation was also at a peak. Major areas of large-scale modern farming were opened up in Kojima Bay on the Inland Sea (Okayama Prefecture), at the mouth of the Shinano river (Niigata Prefecture), on a brackish lagoon, once Japan's second largest inland water area, at Hachirohgata (Akita Prefecture), and on an extensive tract of peat bogs on the Ishikari Plain (Hokkaido). New rice paddy was being created at an annual rate of 30 000 ha in 1959/60 and 15 000 ha ten years later. The expansion of the farmland area actually outstripped the losses to the urban sector, so that the cultivated area reached its all-time maximum of 6 million hectares as late as 1961, and rice paddy peaked at 3.4 million hectares in 1969. With current rice surpluses some 45 000 ha of paddy are annually converted back into dry field. The total cultivated area continues to nudge forward onto the coastal marshlands or into the forest area. In the period 1981–5 new agricultural land was still being reclaimed from unproductive wasteland at an average annual rate of 22 000 ha, which almost made up the whole loss to urban use. Table 6.9 summarizes the net effect of these complex relationships on the cultivated area.

Table 6.9 Trends in cultivated land area ('000 hectares).

Year	Total	Paddy fields	Dry fields Open	Permanently planted
1965	6004	3391	2088	526
1970	5796	3415	1781	600
1975	5572	3171	1774	628
1980	5461	3055	1819	587
1985	5379	2952	1878	540
1986	5358	2931	1889	538

Source: Annual Crop Survey, summary in *Japan Statistical Yearbook* 1987 Table 5–10.

It shows that the total farmed area of Japan is being eroded by some 20 000 ha a year, which might be thought modest for a country of 120 million population with a highly dynamic free-market economy.

Land planning

So at last we arrive at the central concern of this book, the role of the state. In land policy, as in other matters, Japanese government is relatively centralized. Though the letter of the law may attribute autonomy to the 47 elected prefectural assemblies and the 3250 city, town and village councils, their fiscal and administrative dependence on the centre ensures that important decisions fall to the ministries in Tokyo. Local communities obtain access to the credit and the investment programmes of central government through the good offices of political intermediaries who wield influence in the national Diet. Herein lies the secret of the unbroken postwar hegemony of the conservative Liberal Democratic Party, especially in rural areas. The LDP, in essence a big business party, maintains its electoral base in the well-weighted farming vote. Its strong ideology of private property is reassuring to rural proprietors. In a centralized bureaucratic system, LDP politicians act as brokers to get roads maintained, rivers diked, pumps installed, and clinics built. And perhaps most importantly, the network of influence connecting LDP with the farmers' co-operative *Nokyo* has traditionally ensured that agricultural incomes are kept up through the price of rice. Such are the political rules of the game within which rural land planning has developed (Fukutake 1980 ch. 5).

The Japanese land planning system is highly elaborate. Concluding his comparative review of land policy in Japan, Poland, the United States and the United Kingdom, Dawson (1984) grouped it with Poland's as the most all-embracing system of intervention. Its most immediately striking feature is the large number of overlapping designations applied to rural areas. Each designation relates to separate legislation and falls under the purview of a different ministry. A National Land Agency (NLA) exists to co-ordinate the various sectoral elements within an overall policy for the use of land as a national resource. We shall take these elements in turn, beginning with the four principal types of land planning instrument – agricultural, urban, forest and environmental.

The Agricultural Land Act (1952) instituted for the first time a system of control by prefectural governors over transfers of farmland to other uses. Intended primarily to protect the achievements of the 1946 land reform, the legislation allowed governors full discretion and they used it permissively. The Ministry of Agriculture then attempted, in 1959, to define nationally uniform Standards for Permitting the Conversion of Farmland, but they too proved ineffective, given the strong presumption in favour of the farmer's free rights of private property. We have already seen the high rate of building on farmland during the boom years after 1960, when every rural municipality competed to entice industrial investment with tax exemptions, road building, and a free-for-all development climate (Fukutake 1980 p. 178). The frenetic land speculation of those years prompted new and stronger legislation, the Agricultural Promotion Areas Act (1969). This required all prefectural governors to designate Agricultural Promotion Areas (APA), where land conversion of up to 2 ha requires prefectural authorization, and anything larger, approval by the Ministry. Within the APAs, which are extensive rural tracts embracing much forest land as well as rivers, roads and dwellings, a still stronger designation – Agricultural Land Zone (ALZ) – can be applied to the actual cultivated land. In principle, ALZs cannot normally be converted to another use. Currently half the land area of Japan is zoned as APA and about a sixth as ALZ, the latter covering 80% of cultivated land.

The City Planning Act (1968) established for the first time a comprehensive system of control over urban development. Land within designated City Planning Areas is zoned by prefectural authorities either as Urbanization Promotion Area (UPA) or

Urbanization Control Area (UCA). As the terminology implies, the UPA/UCA boundary is intended to define a firm interim limit to urban growth. A quarter of the land area of Japan now lies within a City Planning Area.

Various further pieces of legislation provide the basis for special areas to be designated in the mountains, forest and wild areas. Forest land is, like agriculture, classified by a double-decker system which distinguishes Reserved Forest within broadly defined Forest Zones. Similarly, the National Parks shown in Figure 6.3 contain their own Special Zones and Special Conservation Areas in which development requires permission from the prefectural governor or higher authority, and a comparable system operates for nature reserves under the National Environmental Conservation Act (1972).

Land policy in Japan emerges from the combination of multiple separate systems of zoning, each of which reflects distinct ministerial priorities and local patterns of interest. Matters are made worse by double-decker methods of zoning which allow very extensive designations of a general nature to be applied liberally over the land surface. Dawson (1984) analyses in detail the resulting overlaps between sometimes incongruous zonings. He finds that 40% of the land area of Japan falls into two zones and 7% into three; 4% is classified simultaneously as City Planning Area, Forest Zone and Agricultural Zone!

The National Land Agency (NLA) was established under the National Land Use Planning Act (1974) to bring some central co-ordination to bear, through the preparation of a National Land Use Plan. In its original conception, the plan was part of a system of land market regulation established in response to public outcry at the land price increases of the early 1970s. NLA needed to set land-use priorities as a basis for direct intervention by prefectural authorities in major property transactions. However, the political pressure for market intervention slackened after 1975 as annual increases in land values fell back below 10%. The agency was left with a distinctly more modest role of policy co-ordination and monitoring.

The National Land Use Plan of 1978 set out the basic policy to reduce the land requirement of all users by promoting more efficient exploitation of land through multi-use and intensification. In the urban sector this implied building at higher densities, and reclamation of shallow offshore waters. For agriculture it meant a revival of double-cropping, with a target utilization ratio of 112% set for 1985. For demand that could not be accommodated through better use of existing land the plan set targets for the transfer of uses between categories, both for the country as a whole and for its component regions. Over the plan period 1972–85 cultivated land was to enlarge its share, chiefly at the expense of forest, from 15.2%, and developed land was to grow from 5.3% to 6.9%. These rather precise national targets became fuzzy in the process of translation into land-use plans at a regional scale because of the use of multiple zonings. NLA provides some very complex decision rules for land affected by more than one primary zoning, though the discretionary power of prefectural governors is more important in practice than rational central planning.

As with any plan, what matters is not the intrinsic coherence of NLA's targets but its power to influence events. Like many such co-ordinating bodies, NLA plays a supernumerary role. It has no resources and no positive powers, and the strongly individualistic ethos of the Japanese system of private property has tended to place all forms of planning on the defensive, especially since the election in 1982 of Mr Nakasone, a prime minister known to have close connections to major private development interests, and to be ideologically committed to deregulation. NLA operates indirectly, through a review procedure whereby prefectural plans are submitted to an advisory panel of experts, the National Land Use Council. However, its advice is often overruled by central government. Similarly, the detailed translation of NLA targets and policies is supposed to be ensured by Councils on Land Use Planning which advise the 47 prefectural governors and the 11 big city mayors. They are weak bodies with no enforcement powers.

The trends of land conversion set out in the previous section are increasingly divergent from NLA's stated objectives. The cultivated land area continues its decline and so does the utilization rate. Despite national policy to intensify the use of land within built-up areas, NLA in 1984 reported that the stock of agricultural land within zones designated for urban development (the Urbanization Promotion Areas – UPA) was still 190 091 ha, 14% of the total UPA. Less than 2500 ha per year were being released for development within the three major metropolitan areas over the period 1980–4 (NLA 1985). The planning system has no positive powers to oblige owners to release land for development, nor would there be political support for such moves. So while farmers within the urbanized area sit speculatively upon their land, NLA is inevitably forced to concede further releases of green-field sites as development land (Hebbert 1986, Hebbert and Nakai 1988).

Other aspects of national land policy have met with greater success. Industrial land productivity has intensified, so that the area of land used by manufacturing increased by only 13.7% in 1971–81 while industrial output increased by 70% (NLA 1984). Land reclamation continues apace, with major new schemes in the late 1980s to build in the waters of Tokyo, Osaka and Nagoya bays. Total agricultural output creeps upward at a comparable rate to the decline of farmland area, but vinyl sheeting and solar heating have dramatically intensified land productivity in specific crops such as cucumbers, where a 30% planted area yields 40% more produce than 20 years ago.

The very fact that Japan has an annually monitored national land-use policy sets it impressively apart from other cases discussed in this book. When chalking up its hits and misses we should not attribute too much to the planning process as such. In Japan as elsewhere, land utilization remains an outcome of politics rather than policy. The current political drift is towards deregulation and a greater orientation towards large-scale development interests, possibly at the expense of the traditional connection between the LDP and the farmers. Not even the price subsidy for rice can be regarded as sacrosanct any more.

Recent policy utterances of the National Land Agency cast a question mark on the past 20 years' emphasis on containment and zoning-based approaches to land use, posing an alternative model – reminiscent of William Morris's *News from Nowhere* – in which town and country melt into each other. In part, this approach merely acknowledges the deep-rooted geographical reality analysed by Berque (1982). But it may also represent an increasingly conscious rejection of that predominant OECD-member philosophy of planning for the segregation of town and country, which pervades every other chapter of this book.

Acknowledgements

Though they bear no responsibility for its shortcomings, the chapter could n~t have been written without kind help from Japanese-speaking friends and colleagues. Professor Ichiro Nishimura (Nara Women's University) made some valuable and timely suggestions. Norihiro Nakai (London School of Economics) scrutinized the statistical data with customary acumen and gave much friendly guidance on questions of interpretation. Dr Richard Wiltshire (SOAS) very kindly checked for errors. The author also wishes to record his thanks to Hiroshi Arai, First Secretary at the

Embassy of Japan in London, who obtained English versions of National Land Agency reports and to Gary Llewellyn, who prepared the maps and diagrams. Lastly, a word of grateful acknowledgement to STICERD, the Suntory Toyota International Centre for Economics and Related Disciplines for its generous support of the research project into the metropolitan growth of Tokyo, of which the present chapter is a by-product.

References

Beardsley, R., J. Hall & R. Ward 1959. *Village Japan*. Chicago: University of Chicago Press.

Berque, A. 1982. *Vivre l'espace au Japon*. Paris: PUF.

Dawson, A. 1984. *The land problem in the developed economy*. London: Croom Helm.

Dawson, A. 1985. Land use policy and control in Japan. *Land Use Policy*. January, 54–60.

FAO 1986. *Production Yearbook*. Rome: Food and Agriculture Organization.

Fukutake, T. 1980. *Rural society in Japan*. Tokyo: University of Tokyo Press.

Hebbert, M. 1986. Urban planning and urban sprawl in Japan. *Town Planning Review*, April, 141–58.

Hebbert M. and Nakai N. (1988) *How Tokyo grows: land development and planning on the metropolitan fringe*, Occasional Paper II. London: Suntory Toyota International Centre for Economics and Related Disciplines.

Ishii, M. 1980. Regional trends in the changing agrarian structure of postwar Japan. In Association of Japanese Geographers *The Geography of Japan*. Tokyo: Teikokushoin.

NLA 1984, 1985. *Annual reports on the use of national land: summary* (English version). Tokyo: National Land Agency.

NLA 1987. *Outline of the White Paper on National Land Use for Financial Year 1986* (English version). Tokyo: National Land Agency.

Noh, T. & J. Kimura (eds) 1983. *Japan: a regional geography of an island nation*. Tokyo: Teikoku-Shoin.

OECD 1986. *Urban policies in Japan* (Organization for Economic Cooperation and Development, Group on Urban Affairs). Paris: OECD.

RDPC 1981. *Rural planning and development in Japan*. Tokyo: Rural Development Planning Commission.

Sasaki, H. 1981. Changing patterns of population and land use in the Tokyo metropolitan region. In *Changing agriculture and rural development: the world and Japan*, H. Ishida. Tokyo: International Geographical Union.

Statistical indicators on social life 1984. Tokyo: Management and Coordination Agency, Statistics Bureau.

Trewartha, G. 1965. *Japan – a geography*. London: Methuen.

Yoshikawa, T., S. Kaizuka & Y. Ota 1981. *The landforms of Japan*, Tokyo: University of Tokyo Press.

7 Rural planning in the United States: fragmentation, conflict and slow progress

THOMAS L. DANIELS,
MARK B. LAPPING
& JOHN W. KELLER

Introduction

Rural America consists of nearly 84 million hectares, thousands of administrative jurisdictions, and some 60 million people who live in a diversity of geographic regions, economic conditions and changing land-use patterns. The variety of America's rural areas – from remote wilderness to the rapidly developing rural–urban fringe – has made different planning programmes necessary and a high degree of programmatic idiosyncrasy has been the result. State, local, and federal government policies all have some impact on the use and management of rural land. But the three levels of government have produced considerable fragmentation in the public attempt to foster and yet control rural development. This fragmentation has often frustrated both public officials and private citizens by producing either weak or heavily bureaucratic planning programmes which work against either local interests or the public at large.

Land use in the United States has traditionally involved a minimum of government intervention, and land-use controls have been shaped mainly by local town and county governments. At the heart of the struggle for effective rural planning lies a deep-rooted feeling that a landowner should have considerable discretion over the future of the land. This belief tends to predominate at the local level. By contrast, recent state and federal programmes affecting the rural environment tend to favour the broader public interest, variously defined.

The fragmentation of authority and programmes has underscored the rise in rural land-use conflicts. Policy makers and citizens alike have come to realize that land-use policies, or the lack of such policies, will have important implications for the future vitality and development of rural America. In the 1970s, non-metropolitan counties (counties with no city of more than 50 000 people or with county population of less than 100 000) grew faster than metropolitan counties for the first time in almost 200 years. This 'counterstream' of urban refugees brought some degree of economic prosperity as well as new problems to many rural areas. Population growth and population dispersion resulted in greater land-use conflicts, such as the loss of farmland and open space, toxic waste dumps, industrial plants, and more intensive residential and commercial uses. Although metropolitan counties are growing faster than non-metropolitan counties in the 1980s, returning to the historical pattern, many rural land-use conflicts remain – especially in the rural–urban fringe.

Rural land use and environmental planning are still in their infancy in the United States. Rural people have historically been viewed as politically conservative, traditional, and slow to accept new ideas. While both government and public interest programmes have grown significantly over the past 20 years, American land policies tend to favour the protection of private property rights over the public interest. American rural planning, like its urban counterpart, features a reactive rather than proactive planning style, relying on zoning, building codes and subdivision regulations which seek to protect the public health, safety and welfare. But these methods have often resulted in the failure of local governments to guide development and protect the rural environment. This failure has made evident the need for a more comprehensive approach to land-use planning and greater control in determining land uses. A major challenge facing many rural communities involves finding ways to minimize land-use conflicts so that the rural environment can maintain a diversity of wealth-producing land uses. None the less, rural planners will continue to face a struggle for legitimacy, political acceptance, and effective enforcement of planning programmes.

The federal role: federal lands management, environmental laws and spending programmes

Federal lands

The federal government owns and manages about one-third of the nation's 84 million rural hectares. Most of these federal lands are in the western states and Alaska, and more than half of the land area of several states (Alaska, Idaho, Nevada, Oregon and Utah) is in federal ownership. The states have relatively little input in how the federal lands are managed, even though federal management policies may have a profound impact upon the appearance and functioning of rural areas.

The administration of federal lands falls under a number of federal agencies, headed by the Department of the Interior and the Department of Agriculture. This fragmentation of authority has made coherent federal lands policy difficult. Some lands, such as national parks and wilderness areas, are virtually 'off limits' to any kind of development. Other lands, such as natural forests and acreages under the Bureau of Land Management, are managed according to a policy of 'multiple uses' and 'sustained yield'. Yet, many of these multiple users are likely to result in conflicts between users, especially between industry and environmentalists, and tend to frustrate the achievement of sustained yield in the production of timber, grazing livestock and environmental amenities. Further, some land-based products remain largely unpriced and too seldom receive adequate attention in the decision-making process.

Within the Department of the Interior, the Bureau of Land Management (BLM) administers roughly 190 million hectares or over 60% of all federal lands. About 121 million hectares of BLM lands (mostly tundra) are in Alaska, and nearly all of the rest are in sage-brush located in eleven Western states. BLM lands are generally unsuited for agriculture, except as rangeland, and have not been included in the national forest or national park systems. BLM land uses include outdoor recreation, livestock grazing, timber production, watershed protection, fish and wildlife habitat, industrial development, mining, human settlement and wilderness preservation. But the conservation and productive uses of BLM lands often conflict. Critics of the BLM argue that the agency has favoured ranching interests to the point of overgrazing. Currently, over three-quarters of the BLM's grazing lands are in fair-to-poor condition (US Council on Environmental Quality 1982). Grazing wildlife have been forced to compete with domestic livestock over dwindling supplies of forage, and soil erosion, tramping livestock and herbicide spraying have damaged wildlife habitats.

The US Forest Service, an agency within the Department of Agriculture, oversees the 76 million hectares of national forest lands. There are 155 national forests in 40 states, although over 65 million hectares are concentrated in the Western states and Alaska. About 25 million hectares of national forest lands are open to lumbering and 16 million relatively treeless hectares are used primarily for grazing. Since 1960, the Forest Service has been required to manage the national forest on a multiple use–sustained yield basis; that is, forests are to be managed for many uses which will generate returns, products and incomes over a long and continuous period of time. In the 1980s, the Forest Service has been developing land-use plans for each national forest to provide outdoor recreation, livestock grazing, timber harvesting, some mining, watershed protection, and fish and wildlife habitats.

Each plan for a national forest must include: critical issues facing the forest and its region as identified by the public; an evaluation of different land uses and planning objectives; an inventory of forest resources; an analysis of the present status of forest management; alternatives to meet regional forest output goals; the plan approval process; and a mechanism for the monitoring of the impact of the ensuing forest management policy. The latest federal plans call for near-doubling of the annual timber harvest from 11.6 billion (= thousand million) board feet to 20 billion over the next 50 years, and the construction of thousands of kilometres of logging roads.

In 1964, the Wilderness Act designated 54 natural forest areas containing 3.6 million hectares as the beginning of the National Wilderness Preservation System. As of 1986, wilderness areas contain 34 million hectares, of which 23 million hectares are in Alaska. Certain commercial and industrial uses were allowed on wilderness lands between 1964 and 1983, including timber harvesting and the construction of logging roads, livestock grazing and mineral exploration. Since 1983, only livestock grazing has been permitted. Each new proposed addition to the Federal Wilderness System is the occasion of major debate. Many times the controversy pits local community interests against local and national conservation organizations. It is often the case that local interests are not anti-environment. Rather, the benefits of wilderness are often subtle and widely dispersed while the 'costs' tend to be 'fixed' and located in the community now denied potential benefits from logging or mining, for example, without adequate compensation.

The Fish and Wildlife Service of the Department of the Interior administers the National Wildlife Refuge System which consists of over 700 wildlife refuges and game ranges covering 36 million hectares. Wildlife refuges offer habitats for the protection and conservation of fish and other wildlife that are often threatened with extinction. Game ranges serve as preserves in which herds are managed for present and future public enjoyment.

The National Park Service manages over 9 million hectares of national parks 'to conserve the scenery and the natural and historic objects and wildlife therein as will leave them unimpaired for the enjoyment of future generations'. Outside the national parks, the Park Service is in charge of national monuments and historic sites, national seashores and lakeshores, national rivers, national recreation areas and national trails. In recent years, some of the land and water resources placed under the control of the Park Service have included substantial amounts of privately owned land. The management of these lands has become, in effect, a partnership between federal, state and local governments and private landowners. Protection techniques consist of zoning, co-operative agreements and conservation easements as alternatives to outright fee simple federal purchase. Examples of this novel approach include the Upper Delaware Scenic and Recreational River in Pennsylvania and New York, the new River Gorge National River in West Virginia, and the Santa Monica Mountains National Recreation Area in California.

Federal projects affecting privately owned rural lands most often originate in the Army Corps of Engineers, the Bureau of Reclamation and the Soil Conservation Service. Since the 1930s, the Corps of Engineers has built over 250 dams, mainly for flood control. In some cases, these dams were erected to protect property built in downstream floodplains. The dams have flooded thousands of hectares including farmland, wildlife habitats, wetlands and geologic sites of interest. Another important function of the Corps of Engineers is the authority to grant or deny permits for the dredging and filling of any wetlands for uses other than farming, forestry, or ranching.

The Bureau of Reclamation, like the Army Corps of Engineers, plans and develops water projects which provide flood control, water for irrigation, water-related recreation, municipal and industrial water, and hydroelectricity. These projects may involve the construction of dams, reservoirs, canals and aqueducts. Unlike the Corps of Engineers, the Bureau of Reclamation operates only in 18 states west of the Mississippi River. The Bureau provides irrigation water to about 3.6 million hectares, municipal and industrial water to some 15 million people, and it can generate approximately 8 million kilowatts of electricity.

Within the Department of Agriculture, the Soil Conservation Service (SCS) has sponsored the creation of hundreds of soil and water conservation districts among private landowners. The SCS offers technical assistance to landowners, especially farmers, on practices to control soil erosion. Also, the SCS publishes detailed county soil quality maps indicating the potential for producing crops, erodibility, and limitations for development.

Over half the population of the United States lives in areas adjacent to coastal waters and shorelands, and many rural communities earn their livelihoods from commercial fishing and recreation activities along the shoreline. In 1972, Congress passed the Coastal Zone Management Act, the only nation-wide land-use planning measure ever enacted. Congress found that: 'The increasing and competing demands upon the lands and waters of our coastal zone occasioned by population growth and economic development . . . have resulted in the loss of living marine resources, wildlife, nutrient-rich areas, permanent and adverse changes to ecological systems, decreasing open space for public use, and shoreline erosion.'

The Coastal Zone Act is administered through the National Oceanic and Atmospheric Administration (NOAA) which provides federal funds and technical assistance for the planning and implementation of water and land-use management programmes in 30 states. Federal grants cover up to two-thirds of state planning and implementation costs. State plans must be approved by NOAA; and all subsequent federal actions must be as consistent as possible with the state plans. State plans must include: (a) the boundaries of the coastal zone; (b) permissible land and water uses within the zone; (c) and inventory of sensitive areas of particular concern; (d) state controls to enforce compliance; (e) the priority of uses in different areas of the zone; and (f) a co-ordination system for federal, state, regional and local agencies.

In addition, state plans must consider the national interest in siting developments of greater than local impact, such as electricity generating stations, national defence installations, harbours and ports, and fisheries. Areas of particular concern have helped set management priorities. These areas include unique and scarce plant and animal species and their breeding grounds, hazardous areas subject to flooding or landslides, recreation areas, and commercial and industrial development.

Federal environmental laws

Many rural communities have been lax about the protection of natural areas and enforcing environmental laws. There are many reasons for these shortcomings, primarily financial or in local attitude. Rural areas often lack adequate public funds for the monitoring and enforcement of environmental regulations.

Data bases are often difficult or prohibitively expensive to amass. Moreover, there is a shortage of technical expertise available for the planning and implementation of environmental management programmes. While sustainable economic development coupled with effective management of the environment is a worthy goal, extensive poverty and stagnant local economies cause communities to place economic development efforts far above environmental protection among priorities. But over the past 20 years, natural areas an wildlife have been granted a status of their own in the American legal system. The importance of natural areas has been recognized at the federal level and this has served to make the general public more aware of the environmental consequences of development. At the same time, pollution of air, water and soil has become the focus of major federal legislation.

The National Environmental Policy Act (NEPA) of 1969 requires all federal agencies proposing projects which involve the development of natural resources to prepare an Environmental Impact Statement (EIS) citing: (a) the adverse environmental effects of proposed projects; (b) alternatives to the proposed action; and (c) the long-term impact and irreversible use of resources. In addition, the Federal Water Resources Council has issued 'Standards of Planning Water and Related Land Resources' which apply to federal and federally assisted projects and programmes. These standards are intended to supplement the EIS process and call for broad public participation throughout the project planning stages.

All of these systems have been used to protect natural areas and rare and endangered species. One of the most famous cases occurred in Tennessee where the proposed Tellico Dam was denied under NEPA because of alleged threats to the snail darter, a rare and endangered fish species. In the celebrated 'Mineral King' case, Walt Disney, Inc., proposed a large recreation development in the Sequoia National Forest, but was denied permission because of potential destruction to the natural environment.

The problem of hazardous waste has been a public concern for only a few years, mostly since 1978 when the Love Canal, New York toxic dump site, which had been built over with residences, caused illnesses among local inhabitants. Recently, the awareness of hazardous waste is rapidly emerging as the most urgent environmental problem in rural America.

Today, there are an estimated 10 000 hazardous waste sites that need to be cleaned up. Dumping in rural areas has been widespread because: (a) the areas are sparsely populated; (b) land is relatively cheap; and (c) there is little local regulation or monitoring of dumping. Hazardous wastes pose a particularly severe threat to ground-water supplies because of the difficulty in cleaning up ground water; and rural Americans depend on ground water for about 95% of their drinking water. The pollution of ground water by hazardous wastes has resulted in the closing of wells and bans on certain water supplies. Ultimately, residents may be forced to move away.

In 1976, Congress empowered the Environmental Protection Agency to regulate the disposal of hazardous waste. After the Love Canal disaster, it became apparent that there were thousands of abandoned waste sites that required attention. Congress responded by enacting the 'Superfund' which allocated $1.6 billion (= thousand million) over 5 years for the clean-up of abandoned sites. Another $5 to $10 billion has been proposed for the Superfund over 1986–90. The Superfund allows the EPA to impose liability of those who have abandoned sites, but no compensation is provided for those who have suffered illness. Thus far, EPA implementation and enforcement of hazardous waste controls have generally been weak, featuring a reactive rather than a proactive planning style.

Floodplain management is a pervasive issue in rural America but rural areas receive less attention than urban areas under federal programmes. An estimated 57 to 73 million hectares, or 6–8% of the total land area of the United States, has experienced occasional flooding. Agriculture incurs the majority of flood losses in rural areas, topping $1.6 billion a year. Most other flood damage is inflicted on buildings erected in floodplains. Despite the existence of the National Flood Insurance Program (NFIP), a large amount of property in floodplains is not insured. NFIP provides low-cost flood insurance to over 2 million policy holders owning $100 billion of flood-prone property. In addition, areas of flood hazard in 20 000 communities and rural areas have been identified and mapped (Baker & Platt 1983 p. 250). If a community does not have a floodplain management programme, the NFIP places the community on an 'emergency basis'. This status carries lower levels of insurance coverage on existing properties and more severe restrictions on new development in floodplains, including limits on the type, location, height and design of buildings. If a community fails to adopt a management programme, then property owners can no longer obtain flood insurance. To date approximately 3200 communities have drafted satisfactory floodplain management programmes. In addition, the Flood Disaster Relief Act of 1974 requires states and communities receiving federal disaster aid to prepare a long-range hazard mitigation plan for the disaster area. In sum, the federal programmes emphasize the need to incorporate floodplain management into a community's general planning process rather than treat it as a separate and infrequent problem.

Federal development spending programmes

The US national government has conducted rural development programmes for over 90 years. But large-scale projects and programmes generally began with the New Deal era of the 1930s. Since then, the federal government has poured billions of dollars into improving the economic, social and environmental conditions of rural America. Legal, financial and political limitations of state and local governments have caused much of the reliance upon federal rural development programmes. Many state constitutions restrict state spending actions, such as budget deficits, so that states cannot provide all the services their citizens require. Local governments often have bonding limitations and lack the financial resources, legal authority and technical ability to undertake development projects. Legally, local governments are the creation of the state government and depend upon the state legislature to grant both taxing and law-making authority; but such authority is often inadequate to provide public services or effective land-use ordinances. Local governments depend especially on the generally regressive property tax, and there are fewer people to share the cost of programmes.

Federal rural development programmes carry the advantage of political convenience. A new or expanded federal programme usually applies throughout the nation. Thus, a single federal action is likely to be more efficient than the time and effort spent in duplicating the same programme or law in 50 state legislatures or thousands of local government councils. Until recently, federal rural policy was dominated by farm policy. The two became largely synonymous, but several federal agencies have recently sought to promote non-farm economic development. Still, federal rural policy has lacked coherence and development goals have been couched in abstract terms. Little has been said about the current and future use of privately held resources, particularly the land base.

There are currently some 400 federal rural development programmes administered by 27 different agencies. Not surprisingly, there has often been a lack of co-ordination between the various federal programmes, and some programmes actually work against each other. This tendency has both frustrated orderly rural development and, paradoxically, has actually increased the dependence of rural areas on the federal government.

The 1985 federal budget allocated $7.3 billion for development programmes in non-metropolitan counties along with $1.9 billion in loans. These figures were overshadowed by the $15 billion spent on farm programmes, and farm programme costs soared to $26 billion in fiscal 1986. A common deficiency in many rural development programmes is that they seem to 'throw money at a problem' rather than allocate funds in a systematic way to a particular area to solve an interrelated set of problems: for example, isolation, lack of infrastructure, and the despoliation of natural resources. Two often cited problems with federal programmes are: (a) the lack of an adequate rural data base to guide policy-making and programme design; and (b) fragmented goals coupled with a shortage of financial resources and personnel have resulted in piecemeal action, not a comprehensive planning approach.

The federal government has sponsored the creation of the nation's two major highway networks, the interstate system and the Federal Aid Secondary Highways. Since 1956, 68 000 km of interstate highways have been built, primarily outside urban areas. Interstate highways are expensive to maintain (up to $2 million per mile) and the states have been paying most of the maintenance costs. Meanwhile state highways in many rural areas are receiving low priority for repairs.

The Federal Aid Secondary (FAS) system was built in the 1920s as the first national road network. Even though FAS highways do not have the limited-access or high-capacity design of the interstates, they still provide important connections for many rural inhabitants.

By opening up formerly remote rural areas, federally assisted highways have drawn residential, commercial and industrial development out of urban centres and on to vacant rural land, especially in those areas surrounding urban areas. The result has been sprawl in metropolitan counties and the revival of many non-metropolitan communities. The decentralized pattern of development has obviated the use of mass transportation systems and increased dependency on the automobile and the truck. Decentralized development also makes planning for infrastructure and environmental protection more difficult because of the greater area affected by human activity.

The Housing and Community Development Act of 1974 inaugurated a new concept in federal assistance to communities. Prior to 1974, a rural community might have had to prepare multiple applications under several different federal programmes. The block grant programme replaced several of the categorical grant programmes. Federal block grants are competitively awarded through each state government to rural communities each year. To qualify, each community must have a community development programme which is based upon a locally approved plan. Block grant funds can be used for a variety of public works projects, such as sewer and water lines and streets, among other projects.

Since 1965, the Economic Development Administration (EDA) has targeted communities with high unemployment for the creation of new jobs. The largest portion of EDA funds has been spent on water and sewer lines and roads for industrial development. In addition, EDA money has long been used to support regional planning commissions in many states.

The environmental movement, spurred by Earth Day in 1970, has produced a shift in power away from the industrial domination of nature towards public power in regulating the use of the environment. Historically, America's abundance of natural resources gave little incentive to conserve. Even the utilitarian policies of Theodore Roosevelt and Gifford Pinchot treated the natural environment as the provider of exploitable resources. The environmental movement has successfully made the point that nature is a source of valuable services and benefits – from wildlife habitat to water recharge areas to scenic amenities, as well as the traditional food, fibre and mineral resources. Although many rural areas may appear far removed from an environmental crisis, conflicts over the use of the environment have increased considerably in the last 20 years. Local decisions over the environment have been challenged by newcomers, distantly based corporate headquarters, environmental groups, and state and federal environmental agencies. As more people settle in rural areas, they place greater demands on local water supplies, sewage disposal, and natural areas for recreation. At the same time, newcomers often want to preserve the scenic and environmental qualities which drew them away from urban areas. They may argue for 'quality' development which will both mitigate unsightly and environmentally harmful development patterns and enhance a community's liveability. Rural governments, however, are often slow to respond to these environmental concerns which they often perceive as thinly veiled attempts to curb local economic development. Because rural people tend to experience more poverty and receive lower incomes than urban dwellers, rural people have traditionally given jobs and economic growth higher priority.

Many of the decisions that affect a community's environment are not made at the local level, but by central governments, by corporations, and by urban dwellers seeking recreation and second homes. Central government policies have promoted the construction of over 250 dams, flooding thousands of hectares, and have encouraged the siting of power plants, including nuclear reactors, in rural areas. Resource industries tend to be concerned with short-term profits rather than long-term environmental and aesthetic qualities. The clash of urban and rural interests raises the questions of whose rights to the rural environment should prevail, who should benefit, and who should suffer losses.

Rural communities are witnessing conflicting demands over the environment. Local decision makers must comply with state and federal environment regulations and yet provide for economic development opportunities. Industry has generally acknowledged the need for environmental controls; however, industry often grates at the cost of installing devices to comply with pollution standards, altering the scope or design of a development, delays in obtaining development permits, and associated legal expenses. Moreover, many industries continue to be very powerful in rural areas and attempt to gain the relaxation of environmental regulations to reduce operating costs. There still exist many rural areas where one industry or one firm defines issues and problems, and 'sets the agenda'. Such action may, in turn, lead to intervention by state and federal agencies or national environmental groups. Thus, local land-use and environmental decisions may have greater than local effects, and localities may become the battleground between opposing non-local interests.

Although federal and corporate policies greatly influence rural development, the responsibility for planning generally falls on state, county and town governments. Still, the majority of decisions affecting rural land use are made by private firms and individuals. In recent years, planning efforts by state and local governments have struggled to address: (a) the population resurgence in rural communities; (b) wide-scale concerns about the future of the family farm and agricultural land; and (c) the growing competition between industry, tourists and environmentalists for rural-based resources. It has become apparent that rural communities alone are often poorly equipped to handle the land-use and environmental conflicts involved in personal preferences, federal policies and corporate interests.

Not only is there a clear lack of continuity and co-ordination in rural policy but a fragmentation of power and responsibility exists as well. So far, America has failed to articulate a vision of a 'working rural landscape' which will provide an acceptable quality of life for rural society. Too often, local officials fail to see or anticipate the cumulative impact of many individual planning decisions. Until a broad consensus emerges to deal with the problems and potential of rural environments, the fragmentation, frustration and failure of rural planning policies will remain the rule and not the exception.

Agricultural land retention

Every state and many local governments have enacted programmes encouraging the retention of land in agricultural use. Farmland policy is essentially a state and local matter, yet, it is widely recognized that protecting farmland by itself does not guarantee a farm's financial success. The need for integrated farmland planning and farm income policies has become evident, especially given the current downturn in the farm economy. The federal government lacks a formal farmland protection programme, but some positive steps have been taken. The Department of Agriculture has directed the Farmers' Home Administration to target its funding of rural sewer, water and housing developments away from farming areas. Since 1978, the Soil Conservation Service has been conducting a mapping programme to identify important farmlands. To date, over 500 county maps have been produced to enable local governments to pinpoint their best agricultural lands. In 1979, the Department of Agriculture joined with the Council on Environmental Quality in conducting the National Agricultural Lands Study (NALS). In 1981, NALS issued a widely discussed report which outlined the extent of farmland loss throughout the USA (1.2 million hectares a year between 1967 and 1975), and methods to preserve farmlands. Largely in response to the NALS report, Congress passed the Farmland Protection Policy Act (FPPA) in 1981. The FPPA set out three major programmes. First, the USDA has been directed to ensure that the actions of federal agencies do not contribute to the loss of agricultural land from productive use. Second, the SCS has been authorized to provide technical assistance to state and local governments to develop farmland preservation programmes. Third, both the USDA and SCS have sponsored the use of the Land Evaluation and Site Assessment (LESA) system to rate the quality of land for agricultural uses and to rate farming sites for their economic viability. Sixteen specific criteria have been identified and must be addressed by federal agencies when assessing decisions that may result in the conversion of farmland to non-farm uses. As of 1983, an estimated 400 counties had incorporated an LESA system into their land planning and farmland protection efforts.

In 1985, Congress passed the Food Security Act which included the creation of a Conservation Reserve Program (CRP) aimed at removing highly erodible cropland from production, and thus reducing soil erosion and crop surpluses. An initial 18 million hectares within 5 years was the target of the law when implemented in 1986. As of late 1987, nearly 10 million hectares were enrolled in the programme. The conservation reserve is being amassed through 10-year contract agreements between the US Department of Agriculture and individual landowners. Landowners submit bids based on an annual rent per acre they are willing to accept in order to retire cropland. The Department may accept or reject bids. When a bid is accepted, the landowner receives an annual rental payment for 10 years and up to half the cost of approved conservation measures such as grass seeding and tree planting. The landowner must submit a conservation plan for the enrolled acreage, and the plan must be approved by the local conservation district.

To date the CRP will cost an estimated $1.1 billion a year over a 10-year period. One clear benefit of the programme is that it has established a floor under farmland values, especially in the Midwest and Plains states which contain about two-thirds of the enrolled acreage. Critics point out that monitoring compliance on the 200 000 participating farms will be almost impossible. Some critics predict that the CRP will have little effect on grain surpluses, particularly corn. Farmers have an incentive to use their remaining land more intensively. Moreover, should crop prices rise back to 1970s levels, the incentive to conserve highly erodible cropland could evaporate.

The Food Security Act also included 'sodbuster' and 'swampbuster' provisions to protect fragile grasslands and swamplands from being converted to cropland. Farmers who plough up these sensitive lands will not be eligible to receive any federal farm subsidies.

Differential assessment is the most common farmland retention technique in the United States. Every state has adopted some form of property tax break for farmland. Differential assessment programmes fall into three main categories: (a) preferential assessment in which farmland is assessed for tax purposes on the basis of current use as farmland rather than on the fair market value of the land in its 'highest and best' use; (b) deferred taxation in which preferential assessment is combined with a penalty (often called a 'roll back') to recoup forgone property taxes if the land is converted to a non-farm use; and (c) restrictive agreements in which the landowners and the local government agree to restrict the use of land for a certain period in exchange for preferential assessment, and a penalty is levied for the land if converted before the agreement has expired.

The consensus among land-use analysts is that differential assessment programmes have not been very successful in retaining land in agriculture. This is especially true in rural–urban fringe ares. Differential assessment programmes generally have not dampened the increasing value of farmland for non-farm uses, and they have failed to curb scattered development patterns which fragment the farmland base. Preferential assessment programmes impose no responsibility on the landowner to maintain a working agricultural use of the land, nor is there a penalty for converting farmland to non-farm use. Rollback penalties are rarely large enough to discourage conversion. Farmers in fringe areas are often reluctant to enter restrictive agreements which limit their options to sell land. In many cases, speculators holding agricultural land have benefited from property tax breaks before converting their land to non-farm uses.

Although zoning is the best-known method to influence urban land use, relatively little zoning has been done in rural America. The constitutionality of zoning as a legitimate exercise of local police power has been established in several legal cases, especially *Village of Euclid* v. *Ambler Realty Co.* (1926). But state and local governments cannot use zoning to restrict a landowner's rights unreasonably and purely on the basis of policy. A major barrier to the use of zoning to preserve agricultural land, for example, is the lack of objective standards to determine whether or not property use is being restricted in a reasonable way. While zoning need not permit the most profitable use of the land, agricultural zoning may produce little or no benefit for farmers. When a zoning regulation imposes burdens without any compensating benefits, the regulation might be ruled an unconstitutional 'taking' of property.

Over 400 counties currently have enacted agricultural zoning ordinances, and two states – Hawaii and Oregon – have implemented state-wide zoning programmes. Two main kinds of zoning approaches exist: minimum lot size and exclusive agricultural zoning. Minimum lot size restrictions require that land in an agricultural zone cannot be broken into parcels below a designated size. If lot sizes are sufficiently large, they should be too expensive for residential uses and they should retain agricultural land in big enough blocks to be farmed in a profitable way either individually or as a collection of parcels. Thus, the intrusion of non-farm uses into a farming area is discouraged and the farmland base is not harmfully fragmented. Perhaps the most difficult aspect of the minimum lot size approach involves deciding what the minimum lot size should be. Lot sizes may be too small to support farming and yet too large for low- and middle-income families; such lot sizes could be challenged as exclusionary and discriminatory. In an exclusive agricultural zone only farming is allowed. Hawaii pioneered the use of exclusive agricultural zoning in its 1961 State Land Use Plan, in which agricultural land may be converted to non-farm use, but this land must be contiguous to urban or rural residential districts.

The apparent weaknesses of zoning as a device for agricultural land retention is that even the most carefully prepared zoning maps and ordinances are subject to variances, zoning amendments and special exceptions. As a result, zoning is notorious for its lack of permanence. Zoning decisions are normally made by politically vulnerable local governments, and ordinances are likely to change in the face of development pressures and the desire for an expanded tax base. Moreover, zoning decisions are made on a case-by-case basis. As a consequence, the cumulative effect of zoning changes is not fully recognized. Also, the lack of co-ordination between jurisdictions can easily frustrate comprehensive regional agricultural zoning.

At least 43 states have enacted 'right-to-farm' laws which favour agricultural uses above all others and supersede local nuisance-law-based ordinances. Farmers perceive these laws to be beneficial in providing the freedom to operate and to earn a living. This is especially true where land has been zoned for agriculture use. Most of the laws require that farm operations pre-date competing land uses by at least 1 year and a farm must continue to be managed according to 'good' or 'standard' farming practices. Right-to-farm laws serve to educate a public long separated from the process of food production. The laws emphasize the fact that modern agriculture is an industrial process which needs to be protected from conflicting uses and increasing local population (Lapping et al. 1983).

State forestland planning

Forestland planning is not solely the domain of the federal government. Indeed, the individual states are among the largest forestland owners and managers in the country. With some encouragement from the federal government, states are growing in their involvement in forestland planning. While some of this activity is directed towards the planning of state-owned public lands, state-level forestland planning generally addresses those forest resources managed and owned both by the public and private sectors. By 1982, many states were actively involved in forest resource planning. State-level planning is important to rural communities because local and regional issues tend to drive the process. Unlike the federal approach which seeks to respond to national resource demands and pressures, state forestry planning tends to reflect more accurately the local problems and concerns.

Perhaps the most traditional way in which rural planners participate in forestland planning is through the land-use planning and controls process. The reality is, however, that forested lands have too rarely been the focus of the attention of planners. Where forests have been a concern of local planning they have been dealt with through large lot zoning or 'high' minimum lot size zoning. The assumption has been that large lots preclude use for strictly residential purposes and encourage food and fibre production on the land. The effectiveness of such measures has not been established. California has gone an important step further and instituted timber production zones (TPZ) whereby counties can designate lands for timber production to the exclusion of all other uses, such as housing. Landowners in such designated zones receive substantial tax relief in exchange for a binding agreement to keep their lands in forest land use. A landowner may petition to remove the land from the TPZ but this may be granted only after an extensive public review and hearings. And even then, a landowner must keep the land in question in forest use for a decade after the TPZ designation has been removed. A student of the California approach (Cromwell 1984 p. 158) concludes that:

> Zoning land as TPZ helps control the influence of urban pressure on increasing land values. Land use is restricted, and speculative pressures are dampened because the zone runs for ten years. Available evidence shows that lands zones as TPZ sell for less than lands not so zoned. This is some indication that with TPZ, land can be acquired at a price related to its ability to grow timber.

The planning approach of the State of Maine, the nation's most heavily forested state, is especially noteworthy. While the state has a number of planning initiatives which affect forests, none is more important than the Maine Land-Use Regulation Commission (LURC). The LURC has jurisdiction over the unorganized areas of the state: that part of the state, roughly half of Maine, without a municipal government infrastructure. These lands tend to be owned by such forest products companies as Great Northern, International Paper, St Regis, Georgia-Pacific and Boise Cascade. LURC is a permitting commission with broad powers. It requires permits for the building or placement of any structures, the subdivision of lands, the development of any roads or other structures, and all farming and logging operations in its jurisdiction. Controls over logging roads – and the subsequent creation of backwoods subdivisions –'and actual logging practices fall under the LURC. Even when permits are not required for a particular operation or land use, performance standards may be attached by the LURC. Mountain zones, defined as areas above 2700 feet in elevation, receive special attention from the LURC and all forestry uses in these zones require a permit before operation. Timber harvesting standards applied by the LURC pay particular attention to the mitigation of soil erosion, road and trail placement, skidding techniques, and other silvicultural treatments. Areas such as the 'high mountain' zones or 'aquifer recharge' zones are defined by intrinsic resource factors or limitations rather than development criteria. Taken together, the LURC's policies take a positive approach to forestry while seeking to protect Maine's high environmental quality, perhaps the single greatest reason for the very substantial in-migration to rural areas which the state has witnessed in the past two decades (Lapping 1982a).

Developments of regional impact

One of the main growth issues that small local governments have been unable to handle is the siting, type, design, public service requirements and spin-off development problems posed by developments of regional impact. Often local governments compete with each other for new industrial plants and commercial developments. Typically, one town gets the new businesses and expanded property tax base, while neighbouring towns come under residential development pressure along with rising property taxes. Also, many types of large development can have a major impact on the landscape and environment.

Florida's Environmental Land and Water Management Act of 1972 allowed the state to identify areas of critical concern and charged local governments with protecting state-wide interests when these areas are developed. Also, the state government has some overview of large developments, especially large residential developments, in partnership with regional and local governments. Florida presents a unique planning challenge because of past, present and projected rapid growth, especially for second homes, retirement housing and resort communities. At the same time, Florida features a sensitive, semi-tropical to tropical ecology and permanent or seasonal wetlands cover up to one-third of the state. Water pollution from construction in or near wetlands and crowding of the coastline have been major development problems.

Florida's response was to regulate developments of regional impact and to designate up to 5% 0.6 million hectares of the state as areas of critical state concern. But in Florida the mechanism for regulation fell to regional planning bodies with rather limited authority. The critical areas include (a) environmental or natural areas of regional or state-wide importance; (b) areas that would be affected by major public investment or services; and (c) areas proposed for developments of regional impact. The programme has forced local governments to draft development regulations and eventually administer the regulations. The local government decides whether or not to issue a 'development order' and what conditions must be met. In the process, the regional planning council reviews the developer's application and makes a recommendation to the local government to approve or deny the project.

In May 1985, the Florida legislature passed a broader state planning and growth management law. The law requires each city and county to draft a comprehensive plan which must be approved by the state planning office. To discourage urban sprawl out into the countryside, the law requires cities and counties to fund roads, sewers and schools before new developments are approved, not after. Still, Florida is an estimated $30 billion behind on providing adequate infrastructure.

Three examples of state planning for rural areas

The experiences of New York, Oregon and Vermont provide an insight into the variety of rural planning issues and the diversity of planning responses. In all three states, rural planning efforts were motivated by increasing population pressures in the 1960s and 1970s and the desire to accommodate growth. In New York, planning seemed to be more preservation-oriented, as in the example of the Adirondack Park. In Oregon, planning has sought to control urban sprawl and protect farm and forest lands which are the bases of the state's two leading industries. Vermont's planning response has featured a permit review process to minimize the impacts of large-scale development on the environment and public services. The performance of these programmes is especially important because, given the weaknesses of local planning and disjointed federal programmes, state planning has held the most potential for effective rural planning.

New York

New York State has utilized temporary state-level study commissions to address the problems of rural planning in critical areas. With the exception of the Catskill Mountains region, the Tug Hill and Adirondack commissions have each matured into special planning districts or agencies. Generally speaking, these authorities owe their very existence to perceived threats to environmental quality by massive seasonal home development proposals. Though the agencies do not supersede the county level of government, nor even county or local planning agencies where they exist and function, the Tug Hill Commission and the Adirondack Park Agency tend to represent broader, state-wide constituencies rather than locally based interests. In both the Catskills and Adirondacks, huge tracts of state-owned forestlands, both significant watersheds, were the focus of initial concern. The 'contest' between state and local interests and values may be said to be the operational political reality in which rural planning takes place in New York (Lapping 1982b).

The Tug Hill Commission, founded in 1972, operates in a vast region encompassing nearly 40 townships. It is an area typified by limited and marginal agriculture and forestry, small hamlets and a population base both declining and ageing. The commission adopted a highly participatory approach to planning which has consistently sought to support rather to replace or supplant local governments. Recent activities have tended to shift away from land use to economic development. But in a rural area these matters are, of course, highly integrated. An open, flexible and pragmatic approach typifies the Tug Hill Commission's experience and through the use of 'circuit rider' planners and managers, service in the region has been upgraded and local governments have been more effective (Dyballa *et al.* 1981).

One of the principles which guided the Tug Hill Commission was the strong desire to avoid, where possible, some of the pitfalls of the Adirondack Park Agency (APA), founded in the early 1970s. The need to protect and retain the open-space characteristics of this huge wilderness region, certainly the largest in the northeastern section of the USA, has been the clearest justification of the Agency's approach, which has included the mandatory zoning of both private and public lands within the 2.6 million hectares under its jurisdiction (Liroff & Davis 1981). A number of law suits have sought to challenge the state's authority and the relationship between the Agency and the majority of people living in this traditionally depressed region have been filled with tension and conflict. The Winter Olympics of 1971, headquartered in Lake Placid, one of the region's few economically viable settlements, brought new pressures to balance environmental quality and economic development goals. Since that time the goal of environmentally sensitive economic development has become the focus of the Agency's activities, though structural weaknesses within the region's economic base have not delivered the region from conditions of chronic unemployment, seasonal employment and the out-migration of youth.

Oregon

In 1973 the Oregon legislative enacted a state-wide land-use planning programme that required every city and county to prepare a comprehensive plan consistent with 19 state-wide goals. Each plan must be approved by the state. The programme was a reaction to population growth, most of which was occurring in the fertile Willamette Valley, an area of about 1.3 million hectares with 70% of the state's 2.6 million people. The purpose of the programme was twofold: containment of urban sprawl and protection of farm and forest lands, the bases of the state's top two industries. To limit urban sprawl, the programme has created urban growth boundaries which designate the limit of municipal sewer- and water-line extensions.

The city and county comprehensive plans must identify all agricultural lands and place them in Exclusive Farm Use (EFU) zones. Farmland owners receive property tax deferral; and subdivision restrictions together with minimum lot sizes are employed to retain farmland in large blocks. Some new farm uses are permitted in EFU zones, but farmers are free from nuisance laws which would restrict standard farming practices. In addition, counties may designate rural residential zones to channel rural growth away from farming areas. So far, about 6.4 million hectares have been placed in EFU zones, and the loss of farms and farmland appears to have slowed. However, there has been a sharp increase in the number of hobby farms – farms of less than 21 hectares which produce less than $10 000 in annual sales; and it appears that local jurisdictions have been law in enforcing Oregon's land-use planning laws (Daniels & Nelson 1986 p. 31). The growth in hobby farms could threaten the viability of commercial farms in the long run.

Forestlands capable of producing 20 or more board feet per hectare per year of Douglas fir (the main commercial species) are placed in 'Timber Conservation' zones as part of the county comprehensive planning process. Although just over half of Oregon's 25 million hectares are in state and federal ownership, about 5 million private hectares are now in timber conservation zones. Landowners in forest zones may not be subjected to nuisance laws that would restrict standard forestry practices. In addition, landowners may apply for property tax deferral use-value assessment: both the land and timber are assessed according to forestry value. Harvested forestlands must be restocked for use-value assessment to be maintained. If the forestland is sold for another use, then the seller must pay back taxes at the development value.

In the forest zones counties impose subdivision regulations together with minimum lot size restrictions to retain forestlands in large blocks. Minimum lot sizes vary from 16 to 65 hectares, but most counties employ two sizes. A large size (32 to 65 hectares) applied to areas of prime commercial forestland which already consist of large tracts, tend to be owned by timber companies, and are located at higher elevations or in remote areas. The smaller minimum lot size (16 hectares) applies to areas of mixed farm and forest uses where existing tracts are not large and are closer to developed places.

Outright permitted uses in a timber conservation zone include: (a) the harvesting and processing of forest products; (b) open space; (c) some outdoor recreation on a commercial basis; and (d) the grazing of livestock. Considerable controversy has arisen over the construction of forestry-related dwellings and non-forestry dwellings. The partition of forest lands and the construction of forestry-related dwellings must meet a commercial forestry standard which requires that a new forestry operation must contribute to local markets and at least be of similar size to existing local operations.

Counties may permit some non-forestry uses in forest zones, but only on marginal land and in places where development will not interfere with commercial forest operations. Counties may also conditionally allow non-forestry residential construction on parcels below the minimum lot size. This provision recognizes that high-quality resource lands are often mixed with lands of low productivity. Moreover, the potential for selling some land for non-forestry uses offers an important source of income for small private forest landowners and has increased the political acceptability of forest zoning.

Vermont

The state of Vermont covers 2.2 million hectares of north-west New England. According to the US Census, Vermont is the most rural state in the nation with only one-third of its 525 000 people living in urban areas. In the late 1960s, the completion of interstate highways to the New York and Boston metropolitan areas coincided with a sharp increase in the popularity of skiing. And, with skiing came the 'discovery' of Vermont as a weekend get-away and vacation area. As a result, state-wide real estate activity shot up from just over 5000 transfers in 1967 to over 16 000 in 1968 (Daniels et al. 1986 p. 444).

In 1970 the Vermont legislative enacted a pioneering land-use control programme known as Act 250. The law was created in response to poorly designed and hastily built large-scale developments (particularly groups of second homes in ski areas) that were creating environmental and fiscal burdens on rural towns. Local planning and land-use controls were determined to be woefully inadequate. Act 250 established standards of environmental quality for large-scale developments and large land subdivisions. Projects affected by Act 250 are (a) developments of 10 or more housing units; (b) subdivisions of 10 or more lots; (c) non-residential projects involving 4 or more hectares; and (d) non-residential development of 1 or more acres in towns without zoning.

Prospective developers of large projects apply for a permit from one of nine district environmental commissions, each consisting of three members appointed by the governor. A commission may deny or approve an application with certain conditions.

Between 1970 and 1982, over 4000 permits were granted and only about 100 denied (Daniels & Lapping 1984 p. 505); most permits had one or more conditions attached, but there has been little enforcement to ensure that these conditions have been met.

Prior to 1984, an Act 250 permit was not required for subdivisions of 10 or more lots if the new lots were greater than 4 hectares in size. Also, Vermont Health Department Subdivision permits must be sought when subdivisions of three to nine lots are created. The subdivision permit process requires that sewage site pit tests be performed on lots of less than 10 acres to assure adequate water supplies and sewage facilities. Both the Act 250 '10-acre loophole' and the Health Department subdivision regulations unwittingly encourage the creation of 10- to 20-acre parcels which have limited use for farm and forestry operations. This portends a shift in the land base from commercial agriculture and forestry to low-density residential and leisure-oriented uses.

The widespread subdivision of rural lands into many lots led to the 1973 passage of the Vermont gains tax on land sales. The Vermont tax is aimed at discouraging the resale of land within 6 years of purchase. The tax rates are based on a sliding scale over time, depending on the seller's length of ownership and rate of profit. The tax applies only to the land portion of real estate and up to 10 acres around a primary residence are exempt.

Vermont is the only state with a gains tax on land sales, and the performance of the tax has been mixed. The tax has raised only about $1 million a year. While the volume of land sales has slowed somewhat, the tax does not control the intensity or location of development. Finally, the tax has not been able to prevent rising land values coming from a popular demand for more intensive land uses.

By the mid-1980s, Vermonters began to recognize that Act 250 and the gains tax were ineffective in controlling small-scale development and sprawl. In 1987, Vermont Governor Madeleine Kunin appointed a committee to study ways of achieving adequate growth control. The Vermont experience in land-use regulation is important because it illustrates the shortcomings of a package of techniques (permits and a special tax) which do not include the traditional American land-use control tools of comprehensive planning, zoning and subdivision regulations, and capital improvements plans. The Vermont approach is essentially reactive, rather than proactive, and has limited effectiveness in determining where development should be located and at what density.

Conclusion

Local governments in rural America have traditionally had the most impact on rural land-use planning, typified by the lack of planning and the belief in private property rights. Currently, about 85% of the nation's counties are governed by Republican-dominated county boards. Here, conservative as a political label differs from the concept of conservative toward change and the exploitation of natural resources. Political conservatives generally favour growth through the market system with little government regulation or intervention. In the politically conservative rural South, for instance, many counties lack basic planning and zoning. Other sparsely populated counties in the Midwest and Western states also function without formal land-use plans and zoning ordinances.

Rural planning has been more popular among communities that have experienced rapid growth or felt the threat of rapid, haphazard development. The majority of these rural communities lie within the rural–urban fringe, a band of land stretching from 25 to 67 km outside of major metropolitan centres: for example, techniques to preserve agricultural land and open space were first adopted by towns and counties in fringe areas.

The rise in state intervention in rural planning seems to have peaked in the 1970s with Vermont's Act 250, the Oregon State Land Use Act, the Wisconsin Farmland Protection Act, and Florida's Growth Management Act. Similarly, recent federal programme budget cuts are heralding a reduced federal role in rural planning. The local jurisdictions are again becoming the main focus of rural planning efforts. The struggle between central and local governments for control of land-use and environmental planning has tipped in favour of local control. Part of the reason for this shift is the fragmentation of the federal and state intervention in land-use conflicts and rural development.

References

Baker, Earl J. & Rutherford H. Platt 1983. The management of flood plains in nonmetropolitan areas. In *Beyond the urban fringe: land use issues of nonmetropolitan America*, R. H. Platt & G. Macinko (eds). Minneapolis: University of Minnesota Press.

Cromwell, D. A. 1984. Strategies for dealing with the urban forest interface: the recent California experience. In *Land use and forest resources in a changing environment*, G. A. Bradley (ed.). Seattle: University of Washington Press.

Daniels, T. L. & M. B. Lapping 1984. Has Vermont's land use control program failed?: Evaluating Act 250. *Journal of the American Planning Association* 50, 4, 502–8.

Daniels, T. L. & A. C. Nelson 1986. Is the Oregon farmland protection program working? *Journal of the American Planning Association* **52**, 1, 22–32.

Daniels, T. L., R. H. Daniels & M. B. Lapping 1986. Vermont's land gains tax, a lesson in land policy design. *American Journal of Economics and Sociology* **45**, 4, 441–55.

Dillman, Don A. & Daryl J. Hobbs (eds) 1982). *Rural society in the US: issues for the 1980s.* Boulder, Colo.: Westview Press.

Dyballa, Cynthia, Lyle Raymond & A. J. Hahn 1981. *The Tug Hill program: a regional planning option for rural areas.* Syracuse, NY: Syracuse University Press.

Healy, R. G. & J. S. Rosenberg 1980. *Land use and the states.* Baltimore: Johns Hopkins University Press.

Healy, R. G. & J. L. Short 1981. *The market for rural land.* Washington, DC: The Conservation Foundation.

Healy, R. G. & J. L. Short 1983. Changing markets for rural lands: patterns and issues. In *Beyond the urban fringe: land use issues of nonmetropolitan America*, R. W. Platt & G. Macinko (eds). Minneapolis: University of Minnesota Press.

Lapping, M. B. 1980. Agricultural land retention: responses, American and foreign. In *The farm and the city: rivals or allies*, A. Woodruff (ed.). Englewood Cliffs, NJ: Prentice-Hall.

Lapping, M. B. 1982a. Rural development and land use planning: a forestry perspective. *Journal of Forestry* **80**, 9, 583–4, 602.

Lapping, M. B. 1982b. Upstate – case studies in rural planning. *Journal of the American Planning Association* **48**, 3, 387–9.

Lapping, M. B., G. Penfold & S. MacPherson 1983. The right to farm laws: will they resolve land conflicts? *Journal of Soil and Water Conservation* **38**, 6, 465–7.

Liroff, Richard & G. Gordon Davis 1981. *Protecting open space: land use control in the Adirondack Park.* Cambridge, Mass.: Ballinger.

US Council on Environmental Quality 1982. *1982 Annual Report.* Washington, DC: US Government Printing Office.

Wolf, P. 1981. *Land in America: its value, use and control.* New York: Pantheon Books.

8 Rural land-use planning in Canada

CHRISTOPHER R. BRYANT

Introduction

There are three important points to bear in mind in any treatment of the issues in rural land use and approaches to solutions in Canada. First, Canada possesses a very decentralized system of government which is reflected in the planning function (Audet & Le Hénaff 1983). Furthermore, on top of the different levels of government – municipal, provincial, federal and, in several parts of the country, various forms of regional or quasi-regional government – there are also many special-purpose bodies such as the Conservation Authorities in Ontario which have an interest in the fortunes of rural land.

Second, Canada occupies a considerable land mass, stretching across the North American continent from the Atlantic to the Pacific Ocean and covering over 9 million square kilometres. It is no surprise then that there is a significant regional variation within the country both in terms of jurisdiction and approaches toward government intervention and in terms of the conditions within which various land-use and land-resource conflicts have emerged. There are, of course, some recurring themes because of the existence of some nation-wide processes (e.g. urbanization) and the national significance of resource activities based in rural areas (e.g. agriculture).

Third, and this is as true for Canada as for any other country, conflicts in rural land use and how they are perceived vary temporally. Not all conflicts are perceived as being important enough to act upon at any given time. Thus, the conflicts that are subject to public intervention are only a subset of conflicts. This is not only a function of the absolute magnitude of a conflict or potential problem, but also of the relative importance of other problems and the nature and strength of the various interest or lobby groups involved in a given issue.

Any discussion of rural land-use planning begs the question of what is meant by 'rural'. The residual approach, i.e. defining it as anything that is not 'urban', is not very satisfactory. Statistics Canada has defined 'urban' since 1981 as any place with a population of 1000 or more and a population density of 400 or more people per square kilometre (Statistics Canada 1982) – a population density criterion of 1000 or more people per square mile (2590 per square kilometre) was used from 1961 to 1976 (Statistics Canada 1976). Yet there are many small towns that are functionally part of the rural environment. A more positive approach focuses on the nature of the activities and their interrelationships; thus, a 'rural' area is taken to be an area characterized by resource-based activities that are *land-extensive* in character and which support a network of communities in a close symbiotic relationship with those activities. 'Rural' is thus synonymous with the settled part of the country – and therefore dominated by private property – outside the cities and major towns. Agriculture is the major activity, though forestry is also important in some areas.

Rural Canada has been undergoing rapid changes since the beginning of the century in one way or another. Some have argued that rural Canada is breaking up and is in decline (see Troughton 1986) while others have suggested that it is in fact transforming and adjusting to a new set of realities (see Bryant 1986a) which are tying the rural environment more and more firmly into the urban–industrial complex. The meaning ascribed to 'rural' above helps define a 'rural' environment – of that there is no question – but whether it defines anything approaching a relatively independent system that can be managed independently is quite debatable.

In this chapter, the discussion is focused mainly on the agricultural areas rather than the major forest areas or the Canadian North. First, a brief discussion of land-use planning in rural areas and the nature of rural land-use conflicts is given. Then, to set the stage, some facts and figures on the distribution of the major land uses are outlined. In the following two sections, the major types of rural land-use conflicts are identified and the principal issues synthesized. The emergence of the major conflicts as issues is then dealt with, leading into a discussion of planned intervention in land-use planning in rural areas in Canada; this focuses on a range of agricultural conflicts with a briefer commentary on natural environment-related issues. Finally, some conclusions are offered that emphasize the limitations of traditional land-use planning in rural areas in Canada to cope with the emerging conflicts and issues.

Rural land use and land-use planning

Rural land-use planning is often thought of as the *physical planning* of land uses and as being distinct from rural development planning. The latter is seen as an activity linked to the socio-economic development of communities and intimately tied to regional development and attempts at eliminating regional disparities. The distinction is unfortunate because the conflicts, actual and potential, that land-use planning has to sort out are intertwined with overall community development.

From a similar perspective, it is unfortunate that the distinction is usually made between urban and rural planning. Certainly, some of the approaches developed and applied in urban environments are not necessarily applicable in rural environments – but it is increasingly clear that they are not universally applicable in urban environments either, for example, distinct separation of land uses. Without entering into any discussion, it is suggested that some more fundamental dimensions need to be identified for land-use planning in both rural and urban environments (e.g. involvement of local communities in determining goals and objectives and planning land use to take account of the socio-economic structure of production) which can then be translated into practical terms with sensitivity to fit local or regional circumstances. Thus, it is the specific manifestation of the approach that is different, not the fundamental principles.

It can therefore be argued that 'rural land-use planning' as a distinct entity does not really exist. If 'rural' land-use planning means planning with an orientation to resource-based activities, then what we really have is a sectoral type of planning rather than the more holistic perspective implied by 'rural'. In fact, as we shall see, much of the 'rural' land-use planning in Canada is indeed very sectorally oriented; involvement by federal and especially provincial governments has tended to be almost wholly aligned along sectoral divisions and where there was, or is, a 'regional' component, senior government involvement (e.g. regional development programmes) has usually been quite separate from the more land-use-oriented planning interventions of the same senior government (e.g. vetting of municipal official plans). The same can be said for various special-purpose organizations, such as the

Conservation Authorities in Ontario. It is really only at the local or regional level that there are examples of a *more* integrated approach to land uses in a rural environment. This seems to be greatest in those areas with regional forms of planning administration where jurisdictional areas cover both urban and rural environments – thus underscoring the point made earlier regarding the lack of a clear differentiation between 'urban' and 'rural' land-use planning.

Physical land-use planning in rural Canada has tended to deal only with part of the phenomenon of land-use conflicts. *Land use* actually incorporates several distinct dimensions (Scace 1981). To capture the essence of *land use*, it is necessary to ask questions regarding:

(a) *what* land-use activity or cover is involved, as well as what are the attributes of the land resource;
(b) *where* is the land under investigation.
Both (a) and (b) are the stuff that land-use planning has traditionally been aimed at, especially in rural environments;
(c) *how* is the land resource used in combination with other inputs, for example, labour and capital (one could, of course, subsume this under *what*-type questions by considering every possible combination of land, labour and capital as a different land use); and
(d) *by or for whom* is the land being used (tenure characteristics of land ownership, including resident or non-resident ownership, may indicate something about such questions as the motivation for ownership of land and the productivity of the land).

Clearly, *land use* is not a purely physical phenomenon. It is therefore interesting to enquire to what extent there is any integration between the physical aspects of planning land use and the other dimensions of land use.

Land-use conflicts involve changes in one or more of the above dimensions that reduce the ability of the 'system' to fulfil the community's needs and objectives. 'Community' is used in the broad sense here to include not just local community but any segment of the population which has some interest in the use of land. Land-use conflicts involve tension between different values that are held with respect to the land; they can arise because of negative externalities spilling over from one property to other adjacent or close-by properties, and/or because of individual versus collective values held with respect to the land resource. Thus, land-use conflicts, even when there is a physical manifestation of the problem, reflect more fundamental conflicts involving people's values and the socio-economic organization of production in society.

Frequently, land-use planning in rural Canada has been preoccupied by the symptoms rather than the causes of conflict. Furthermore, it is often separated from other planning-related activities such as local economic development initiatives (Bryant & Preston 1987). The potential then for different approaches to land-use planning in rural areas to deal effectively with the range of values involved in land-use conflicts varies tremendously, even within a country such as Canada. Overall, however, land-use planning in rural Canada has had a strong focus on the land resource and only in the last decade or so have any significant moves been observed to integrate this with the socio-economic dimensions of the issues – and then only partially.

The rural land base

The popular image of Canada is still that of a country with vast open spaces and huge reserves of untapped resources. With 9.2 million square kilometres, and a 1986 population of 25.3 million, Canada does indeed appear to be a sparsely settled country. Even the high level of urbanization (65% of the population in 1981 lived in settlements of 10 000 or more) and the high levels of population increase in the 1950s and 1960s (Table 8.1) have not changed the overall impression of a country with vast land resources. Non-Canadians therefore still express surprise when Canadians speak of conflicts of land use and land resource scarcity.

Canada exhibits, however, a marked geographic differentiation with respect to its rural resource lands and population, and, moreover, its rural resource lands represent only a small portion of the total national territory. Best (1981), in an international comparison of data from the early 1970s, estimated that only 7.5% of Canada's land was devoted to agriculture (compare 56.3% for the USA), 0.6% to urban uses, 53.5% in wooded areas and 38.4% in other uses; the only country in Best's comparison that came close to the distribution of broad land uses in Canada was Sweden, thus emphasizing the significance of the northern latitudes in both countries in the national land-use distribution.

There are strong regional variations in quality and volume of land resources. For example, a major portion of the country's best agricultural resources is located within the highly urbanized

Table 8.1 (A) Distribution of Canada's agricultural land resources by province.

% national area included in the Canada Land Inventory in each	% of Canada Land Inventory land capability for agriculture soil classes in each province Classes (1 = first class)						
	1	2	3	4	5	6	7
Newfoundland	3.83	—	—	0.02	0.24	1.15	15.73	6.10
Prince Edward Island	0.30	—	1.60	0.56	0.20	0.22	–	0.05
Nova Scotia	2.80	—	1.02	3.86	1.67	0.24	0.08	5.73
New Brunswick	3.73	—	0.98	4.53	8.01	5.03	0.06	3.00
Québec	14.73	0.47	5.56	5.04	10.19	4.91	0.06	33.89
Ontario	13.09	51.41	13.56	11.44	10.35	5.66	6.21	18.32
Manitoba	6.97	3.87	15.47	9.59	9.43	6.62	11.36	1.69
Saskatchewan	17.07	23.83	35.91	37.02	14.91	25.20	15.90	0.06
Alberta	21.24	18.75	23.47	24.02	36.60	32.82	21.42	6.84
British Columbia	16.22	1.67	2.43	3.93	8.40	18.15	29.18	24.32
Total	100.00				100.00			

(B) Population distribution by province, 1951 to 1986.

	Population ('000)				
	1951	1961	1971	1981	1986
Canada	14 009.0	18 238.2	21 568.3	24 343.2	25 309.3
Newfoundland	361.4	457.9	522.1	567.7	568.3
Prince Edward Island	98.4	104.6	111.6	122.5	126.6
Nova Scotia	642.6	737.0	789.0	847.4	873.2
New Brunswick	515.7	597.9	634.6	696.4	709.4
Québec	4055.7	5259.2	6027.8	6438.4	6532.5
Ontario	4597.5	6236.1	7703.1	8625.1	9101.7
Manitoba	776.5	921.7	988.2	1026.2	1063.0
Saskatchewan	831.7	925.2	926.2	968.3	1009.6
Alberta	939.5	1331.9	1627.9	2237.7	2365.8
British Columbia	1165.2	1629.1	2184.6	2744.5	2883.4
Yukon	9.1	14.6	18.4	23.2	23.5
Northwest Territories	16.0	23.0	34.8	45.7	52.2

Source: Canada Land Inventory Land Capability for Agriculture and Census of Canada.

provinces (Table 8.1) of Ontario and Québec. More generally, the urban field across the country contains a significant share of Canada's agricultural land resources, farms, farm capital and farm population (Gierman 1977, McCuaig & Manning 1982, Bryant *et al.* 1984, Russwurm & Bryant 1984). It is important to remember as well that agricultural production contributes significantly to GNP and the country's balance of payments. For instance, in the period 1978 to 1982, 'agri-food' exports (primary agriculture products, food and beverage, fish products, and tobacco) accounted for 12% of all Canadian exports and 19% of the total trade surplus, and the agri-food sector was only second to the forest sector in terms of positive trade balances (Singhal 1985).

Forestry, another extensive land-based activity, is also extremely important to the country's economic health, but is not located primarily within the main urbanized parts of the country (New Brunswick 1981). Other important uses of land in rural areas (the rural parts of the urban field and the agricultural regions) include recreation, aggregate mining and urban/industrial land uses dispersed through the countryside or in the smaller settlements. No reliable data exist on these categories of land use. For instance, recreation land uses can be quantified when land-intensive uses are involved, but so much of the recreational use of rural land is land-extensive and multi-purpose in character.

Agriculture has probably undergone the most complex and dramatic changes of all uses of rural land in Canada in the last 30 years. The total volume of land incorporated into census farms has declined nationally since the 1950s; however, this hides some very significant regional variations reflecting very different processes (McCuaig & Manning 1982). There has been a general contraction of the farmed area in the eastern half of the country (the 'receding agricultural margin') and an expansion in the west, e.g. the Peace River area in Alberta and British Columbia (the 'expanding agricultural frontier'). During the 1960s and 1970s, the removal of land from agricultural production was very important – census farmland declined by 1 166 481 ha (or −1.2%) between 1961 and 1971, compared to −0.8% from 1951 to 1961 and −4.0% from 1971 to 1981. Within a radius of 50 km of urban centres with a 1976 population of over 40 000 (and including in addition Charlottetown in the Maritime Provinces and Granby for Québec), the loss of census farmland between 1966 and 1971 was 2447 ha for each 1000 increase in population in these urban regions for the Maritime Provinces, 1201 ha for Québec and 522 ha for Ontario (data comparability problems prevent similar data being given for the West (Bryant *et al.* 1981)).

Only part of these land 'losses' are due to conversion to non-farm land uses, however. This is highlighted by sequential air-photo analyses in which the volume of *rural* land actually converted to urban uses around urban centres of more than 25 000 in population (1976) was estimated at only 60 ha per 1000 urban population increase from 1966 to 1971 and 72 ha from 1971 to 1976 (Warren & Rump 1981).

Rural land-use conflicts

The major uses of rural land are agriculture, forestry, recreation and various categories of 'urban' uses (e.g. residences, industry, infrastructure). In the Canadian context, the majority of rural land-use conflicts that have been recognized have to do with agriculture. There appear to be three principal factors that account for the attention given to agricultural issues: first, agriculture's important role in the national economy; second, because of its locational structure, agricultural activity is frequently in contact with other land uses; third, agricultural activity supports a much more widespread settlement system than any other rural resource activity such as forestry. Thus, the impact of changing agricultural land use is seen as having implications for an economically and geographically significant part of the nation. This is in contrast to forestry, which, although being important economically, is much less so in terms of the rural settlement system.

The most important land-use conflicts involving agriculture are:

(a) conflicts associated with the conversion of agricultural-based land to non-farm uses (i.e. actual conversion to urban development, scattered residential development and so forth as well as indirect effects associated with impacts 'transmitted' by the urban uses to the continuing agricultural structure, e.g. land-use incompatibilities, higher property taxes and servicing costs, etc. (Bryant & Russwurm 1979);

(b) changes within agriculture that affect the long-term productivity of the land resource, e.g. technological change and changing cultural practices;

(c) changing tenure patterns (e.g. increasing non-farm and non-resident ownership of farmland, and associated land rental issues);

(d) the transference of agricultural land at the 'extensive' margin to forestland which, in most cases, reflects abandonment of agriculture.

In addition, a number of conflicts have been recognized with recreation land uses. These include impacts on agriculture, non-resident (especially out-of-province) ownership of recreational properties (e.g. PEI Land Use Service Centre 1978), and public access to recreational resources. Other conflicts exist within forestry, essentially in terms of the impact of management practices (or lack of) on the long-term sustainability of production. The recreational concerns have been dealt with at different levels, but not as systematically as the agricultural issues, while the forestry issues essentially have been handled as sector-specific resource planning/management problems. Neither the recreational nor the forestry conflicts are pursued in this chapter.

Cutting across many of the land-use conflicts mentioned above is a *natural environment* dimension. It is difficult to label this as a 'use', because there are many different aspects to it: inherent productivity of the land resource; links to water supply and quality; wildlife habitat; and a landscape component. There are conflicts between various uses of rural land, for example, farming or recreation, and maintenance of natural environment qualities, and some of these, in turn, may affect the potential of an environment to support further development, for example, water quality and quantity. Because of the potentially integrating nature of natural environment components, these are discussed in more detail below.

The principal issues

Four sets of preoccupations exist in rural land resource conservation in Canada, all of which can be illustrated with respect to agriculture. Of course, not all have received equal attention from land-use planning efforts in rural areas. Two of the preoccupations involve productivity relationships, one involves cost at the community level and the other involves interrelationships between rural resource activities and other functions of the land (amenity/landscape support, and links to natural environment elements).

The sufficiency and sustainability of resource production capability

This set of preoccupations is linked to the volume and quality of the physical resource base. In the agricultural arena, the conflicts involving the conversion of agricultural land to nonagricultural uses and the impact of agricultural technology upon long-term resource values have been the main conflicts singled out. Concerns also exist over the ability of the forest land to sustain production in the face both of specific industry practices and in terms of environmental change (e.g. climatic change and acid rain). In the natural environment domain, the capacity of the natural environment to perpetuate itself and support and withstand human development has also received much attention in the main settled part of the nation, but not to the same degree as the agricultural issues.

Viability of the socio-economic structure of the production system supported by the resource base

In agriculture, this is linked to the larger concern for sustainability of the total food production system. The principal manifestation of these concerns has been over the presumed degeneration of agricultural structure related first, to the indirect effects of urban development on farming such as higher property taxes and land prices and farmland fragmentation (e.g. Krueger 1959, 1978, Bryant et al. 1982) and second, over the potential ramifications of non-resident farmland ownership on farming (e.g. Mage & Stock 1981).

Community costs associated with alternative settlement forms

This is a preoccupation that is felt both by individuals (as taxpayers) and by local municipalities. For agriculture, this preoccupation has developed primarily in rural municipalities in the urban field which have experienced non-farm development. More scattered forms of residential development create higher servicing costs, and, because of the nature of the agricultural landholdings, the farm population ends up carrying a higher proportion of property taxes than comparable farmers in municipalities which have not experienced the same level of non-farm development (Krueger 1957, Bryant et al. 1982).

Amenity and natural environment concerns

This is a complex set of preoccupations. The amenity concerns which relate mainly to landscape are not especially well developed in Canada in the main rural areas (Troughton 1976) (except in some very special circumstances, e.g. the Niagara Escarpment in southwest Ontario). These values have received much more attention in the development and management of parks in wilderness areas and in sparsely settled areas of the country (Theberge 1987). The concerns which relate to the conservation and management of natural environment elements that influence development options, for example, flood control and water quality control, or that relate to recreational resources for nearby urban populations have received more attention in the main settled areas. Usually, these have been addressed in the form of sectoral approaches to management.

In addition to these preoccupations, there are two important considerations that land-use planning in rural areas has to deal with. First, the development of planned intervention presupposes, in an ideal situation, that the impacts and conflicts have been properly analysed and the evidence carefully weighed. Many of the rural land-use conflicts noted earlier have not received such scrupulous attention, especially in agriculture where we are faced with a multitude of pressures and actors (Bryant 1986b). When intervention has occurred, it seems to owe as much to the strength of different interest groups as to any 'objective' weighing of evidence.

Secondly, most of the preoccupations involve complex scale issues. Many of the concerns are focused upon collective values in the resource base that cannot be internalized easily within a municipality. As rural areas have become integrated increasingly into a broader and more open social and economic system, rural municipalities have been faced with more and more situations where they are called upon to take action to maintain or develop resource values to benefit the larger collectivity, both present and future. This is particularly troublesome given the distribution of land-use planning powers in Canada whereby provinces have tended to delegate considerable powers to the local level (Audet & Le Hénaff 1983). This delegation of powers is appealing in a democratic system, but raises questions about municipalities' abilities to recognize the root causes of conflicts and to evaluate costs and benefits effectively without some sort of broader framework.

Emergence of conflicts into the political area

It is not enough for a problem or conflict to exist for it to be subject to planned intervention. It has to be recognized and brought into the political arena at some level or another, and then has to be seen as sufficiently important to be acted upon. In the rural land resources domain, the process by which the conflicts emerge as issues is complex because often not all the 'stakeholders' are *directly* involved in the conflict and also because the stakeholders vary from one issue to another.

Land-use conflicts that end up as issues can be thought of as going through a series of stages, though it is not claimed that there is any unique or simple linear sequence of stages. Obviously, where the costs involved in a particular land resource use conflict are internalized rapidly within a community, directly concerned local community groups have often been instrumental in bringing problem situations into the political arena. Crisis situations such as those prevailing on the Prairies in the 1930s, a combination of economic conditions and drought, quickly gave rise to political pressure groups and action (e.g. the Prairie Farm Rehabilitation Act of 1935, designed to support projects for the rehabilitation of drought-stricken and soil drifting areas in the three Prairie provinces – Troughton 1981). However *ad hoc* such action may be, the institutional structures so created have a tendency to stay around a long time.

At an early stage, however, early indicators of an actual or potential rural land-use conflict in Canada have often been brought to light through various research efforts within post-secondary education institutions or other research agencies. When the interest groups are powerful enough, or the public interest is clearly evident, particular problems or conflicts may be taken on as a 'cause' by a political party. Public debate and heightened interest in the specific issues may lead to government intervention. The emergence of other problems and conflicts as issues into the political arena at any level can alter the course of events significantly for a particular issue. Even when government action is taken, this is no guarantee of a solution, because the emergence of other issues with claims on public resources (personnel and finances) can deflate attempts at management and control.

Before providing examples, it is well to emphasize again that in addition to various groups (e.g. farm groups, environmental groups, citizen groups) and special-purpose agencies, Canada has at least three levels of government. The *federal* government has little direct control over land use and natural resources, except of course over the lands it owns itself – and most of these are located north of the 60° parallel – and in the Northwest Territories and the Yukon (Swan 1978, Canada 1984). However, the federal government should not be discounted for it can influence land use in various ways (see, e.g. McCuaig & Manning 1980, Canada 1984, Kerr *et al.* 1985, Bond *et al.* 1986). Furthermore, it has various agencies which have played a very important role in research related to specific conflicts (e.g. the efforts of the Lands Directorate of Environment Canada). The *provinces* hold the main powers with respect to the regulation of land use and resources, but much of this has been delegated to local and regional municipalities under various provincial planning acts. The provincial presence, however, does vary; thus, in the Atlantic provinces, it tends to be stronger and local planning is much more weakly developed than in Ontario.

The planning of rural land use

Four basic approaches to the planning of rural land use can be identified: negative-regulatory, persuasive-regulatory, positive-regulatory and integrated (Bryant et al. 1982, Bryant & Russwurm 1982). The earliest attempts at regulating land use were negative-regulatory, and this approach still characterizes many rural municipalities. The basic thrust was to protect public welfare and to safeguard individual property rights – still important cornerstones of planning in Canada today (Gomme 1984).

Local municipal zoning is the classic example of the negative-regulatory approach and many of the so-called planning documents frequently simply confirm the existing patterns of land use. Intervention in the market allocation process is minimal under this approach and this undoubtedly reflects the individualistic pioneering spirit that helped launch this country (Troughton 1986). The local orientation of this approach tended not to take into account negative externalities at a broader scale and thus made long-term policy development difficult – and still does so! Furthermore, this local orientation is frequently 'local' in the sense of scope and horizons rather than in terms of the full involvement of local populations in planning their own environment.

Rapid urban growth in the 1950s and 1960s around many of the country's major urban centres underscored the difficulties of this early approach. In several parts of Canada, the response was the development of broader regional-scale persuasive-regulatory approaches. This involves a more co-operative and voluntary approach to planning which seemed better suited to Canada's cultural context where municipal powers and private property rights were jealously guarded. Hence, this period saw the development of various voluntary associations of adjacent municipalities, for example, the Joint Planning Boards in Ontario, the Regional Commissions in Alberta and the Regional Districts in British Columbia, all during the 1950s and 1960s (Bryant et al. 1982, Audet & Le Hénaff 1983, Simpson & Baldwin 1983).

It became clear, however, that in the most intensely urbanizing areas, these persuasive-regulatory approaches were not able to handle the complex system of values in land around the urban periphery. Thus, more positive-regulatory approaches began to evolve. This is characterized by a broader geographic scale of intervention, for example, the Regional Municipalities in Ontario around most of the major metropolitan areas (late 1960s and early 1970s); this positive-regulatory thrust has been reinforced under the recent 1983 Planning Act in Ontario since these regional bodies now have regulatory powers over zoning and subdivision control after their official plan has been approved. Other examples are the sectorally specific approaches in agricultural land conservation adopted by British Columbia, Québec and Newfoundland.

In understanding the types of responses, however, it is not enough to look at the severity of the presumed land-use conflicts. Cultural acceptability has a significant influence too. It is interesting that the movement towards greater regionalization in Québec had to await the late 1970s (Québec 1979a) despite the obvious problems created by the considerable fragmentation of the local government administrative structure in that province. And Ontario, because of its history of strong local powers and an image of being a bastion of individual rights, is most unlikely ever to adopt the type of positive-regulatory approach with respect to agricultural land conservation that British Columbia did in 1973.

In all of this, the closest examples of integrated approaches to rural land-use planning are found within some of the regional structures based on a major urban concentration. Even here, however, the integration of the spatial planning of land uses with other interventions, for example, property taxation measures and aid to farming, has not progressed very far. There are links, of course, between planning activities at this regional level and provincial levels (e.g. the provincial approval process for municipal official plans in Ontario) which is only natural given that many of the costs and benefits of alternative development options are realized at an even broader scale than the urban region. Unfortunately, much of the senior government involvement remains itself very sectorally organized and some of the key variables such as regional patterns of investment have not been effectively tackled.

Rural land-use conflicts: examples

Conflicts associated with the conversion of agricultural land to non-farm uses

The conversion of agricultural land to non-farm uses did not just begin in the 1960s – so why was it in that period that concern began to mount? First, non-farm development in Canada entered into a rapid phase during the 1960s both in terms of accretionary urban growth and scattered development in the countryside. The process thus became more noticeable. Second, during the 1960s, a greater awareness began to develop about environment and natural resource values, including the range of values associated with the agricultural land resource. The Resources for Tomorrow Conference in the early 1960s produced major evaluations of changing agricultural resources (Gertler & Hind-Smith 1961, Crerar 1961) that helped direct thinking in Canada about agricultural resources for the next 20 years; it also reinforced the decisions to undertake and complete a major inventory of the capability of the land resource for agriculture and other uses (the Canada Land Inventory – CLI) which has served as an important planning tool in rural areas to the present time (Rees 1979).

While urbanization and industrialization were contributing to a substantial decline in farm numbers because of the attractive pull of agricultural labour into growing non-farm employment in the 1960s and 1970s, non-farm development impacts on agriculture were receiving the bulk of the attention. Ontario and British Columbia both experienced an intensification in geographic research on the subject. In Ontario, for example, the Niagara Fruit Belt was the scene of much research (Reeds 1969, Ontario Department of Treasury and Economics 1972, Krueger 1978) building upon earlier work by Krueger (1959). This specialized fruit (peaches and cherries) and vine area possesses a special combination of edaphic and climatic conditions unique in Ontario, and, indeed, in Canada. It was also well located in the 1960s to benefit from urban and industrial development. The concerns raised by the early research was not just over the conversion of special quality farmland, but also over the indirect effects of non-farm development on the viability of the ongoing farm structure. Krueger (1959) suggested that for every hectare converted, another two hectares were ruined for agricultural production because of these indirect negative effects. *The real effect of such indirect impacts has yet to be measured properly* – and not just in Canada (Bryant 1986b) – but none the less, the research that was started in the Niagara area in the late 1950s and in the 1960s has influenced geographic and planning research in Canada in this domain to the present day.

During these early beginnings of the agricultural land conservation movement in Canada, it is interesting to note that another preoccupation paralleled the agricultural concerns, namely, *concern over costs to the community and to farmers as taxpayers arising from the scattered form of non-farm development in the countryside* (Lower Mainland Regional Planning Board 1956, Krueger 1957). Some of the initial attempts at planned intervention were more likely concerned with these aspects than with the land conservation aspect, especially given the growing capacity of the agricultural system to over-produce in relation to the effective market (Ontario Ministry of Agriculture and Food 1969, Craddock 1970). Hence, various attempts in a largely negative-regulatory vein were made, for example, the setting of minimum lot sizes for severances (new properties created by subdivisions of existing parcels of land). Even the regional government structures in Ontario and other regional structures elsewhere were more concerned with efficiency in service delivery and in government than with any conservation movement; however, the development of the regional official land-use plans usually contained provisions to avoid 'unnecessary' urban development on the best farmland and to control severance development. Although the urban pressures were strong in Ontario on the agricultural land base, Ontario was not fast off the starting blocks in developing any systematic intervention aimed at land conservation.

Thus, although the creation of regional government structures in Ontario did herald a move towards a more positive-regulatory stance that allowed the development of more coherent policies with respect to non-farm development in rural areas, one has to cross the country to British Columbia to witness the first real effort to develop a coherent provincial position with respect to the agricultural land preoccupations (Manning & Eddy 1978, Pierce 1981, Furuseth & Pierce 1982). It is no coincidence that this first real agricultural land conservation effort came in a province where the small area of high quality farmland is highly correlated with strong urban development pressures in the Lower Fraser Valley.

Following considerable pressure from various groups, the preservation of prime agricultural land formed part of the platform of the New Democratic Party, elected in 1972. In 1973, the Land Commission was created in British Columbia, which involved the establishment of a system of Agricultural Land Reserves based primarily upon the quality of the land resource as well as a system for monitoring and evaluating requests for exclusion and inclusion in the Agricultural Reserves. This was a strongly positive-regulatory move, especially in the Canadian context, as well as being very sectoral. Evidently, drastic steps were thought appropriate for what appeared to be a drastic situation. The dominant perspective of the agricultural land resource base was of agricultural land as a special resource that required special attention.

Certain farm business considerations were also taken into account in the delimitation of the reserves.

In Ontario, despite all the research and the high level of urbanization, movement towards any provincial involvement was much slower. This was undoubtedly related to strong attitudes concerning private property rights (farmers have often been against systems of reserves, at least initially, because it restricts their ability to sell their land), the continuing excess production capacity in many agricultural sectors and the conservative tradition of the government until the early 1980s. Nevertheless, during the provincial elections of 1975, the New Democratic Party (NDP) endorsed mounting concerns from various interest groups including farm groups. The NDP became the official opposition party to a minority Conservative government in 1975 (Troughton 1981), and the provincial government finally adopted a strategy (Ontario Ministry of Agriculture and Food 1977), the *Foodland Guidelines*, which has been revised somewhat recently (Ontario Ministry of Agriculture and Food 1986), although the revisions are still awaiting formal approval. It was still quite sectoral, but compared to the British Columbia (BC) legislation, the Ontario move was much more persuasive-regulatory in character and has sought to:

(a) persuade municipalities to identify the best agricultural lands, to control the fragmentation of agricultural properties through severance control and to address the problem of incompatibility between farm and residential land uses, e.g. through ensuring that minimum distances separate new residences from certain types of farming operations (minimum distances can be calculated for different types and sizes of farm operations such as hogs using criteria and formulae set out in Ontario's *Agricultural Code of Practice*); and

(b) to assist municipalities through a network of field consultants within the Ministry of Agriculture in the preparation of official plans, amendments to plans, and requests for severances from agricultural properties.

Evaluations of the efficacy of these provisions have not been overly optimistic (see Johnston & Smit 1985) but it is not clear that a more positive-regulatory mechanism would be accepted in Ontario in any case, given prevailing attitudes.

Practically at the same time, another major piece of provincial legislation was enacted in Québec in 1978, modelled partly on the BC experience (Québec 1979b). Once more, endorsement of the conservation ethic by the Parti Québecois which became the governing party from 1976 to 1985 was important in bringing about the change. Agricultural land represented part of the 'national' heritage of Québec and so its protection was a theme that seemed to fit in well with the Parti Québecois's political preoccupations. The Commission de Protection du Territoire Agricole was established to oversee the creation of agricultural land reserves within local land-use plans based on the best agricultural lands, to adjudicate requests for inclusion and exclusion from the reserves, and to control farmland fragmentation. Recent evaluations of this have been optimistic (Thibodeau 1984, Thibodeau et al. 1986). Subsequently, other provinces have responded to similar preoccupations, for example, Newfoundland's Development Areas (Lands) Act, and other attempts to influence development which has an impact on farmland have appeared, such as in Alberta, Manitoba, New Brunswick, Nova Scotia and Prince Edward Island (PEI) (Furuseth & Pierce 1982).

During the 1970s, a new set of research thrusts were developed, aimed at uncovering the complexities of farm and farmland change around cities. Processes other than land conversion were highlighted in the removal of land from agricultural production, even in the most urbanized regions (e.g. Gierman 1977, Warren & Rump 1981, Bryant et al. 1981); regional variations in the nature of agriculture–urbanization interactions were emphasized (see Bryant & Greaves 1978); and the magnitude of the negative indirect impacts of non-farm development was questioned and positive impacts studied such as the rental of land from non-farm landowners and market opportunities (e.g. Ironside 1979, Bryant & Fielding 1980, Joseph & Smit 1981). This did not mean that the negative impacts were being denied, but rather attention was being drawn to the real complexities of farm change around cities, drawing upon the recognition of other processes, and the adaptive behaviour of farmers as explanations (see Bryant 1984, Johnston & Bryant 1987). The real complexity of change means that the challenge for planning is greater, and that, if agricultural land-use problems are influenced by the state of the agricultural economy, in addition to development pressures, attempts at planning based on controlling urban growth alone are illusory (see, for instance, Ontario Federation of Agriculture 1974).

Furthermore, in many of the regulations developed to control scattered non-farm development, for example, minimum lot sizes for severances in many parts of Ontario and in Québec under the *Loi pour la Protection du Territoire Agricole*, it is clear that particular images of agriculture have permeated planning. The dominant assumption is of a full-time, relatively land-extensive farming system, an image that most certainly reflects the agricultural lobby group and the influence early on of the respective ministries of agriculture. It tends to sidestep the positive contributions of very intensive farming in some areas and of part-time farming which accounts for a very important proportion of farms in many parts of the country.

Despite the emergence of other problems in Canada towards the end of the 1970s and the 1980s, notably an economic slow-down and increasing unemployment, the debate over and research into the conversion of agricultural land has continued (see Yeates 1985). The debate does not have the same profile it once had, but the momentum of the early and middle 1970s has carried it through. The conservation movement has even managed to 'win' some important battles, for example, in the Niagara Fruit Belt, a strong lobbying effort by various individuals and groups – especially a citizens' group known as PALS (Protection of Agricultural Land Society) (Gaylor 1979, Krueger 1982) – led to a provincial decision to reduce considerably the urban development zones in the land-use plan around St Catherines, Niagara Region. On the other side, however, this decision has to be seen in the context of a relatively much slower rate of growth in the region than was initially anticipated in the land-use plan.

Non-resident ownership of farmland

The roots of the concerns here are to be found partially in the agriculture–urban development debate. One of the negative impacts of urban development frequently noted – but rarely studied in depth – is the non-farm ownership of farmland. In the urban fringe, this has also often been associated with land speculation and land development companies. Negative impacts cited include pressures on land prices and the creation of an environment of uncertainty.

During the 1970s, similar concerns began to be expressed over non-resident ownership of farmland generally, especially foreign ownership. The concerns were often expressed in areas outside the main urbanizing regions, for example, Prince Edward Island in the Maritimes and Huron County in south-west Ontario. In Prince Edward Island, the concerns were related to the premature subdivision of farmland for recreational properties; in Ontario, the concern was over the impacts on farmland prices and farmland upkeep.

In several provinces, actual legislation has been adopted either to control non-resident ownership (including foreign ownership and out-of-province ownership) of farmland, such as in Prince Edward Island (Kienholz 1980) and Québec, or to monitor it through disclosure and registration, as in Nova Scotia and Ontario (Ward & Reid-Sen 1984).

In Ontario, studies were undertaken (e.g. Mage & Stock 1981); evidence regarding the negative impact of foreign ownership in Ontario and especially Huron County was not impressive – in fact, the 'problem' hardly seemed to exist. Not surprisingly, the Ontario government has only adopted legislation that requires registry of foreign-owned farmland.

The non-resident ownership question, although it led to legislation in several provinces, has not maintained a high profile. This is undoubtedly partly due to the lack of evidence of a real 'problem', but it also probably reflects a strong feeling especially during the 1980s over not discouraging foreign investment, of whatever kind. This conflict thus experienced a very short-lived public profile and has not given rise to any significant widespread impacts in terms of directions in rural planning.

Agricultural resource degradation and agricultural technology

Unlike the short-lived profile of non-resident ownership, the relationship between agricultural technology, the environment and the long-term capacity of the agricultural resource base has been gathering momentum. The negative impacts of agricultural technology (e.g. pesticides and fertilizers) on water quality, both in rivers and the Great Lakes, was the subject of many studies in the context of the Joint Commission on the Great Lakes although attempts at improving the situation have been limited. More generally, the negative impacts of modern agricultural technology on long-term soil productivity has been recognized in certain quarters for some time (especially in circles of agrologists and other research scientists); for example, erosion and compaction problems related to monocultural grain corn production in south-west Ontario (Sparrow 1984), and erosion and salinization in parts of the Prairies (Bircham & Bruneau 1985).

In some parts of the Prairies, the recent series of poor climatic years underscored the urgency of the degradation problem. It was sufficiently important for a series of hearings and a report to be undertaken by the Standing Committee of Senate on Agriculture, Fisheries and Forestry (Sparrow 1984). Although the exact figures are subject to debate, the Senate report conclusions suggest that the soil degradation problem could be a much more serious problem than the effects of urban development on agricultural production. Thus, in the 1980s, the public profile of this conflict within agriculture has been high, witness the increasing number of publications and conferences on the subject (Coote et al. 1981, Sparrow 1984, Bircham & Bruneau 1985). This increasing preoccupation with the impact of agricultural technology and cultural practices on long-term agricultural productivity is reminiscent of debates in the UK (e.g. Munton 1983) although there the debates have also incorporated concerns over landscape quality and the historical, cultural and ecological values associated with agricultural landscapes (e.g. Nature Conservancy Council 1977).

This conflict is still at the stage of increasing awareness and information about the issues. Already, however, attention is being given to ways of combating the problems (e.g. the SWEEP programme of Agriculture Canada in south-west Ontario to support research into conservation practices in agriculture). However, this conflict falls outside the role of traditional land-use planning in rural areas, although there may be ways of developing agreements with farmers to engage in certain types of practices and linking these with certain aspects of physical land-use planning. In Ontario, the Conservation Authorities clearly have a potentially important role to play through research and counselling. We must await the future to see what approaches will be taken, although they are likely to involve a strong dose of persuasion and voluntary co-operation.

Amenity and natural environment issues

Conflicts involving amenity and natural environment issues are complex. Some have already been touched upon because they cut across many of the other conflicts. Landscape amenity concerns in Canada in the urban field and rural/agricultural regions have not tended to be very strong or well articulated. The germs of the notion are seen in the increasingly frequent mention of 'preserving rural character' in official land-use plans dealing with rural settlements, but the best examples of landscape concerns are found in the debates and intervention along the Niagara Escarpment in south-west Ontario (Gertler 1968, Niagara Escarpment Commission 1979). This prominent geological feature, cutting through the urban field of several large conurbations, was singled out in the late 1960s as a significant provincial resource meriting protection from urban development and aggregate mining so as to maintain it as a scenic and recreational resource for the whole province. The Niagara Escarpment Commission, created in 1973 to develop a plan for this 725 km length feature, has had a long and rocky battle, coming up against not only individuals trying to safeguard their property rights but also the jealously guarded acquired powers of local municipalities in terms of planning. Over the years, the area of protection over which the Commission has jurisdiction has become smaller as the result of such confrontations.

The management of other natural resource elements generally is sectorally oriented, for example, in Ontario the Conservation Authorities and their involvement in the management of water, certain wooded areas and floodplains. None the less, in official land-use plans, there is an increasing tendency to set aside, in consultation with other more sectorally oriented agencies, various types of natural environment zone. 'Natural hazard zones' and the like are identified where environmental conditions create a potential threat to property and health – floodplain zones and steep, potentially unstable slopes are both good examples. 'Environmentally sensitive areas', on the other hand, are areas identified where the ecosystem is particularly sensitive or fragile with respect to any change in uses. Again, there are a variety of motivations for such areas, for example, protection of a ground-water recharge area as part of the water management system and protection of an interesting ecological system for recreational and/or educational purposes. All of the concerns have now become generally acceptable as part of the physical planning of rural areas whereas 20 years ago this would not have been so.

Conclusions

Land-use planning in rural areas in the final analysis is concerned with people – their values and objectives. The physical planning of land uses tends to deal only with part of the attributes of land use, and, unfortunately, tends to deal frequently with symptoms rather than causes, unless it is placed in the broader context of community development. In Canada, as in many countries, this is frequently not the case.

A number of conflicts in rural land use have been discussed in this chapter. Those discussed are only a subset of all the conflicts, but they were chosen to represent the major debates that have developed in Canada in the last 20 years. Others could have been selected. For example, the abandonment of agricultural land to bush and forest at the 'extensive' margin has been an extremely important phenomenon in the eastern part of the country (Parsons 1977, McCuaig & Manning 1982, Mandale 1984, Fox & Macenko 1985, Lamoureux 1985). However, it has not been generally singled out as a phenomenon that requires tackling, except indirectly in so far as it reflects the declining fortunes of some rural communities. Another example is the conflict between aggregate (sand and gravel, etc.) resources and alternative uses of the land; these problems have given rise to specific provincial initiatives especially in Ontario (Marshall 1982, Bryant et al. 1982), but naturally, the conflicts tend to be much more localized than the agricultural issues.

The most widespread and most coherently articulated rural land-use conflicts in Canada concern agriculture. Some of these fall clearly into the domain of traditional land-use planning, for example, agricultural land conversion. The primary forces behind such problems are often to be found at a broader scale than that at which land-use planning has traditionally been carried out. In addition, the values and costs involved in such conflicts are not easily internalized within the local or even the regional municipality. Therefore, it is no surprise to see that provincial-level involvement has been an important component in tackling the problems. Even so, the nature of this provincial involvement varies from one province to another as a function of the nature and magnitude of the problem and the cultural and political acceptability of different approaches. Despite all the activity in this domain in the last 20 years in Canada, there are still debates about the seriousness of the 'problem'.

Other agricultural conflicts are not so easily integrated into traditional physical land-use planning. The non-resident farmland ownership issue received attention at the provincial level in several provinces but has lost its short-lived profile. On the other hand, the land degradation issue, intimately connected to environmental concerns, is enjoying a substantial profile and is increasingly recognized as a problem requiring urgent attention. It falls outside traditional approaches to land-use planning in rural areas, and solutions will probably have to be found in more persuasive, voluntary approaches, perhaps integrated with physical planning. Curiously enough, this concern for the conservation of soil quality has some potential conflicts with the land protection movement. In the latter, more attention is being given to the 'right-to-farm' perspective which would almost outlaw complaints from non-farmers about farming practices; the danger, of course, is if this results in giving *carte blanche* to farmers and farm technology. Finally, of course, both the soil and land conservation movements have to contend with the perennial problem of excess production capacity. This emphasizes the importance of a future-oriented perspective in conservation; in this respect, the type of scenario-building research undertaken by the land evaluation group at the University of Guelph may prove to be invaluable in forcing decision-makers' attention towards the future (Land Evaluation Project 1981).

In Canada, given the geographic diversity of the country, the very decentralized system of administration and the diversity of the issues, there has been no uniform system of handling the issues. To an outsider, a curious mosaic appears: a federal government with few powers in the area of rural land and resource use but with a significant research function, some provincial governments with strong positive-regulatory sectoral programmes and others with persuasive approaches, regional structures with strong co-ordinating powers and other municipalities with poorly developed planning functions. The two keywords for the future would appear to be:

(a) *integration*, not just within a given municipality or between adjacent municipalities, but also (i) between different levels of government, to recognize the complementarity of different levels in dealing with rural land-use/resource-use conflicts, (ii) 'integration' between different conservation movements as well as other uses of the land and (iii) involvement of local populations more fully in all stages of land-use planning in rural areas so that greater sensitivity to local and regional conditions can be achieved; and

(b) *flexibility* in terms of recognizing the need to combine traditional land-use planning actions with other forms of social and economic involvement.

Acknowledgements

Much of the personal research noted in the text has been undertaken in the past 10 years under various research grants from the Social Sciences and Humanities Research Council of Canada, which is gratefully acknowledged. I would also like to acknowledge the invaluable discussions on rural planning in Canada with my colleague and friend, Lorne Russwurm, before his untimely death early in 1987. The work specifically on rural planning has been complemented as well recently by a NATO grant for international collaborative research to undertake comparative work on the integration of local community in the planning and management of agricultural and natural environment areas in Ontario and France, and this is gratefully acknowledged.

References

Audet, R. & A. Le Hénaff 1983. *The land planning framework of Canada: an overview*. Lands Directorate, Environment Canada, Ottawa, Working Paper no. 28.
Best, R. H. 1981. *Land use and living space*. London: Methuen.
Bircham, P. & H. Bruneau 1985. *Degradation of Canada's prairie agricultural lands: a guide to literature and annotated bibliography*. Lands Directorate, Environment Canada, Ottawa, Working Paper no. 37.
Bond, W. K., H. C. Bruneau & P. D. Bircham 1986. *Federal programs with the potential to significantly affect Canada's land resource*. Land Directorate, Environment Canada, Ottawa.
Bryant, C. R. 1984. The recent evolution of farming landscapes in urban-centred regions. *Landscape Planning* **11**, 307–26.
Bryant, C. R. 1986a. Les transformations récentes de l'agriculture canadienne et les problèmes d'aménagement des ressources agricoles dans les régions métropolitaines. In *La géographie du Canada*, P. George (ed.), 185–98. Bordeaux: Les Presses Universitaires de Bordeaux.
Bryant, C. R. 1986b. Agriculture and urban development. In *Progress in agricultural geography*, M. Pacione (ed.), 167–94. London: Croom Helm.
Bryant, C. R. & J. A. Fielding 1980. Agricultural change and farmland rental in an urbanising environment. *Cahiers de Géographie de Québec* **24** (62), 277–98.
Bryant, C. R. & S. M. Greaves 1978. The importance of regional variations in the analysis of urbanisation–agriculture interactions. *Cahiers de Géographie de Québec* **22** (57), 329–48.
Bryant, C. R. & R. E. Preston (eds) 1987. *Papers in Canadian economic development. vol. 1: local initiatives in economic development*. Faculty of Environmental Studies, University of Waterloo, Ontario.
Bryant, C. R. & L. H. Russwurm 1979. The impact of nonagricultural development on agriculture: a synthesis. *Plan Canada* **19** (2), 122–39.
Bryant, C. R. & L. H. Russwurm 1982. North American farmland protection strategies in retrospect. *GeoJournal* **6**, 501–11.
Bryant, C. R., L. H. Russwurm & A. G. McLellan 1982. *The city's countryside: land and its management in the rural–urban fringe*. London: Longman.
Bryant, C. R., L. H. Russwurm & S. Y. Wong 1981. Census farmland change in Canadian urban fields, 1941–1976. *Ontario Geography* no. 18, 7–23.

Bryant, C. R., L. H. Russwurm & S. Y. Wong 1984. Agriculture in the Canadian urban field: an appreciation. In *The pressures of change in rural Canada*, M. F. Bunce & M. J. Troughton (eds), 12–33. Atkinson College, York University, Geographic Monograph no. 14.
Canada 1984. *Federal policy on land use*. Minister of Supply and Services Canada, Ottawa.
Coote, D. R., J. Dumanski & J. F. Ramsey 1981. *An assessment of the degradation of agricultural land in Canada*. Land Resource Research Institute, Agriculture Canada, Ottawa, Contribution no. 118.
Craddock, W. J. 1970. *Interregional competition in Canadian cereal production*. Economic Council of Canada, Special Study no. 12, Ottawa.
Crerar, A. D. 1961. The loss of farmland in the growth of the metropolitan regions of Canada. In *Resources for tomorrow: supplementary volume*, 181–96. The Queen's Printer, Ottawa.
Fox, M. F. & S. Macenko 1985. *The agriculture–forest interface: an overview of land use change*. Lands Directorate, Environment Canada, Ottawa, Working Paper no. 38.
Furuseth, O. J. & J. T. Pierce 1982. A comparative analysis of farmland preservation programmes in North America. *The Canadian Geographer* 26 (3), 191–206.
Gaylor, H. 1979. Political attitudes and urban expansion in the Niagara Region. *Contact, Journal of Urban and Regional Affairs* 11, 43–60.
Gertler, L. O. 1968. *The Niagara Escarpment Report*. The Queen's Printer, Toronto.
Gertler, L. O. & J. Hind-Smith 1961. The impact of urban growth on agricultural land. In *Resources for tomorrow: supplementary volume*, 155–80. The Queen's Printer, Ottawa.
Gierman, D. M. 1977. *Rural to urban land conversion*. Lands Directorate, Environment Canada, Occasional Paper no. 16, Ottawa.
Gomme, T. 1984. Municipal planning in Ontario. *Plan Canada* 24, 102–14.
Ironside, R. G. 1979. Land tenure, farm income and farm practice in southern Ontario. *Ontario Geography* 14, 21–39.
Johnson, T. R. R. & C. R. Bryant 1987. Agricultural adaptation: the prospects for sustaining agriculture near cities. In *Sustaining agriculture near cities*, W. Lockeretz (ed.). Tufts University, Mass.
Johnson, T. R. R. & B. Smit 1985. An evaluation of the rationale for farmland preservation policy in Ontario. *Land Use Policy* 2 (3), 225–37.
Joseph, A. & B. Smit 1981. Implications of exurban residential development: a review. *The Canadian Journal of Regional Science* 4 (2), 207–24.
Kerr, M. A., E. W. Manning, J. Séguin & L. J. Pelton 1985. *Okanagan fruitlands: land-use change dynamics and the impact of federal programs*. Lands Directorate, Environment Canada, Ottawa, Land Use in Canada Series no. 26.
Kienholz, E. (1980). *The land-use impacts of recent legislation in PEI: an analysis of the Land Development Corporation and non-resident ownership*. Lands Directorate, Environment Canada, Ottawa, Land Use in Canada Series no. 18.

Krueger, R. R. 1957. The rural–urban fringe taxation problem: a case study of Louth Township. *Land Economics* **33**, 264–9.

Krueger, R. R. 1959. Changing land use patterns in the Niagara fruit belt. *Transactions of the Royal Canadian Institute* **32**, 39–140.

Krueger, R. R. 1978. Urbanization of the Niagara fruit belt. *The Canadian Geographer* **22**, 179–94.

Krueger, R. R. 1982. The struggle to preserve specialty crop land in the rural–urban fringe of the Niagara Peninsula of Ontario. *Environments* **14** (3), 1–10.

Lamoureux, D. 1985. *The abandonment of agricultural land in Gaspé, Québec: the causes and impacts on land use.* Lands Directorate, Environment Canada, Ottawa, Working Paper no. 29.

Land Evaluation Project 1981. *Effects of urban expansion on land needs for agriculture in Ontario.* School of Rural Planning and Development, University of Guelph, Guelph, Ontario, Report no. 2/81–83.

Lower Mainland Regional Planning Board 1956. *Urban sprawl in the Lower Mainland of BC.* Lower Mainland Regional Planning Board, New Westminster, British Columbia, Technical Report.

McCuaig, J. D. & E. W. Manning 1980. *The effects on land use of federal programs in the Windemere Valley.* Lands Directorate, Environment Canada, Ottawa, Working Paper no. 8.

McCuaig, J. D. & E. W. Manning 1982. *Agricultural land use change in Canada: process and consequences.* Lands Directorate, Environment Canada, Land Use in Canada Series no. 21.

Mage, J. & G. Stock 1981. *Absentee land ownership in the Huron–South Bruce Area of Ontario.* Rural Development Outreach Project, University of Guelph, Ontario.

Mandale, M. 1984. *Marginal land utilization and potential, Kent County, New Brunswick.* Lands Directorate, Environment Canada, Ottawa, Working Paper no. 31.

Manning, E. W. & S. S. Eddy 1978. *The agricultural land reserves of British Columbia: an impact analysis.* Lands Directorate, Environment Canada, Ottawa, Land Use in Canada Series no. 13.

Marshall, I. B. 1982. *Mining, land use and the environment.* Lands Directorate, Environment Canada, Ottawa, Land Use in Canada Series no. 22.

Munton, R. J. C. 1983. Agriculture and conservation: what room for compromise? In *Conservation in perspective*, A. Warren & F. B. Goldsmith (eds). Chichester: Wiley.

Nature Conservancy Council 1977. *Nature conservation and agriculture.* Nature Conservancy Council, London, England.

New Brunswick, Province of 1981. *New Brunswick: forest inventory.* Department of Natural Resources, Forest Management Branch, New Brunswick.

Niagara Escarpment Commission 1979. *The proposed plan for the Niagara Escarpment.* Toronto: The Queen's Printer.

Ontario Department of Treasury and Economics 1972. *Niagara Escarpment Study: Fruit Belt Report.* Toronto: The Queen's Printer.

Ontario Federation of Agriculture 1974. *Agricultural land use policy of the Ontario Federation of Agriculture.* Policy statement adopted at the Ontario Federation of Agriculture Annual Convention, 27 November.
Ontario Ministry of Agriculture and Food 1969. *The challenge of abundance.* Toronto: The Queen's Printer.
Ontario Ministry of Agriculture and Food 1977. *Foodland guidelines.* Toronto: The Queen's Printer.
Ontario Ministry of Agriculture and Food 1986. *Proposed foodland preservation policy statement.* Toronto: The Queen's Printer.
Parsons, H. E. 1977. An investigation of the changing rural economy of Gatineau County, Québec. *The Canadian Geographer* 21 (1), 22–31.
PEI Land Use Service Centre 1978. *Non-resident land ownership legislation and administration in Prince Edward Island.* Lands Directorate, Environment Canada, Ottawa, Land Use in Canada Series no. 12.
Pierce, J. T. 1981. The BC Agricultural Land Commission: a review and evaluation. *Plan Canada* 21 (2), 48–56.
Québec, Government of 1979a. *Projet de loi no. 125: loi sur l'aménagement et l'urbanisme.* Québec: Editeur Officiel du Québec.
Québec, Government of 1979b. *Loi sur la protection du territoire agricole: renseignements généraux.* Québec: Commission de Protection du Territoire Agricole du Québec.
Reeds, L. G. 1969. *Niagara Region: agricultural research report.* Ontario Department of Economics, Treasure and Intergovernmental Affairs, Toronto.
Rees, W. E. 1979. The Canada Land Inventory and its impact on regional planning. In *Urban and regional planning in a federal state – the Canadian experience*, W. T. Perks & T. M. Robinson (eds), 159–71. Stroudsburg, Pa.: Dowden, Hutchinson & Ross.
Russwurm, L. H. & C. R. Bryant 1984. Changing population distribution and rural–urban relationships in Canadian urban fields 1941–1976. In *The pressures of change in rural Canada*, M. F. Bunce & M. J. Troughton (eds), 113–37. Atkinson College, York University, Toronto, Geographical Monograph no. 14.
Scace, R. C. 1981. *Land use classification systems: an overview.* Lands Directorate, Environment Canada, Ottawa, Working Paper no. 14.
Simpson, J. A. & T. W. Baldwin 1983. *Joint municipal plans: the Peace River region experience.* School of Urban and Regional Planning, Ryerson Polytechnical Institute, Toronto, Occasional Paper no. 11.
Singhal, I. 1985. Fiscal framework and agricultural expenditures in Canada. *Canadian Farm Economics* 19 (1), 17–31.
Sparrow, H. O. (Chairman) 1984. *Soil at risk – Canada's eroding future.* Standing Committee on Agriculture, Fisheries and Forestry, Report on Soil Conservation to the Senate of Canada, Ottawa.
Statistics Canada 1976. *Profile studies: the urban and rural composition of Canada's population.* Ottawa: Statistics Canada Census of Canada Catalogue V, 99–702, Bulletin 5.1 - 2.

Statistics Canada 1982. *Population: geographic distributions.* Ottawa: Statistics Canada Census of Canada Catalogue 2, 93–906.

Swan, H. 1978. *Federal lands: their use and management.* Lands Directorate, Environment Canada, Ottawa, Land Use in Canada Series no. 11.

Theberge, J. (Chairman) 1987. *Our parks – vision for the 21st century.* Task Force on Park Establishment, Report to Environment Canada, Ottawa.

Thibodeau, J. C. 1984. Une urbanisation mieux contenue, une agriculture qui se regénère. *Cahiers de l'IAURIF* **73**, 238–58.

Thibodeau, J. C., M. Gaudreau & J. Bergeron 1986. *Le zonage agricole: un bilan positif.* Institut de la Recherche Scientifique – Urbanisation, Montréal, RR9.

Troughton, M. J. 1976. Agriculture and the countryside. In *The countryside in Ontario*, M. J. Troughton, J. G. Nelson & S. Brown (eds), 45–77. Department of Geography, University of Western Ontario, London.

Troughton, M. J. 1981. The policy and legislative response to loss of agricultural land in Canada. *Ontario Geography* **18**, 79–109.

Troughton, M. J. 1986. *Rural Canada: what future?* Paper presented at the conference 'Integrated Development beyond the City', Mount Allison University, Sackville, New Brunswick.

Ward, E. N. & S. J. Reid-Sen 1984. *Foreign ownership of land and real estate in Canada.* Lands Directorate, Environment Canada, Ottawa, Working Paper no. 30.

Warren, C. L. & D. Rump 1981. *The urbanization of rural land in Canada: 1961–1971 and 1971–1976.* Lands Directorate, Environment Canada, Land Use in Canada Series no. 20.

Yeates, M. (1985). *Land in Canada's urban heartland.* Lands Directorate, Environment Canada, Ottawa, Land Use in Canada Series no. 27.

9 Rural land-use planning in Australia

GEOFFREY T. McDONALD

Introduction

Australia's rural land-use planning is dominated by its colonial past, its location in a remote corner of the world and its very low rainfall. The history of Australia since European colonization is short; the Commonwealth of Australia was formed in 1901 from the federation of six separate colonies, now states, which retained most powers over land.

Much of the better land in Australia was colonized at a time when Europeans thought they had an evolutionary right to take over from the non-productive indigenous occupants, the Aborigines (*terra nullius*). In common with other European ex-colonial countries, Australia now has areas of land reserved for the surviving native peoples.

Australia is at the extensive margin of the world's trading system with a very small population and market of only 16 million people. Land has a near zero rent and most Australian land-use planning policy has been directed to promote economic activity and to minimize locational disadvantage. Conservation policies have not had a high priority, at least until recently.

The following sections describe some important overarching factors that have influenced the development of Australia's land resources and its land-use planning systems.

Dependence on rural exports

Australia has been extremely dependent upon international trade to generate economic activity and this trade has been dominated by primary product exports and manufactured imports. In 1985 Australia's total export trade was $30 634 million, of which $10 196 million (33%) was in farm products and $13 303 (43%) in primary energy and mineral products, all having very low levels of transformation. Only 23% of the nation's exports was fabricated products. Even with a history of government intervention in the trade in manufactured products, the Australian economy is still resource-extractive.

In the years since 1950, national dependency on rural exports has fallen from 82% to 33%; nevertheless, Australia exported 69% of its rural production in 1985 and it is extremely sensitive to world trading conditions in agricultural commodities. Farm incomes fluctuate widely.

In recent years Australia has been a leader in opposing protectionist agricultural policies in Japan, Europe and elsewhere because they have resulted in depressed world prices for many agricultural products. The terms of trade for agricultural exporters have been declining for many years but the decline since 1984 has been so sharp that Miller (1986) claims that it represents an agricultural crisis comparable with the depression of the 1930s.

The realignment of Australia's agricultural marketing and rural production since the formation of the EEC and particularly since the UK joined has been substantial. Some industries have contracted from major export industries to just supplying local demand, for example, frozen lamb, processed dairy products industries and deciduous fruit, whereas others have risen dramatically to supply new markets in the Pacific Region and Asia including cotton and coarse grains and live sheep. The staples (wool, wheat, sugar and beef) still account for 70% of rural export earnings and half of the total value of rural production. It is for these commodities that Australia's concern about export prices is greatest.

From a land-use policy perspective the highly export-oriented nature of rural industry is of critical concern because the variations in export earnings has widespread implications for farm viability, farmland management and land resource use. It sets the economic context in which agriculture competes with other uses for land, and land-use priorities must be set. This context is quite different from many of the developed nations where, for example, there may be justified concern about conversion of farmland to other uses, an issue of minor significance in Australia at least from an agricultural perspective (see McDonald & Rickson 1987).

Private enterprise and agrarian socialism

In Australia, there is still a peculiar coexistence of a belief in free enterprise, in individual landowners' rights to do what they choose with their businesses and land resources at the same time as a dependence upon agrarian social policies in the form of programmes to protect rural enterprises by regulated marketing and subsidized infrastructure. In Australia governments socialize many of the losses, high costs and risks for the landowning class and in reality there is a high dependence on the public sector.

Dependence on imported capital

Australia has always depended to a large extent on imported capital for resource development. This is as true for mining and real-estate development in the 20th century as it was for pastoral development in the 19th century. In an exploitive economy very little domestic capital is available; profits on these resources are made in metropolitan centres well away from the resource extraction districts, notably London, New York and Tokyo. Of the limited local 'capital' much of it is tied up as natural resources *in situ*. These resources can be bartered by government for development.

Perception of resources

In Australia, the low intensity of land use gives an impression to many residents that there is an unlimited supply of land, thus creating a number of misconceptions. First, it creates an urgency to 'develop' the land, on the grounds that if this obligation is not met the land should be relinquished to others who will. In some instances there is an expressed desire even now to close the frontier and have some development presence in remoter regions. The only commercially successful cultivation in that one-third of the country lying north of the Tropic of Capricorn is sugar cane and horticulture on a very limited coastal strip on the east coast; 400 000 ha of cultivation in a region of 250 million ha. Very extensive livestock grazing and mining are the predominant activities on the remaining land.

Secondly, attitudes based on a view of unlimited resources leave relatively little room for conservative land management and sustainable use, and promotes haste in the planning of new development.

Grossly over-optimistic appraisal of resources produced many problems in Australia's development. It led to destruction of forests for timber and agriculture, over-commitment of underground and surface water supplies, overstocking of semi-arid grasslands, cultivation of lands too steep or with soils too thin for long-term agricultural use, and so on (see Donald 1965, Heathcote 1970, Powell 1976, 1986).

In addition to a lack of knowledge about the environment was an indifference to it, a belief that the landscape could only be improved by the works of Europeans (see also Seddon and Davis 1976).

> Possibly deriving from this desire to improve on nature was the indifferent regard for the natural landscape itself. The scale of the land was so large that there was no need of care in its use. If the aim was to transform it, the quicker the better.
> (Heathcote 1970 p. 90)

Australia's land resources and their use

Land resources

There has always been great debate about the limits to settlement posed by Australia's land resources. From the early days of European colonization to the present day the argument has raged as to what are the spatial and quantitative limits to the agriculture. It has not always been a rational debate and there have been misguided attempts in most states to create farms far too small to be viable or carrying out farming practices that just could not be sustained (see Meinig 1962). Despite the massive improvements in the efficiency of land resource science and the excellent work of organizations such as the Commonwealth Scientific and Industrial Research Organization (CSIRO) which pioneered techniques of land assessment (land systems) to assist in the evaluation of large tracts of land, to this day there remains considerable uncertainty about the supply of potential agricultural and grazing land in Australia. 'Until adequate information on land attributes and land use models are available and used in land assessment, widely divergent estimates of Australia's agricultural and pastoral resources will continue to be made', Gifford et al. (1975 p. 212).

The margin of error is somewhat smaller than predictions made early this century which suggested that the country might accommodate hundreds of millions of people.

The compound effects of climate, terrain and soil type in Australia limit agricultural development to a very small fraction of the country's large land mass of 768 million hectares. Scientists agree that there are about 230 million hectares that are climatically suited to arable agriculture – about 30% of the country. The moisture factor is by far the most limiting. Two key criteria are that the ratio of actual to potential evapotranspiration should exceed 0.4 for at least 13 consecutive weeks during which time total incident solar radiation exceeds 40 kcal/cm^2 (see Gifford et al. 1975 p. 213). Once terrain is taken into account by deleting areas which have steep slopes (and unfortunately by an accident of geography most of these areas are in high rainfall zones) and those problem soils such as saline soils, sand dunes, or rock outcrops, only 77 million hectares (10%) of the country can be regarded as suitable for intensive agricultural and pastoral use. Some of that is already set aside for other uses and the balance is 70 million hectares (see Figs 9.1 and 9.2).

This leaves 19 million hectares that are potentially available for more intensive agricultural and pastoral pursuits, most of that land being in northern Australia where there are many unconquered technical and economic problems including unreliable rainfall, very high erosion rates, tropical pests and diseases, and high costs of production and marketing due to remoteness (see Davidson 1966, Isbell 1986). It is not that development has not been attempted; many agricultural schemes have been tried and have failed in this region for a variety of reasons (Courtenay 1978).

This very rough estimate of the quantity of land for agriculture has overlooked the quality dimension. There are small areas of the highest quality volcanic and alluvial soils in Australia but most of the cropland that is used suffers from low fertility and an unreliable climate which is reflected in the low yields and low carrying capacities on most of the country: 1.61 tonnes per hectare for the nation's cereals crop in 1985 which contrasted with the EEC average of 5.90 tonnes per hectare and the USA's 4.38 tonnes per hectare

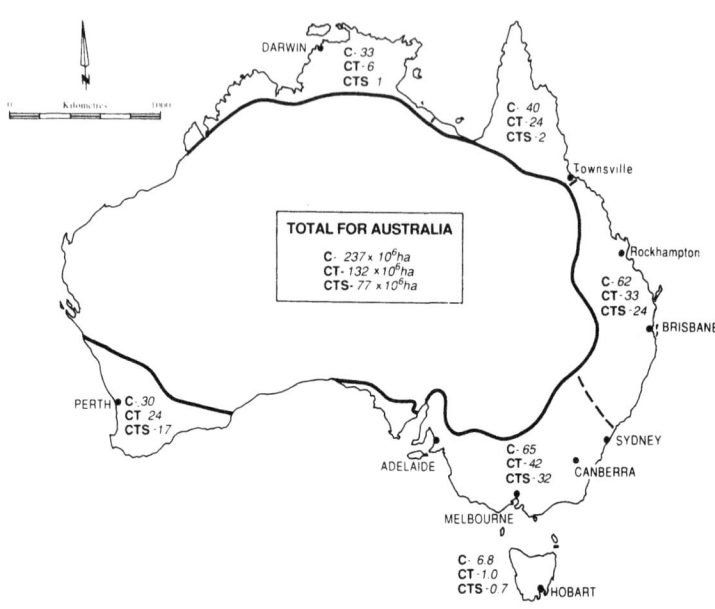

Figure 9.1 Areas suitable for dryland arable agriculture in Australia (Nix 1974). C – climatic constraints only; T – terrain constraints; S – soil constraints. Unit: 10^6 ha.

(FAO 1986). Irrigation is an important activity in Australia and 1.7 million hectares are irrigated, although surface water supplies are very limited and not well distributed in relation to the land which might use it. Development of these limited resources has been an important element in Australia's rural development strategy. These developments are concentrated in the south-east of the country (87%) and in the Murray–Darling Basin where some 85% of the basin's exploitable yield has now been used (Australia Department of Resources and Energy 1983, Pigram 1986.

Land use

The non-arid zone occupies only 30% of Australia and yet it contains all the crop and forest land, 75% of the country contains the semi-arid pastoral lands together with unused deserts. Economically, mining is the most important activity in the arid

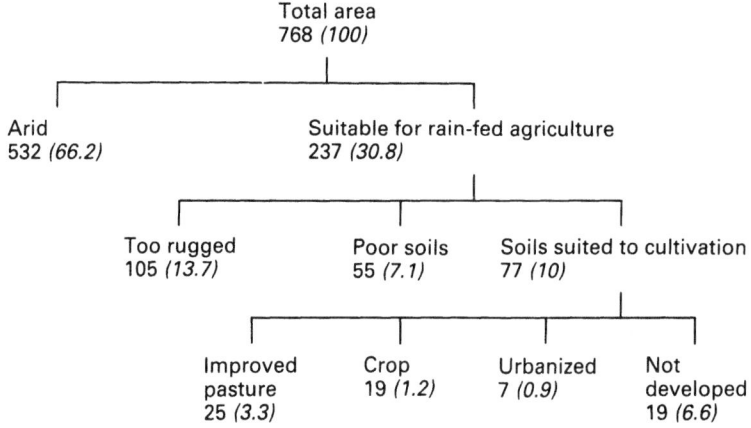

Figure 9.2 Estimates of the amount of land in Australia suitable for dryland agriculture; millions of hectares (%)
Sources: Gifford et al. 1976 p. 212, Bureau of Agricultural Economics 1983 p. 25, Chittleborough 1986 p. 492.

zone with centres such as Kalgoorlie (gold, nickel), Broken Hill (silver, lead, zinc), Mount Isa (copper) and the Pilbara (iron ore). Soils and climate are the principal determinants of the use of land in the non-arid zone.

As a result of climatic limitations, only 9% of Australia supported forests at the time of European colonization and this original cover has been reduced by half (Wells et al. 984). The most ubiquitous native forests are the eucalypt-dominated open forests found in all parts of the forested regions of the country and important for hardwood sawlog and pulp production. Rainforests, although small in area (only about 1.8 Mha), are valued out of all proportion to their area for quality timbers, recreational and scientific value and for nature conservation purposes. Native forests are fully if not over exploited at this time. At present native and exotic pine plantations forests contribute equally to sawn and pulp wood production, but by the turn of the century plantation forests will contribute about double their present output.

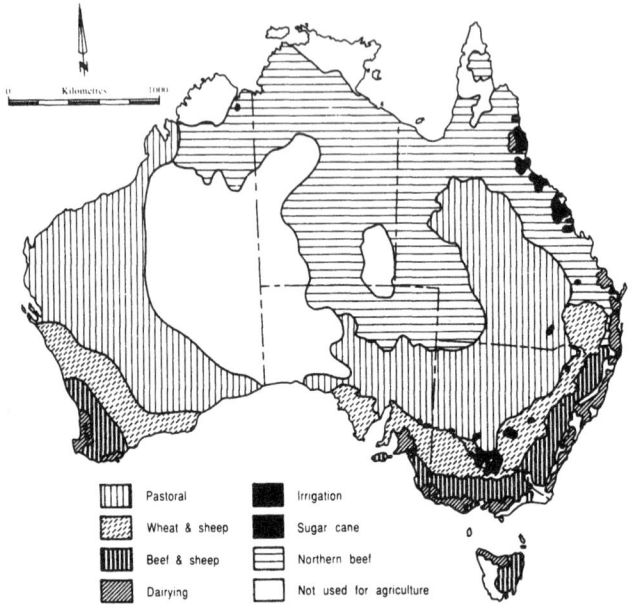

Figure 9.3 Dominant land uses.

Land-use issues

Given the relatively low population densities in Australia and the small domestic market for locally produced food and fibre, the predominant issue facing managers of Australia's land resources has been to find rural activities with viable international markets. Competition between rural uses of a rather limited land base has not been common. Conflicts arise more commonly due to degradation of the land base and off-site problems.

Many of these issues result from European settlers learning to understand the Australian environment. It was inevitable that they would make errors and misjudgements in adapting to the land and some of these problems have only emerged in serious form in recent years (see Table 9.2.)

Irrespective of the spatial extent of a territory and the quality of its land resources, wherever there are substantial metropolitan centres, as there are in Australia, strong competition will exist for land for urban-related uses. Locational factors will always produce land scarcities and land-use problems. Given that 64% of Australia's population lives in cities of more than 100 000 these issues are many

Table 9.1 Percentage of the total area of Australia devoted to each major land use.

Use	Area (Mha)	%
Urban and transport	7.7	1.3
Nature conservation	26.9	3.5
Forestry	15.4	2.0
Agriculture		
Cropping	19.0	2.5
Improved pasture	25.0	3.3
Grazing		
Non-arid	136.4	17.8
Arid	335.6	43.7
Unused mainly desert	199.7	26.0
Total	768.0	100.0

Sources: Bureau of Agricultural Economics 1983 p. 25, Australia, Department of Arts, Heritage and Environment 1986 p. 2.

and recurrent and to that extent Australia is no different from the other developed countries.

In terms of public debate it is possible to group the recent land-use problems according to the two main regions of change, namely, the rural–urban fringe where there is conflict between the expansion of urban-related uses on to farmland and perhaps on to undeveloped open space areas, and the extensive margin of agriculture/forestry where there is still undeveloped wilderness that is now coming under pressure for logging, water resources developments, or mining.

In Australia public inquiries and special commissions are ritualistically established to deal with problems of land-use planning (for example, Australia Senate Standing Committee 1984, Australia Department of Resources and Energy 1983, Australia Parliament Senate Standing Committee on Science, Technology and the Environment (1984), FORWOOD 1974) and countless 'inquiries' about issues such as Fraser Island, Ranger uranium, Lake Pedder, woodchips, soil conservation, land-use policy, the coastal zone, and so on. The issues are presented in Table 9.2 in terms of the land allocation and land management issues identified. A more comprehensive treatment is given in Cocks *et al.* (1980).

Table 9.2 Land-use planning issues in Australia.

URBAN-RELATED USES

A Land-use allocation issues
- expansion of residential subdivisions and services on to the good farm land that surrounds most cities and towns
- decentralization and growth centres in rural areas

B Land-use management issues
- subdivision standards in relation to sewerage, water supply and roads around almost all cities and towns
- bush fire hazards especially in the southern summer-dry regions
- aesthetic effects of uncontrolled development in semi-rural areas

NATIONAL PARKS AND CONSERVATION

A Land-use allocation issues
- acquiring land to provide an adequate estate of representative ecotypes
- with forestry in the Queensland and NSW rainforests, SW Tasmania
- with mining in Kakadu, Fraser Island, Myall Lakes
- with tourism and recreation, for example, Kosciusko NP
- with agriculture and pastoralism on coastal wetlands

B Land-use management issues
- recreational use pressures on limited areas causing degradation of the resource, overcrowding and rationing of access, e.g. Kosciusko NP
- the environmental effects of providing recreational facilities in Parks
- determining fire management strategies that do not disrupt natural processes
- management of faunal species considered as pests by agriculturalists

RURAL INFRASTRUCTURE

Land-use management issues
- providing efficient commodity transportation and handling systems for grains, sugar and meat
- providing low-cost and reliable irrigation water in a region of unreliable rainfall especially in the Murray–Darling Basin
- providing high-standard and low-cost domestic services such as health, education and communication for rural dwellers in the remote areas of inland and northern Australia
- provision of adequate rural roads over large distances

RURAL RECREATION

A Land-use allocation issues
- supply of sufficient land for public outdoor recreation in the vicinity of the metropolitan areas and along the closely settled south-east coastal strip in conflict with productive forestry, water resources management for agriculture and nature conservation

B   Land-use management issues
   - managing the environmental effects of off-road vehicles in environmentally sensitive areas especially beaches and forests near to urban areas

Forestry

A   Land-use allocation issues
   - with nature conservation especially of rainforests in Queensland and northern NSW
   - replacement of agriculture with plantations
   - insufficient attention to multiple use of forests especially the recreation and conservation components

B   Land-use management issues
   - whether Australia should be self-sufficient in wood products and consequently have public investment in plantation forests and stronger protection of the wood values of native forests
   - determining the sustainable yield of native forests to define logging rates and timber requirements. This is especially controversial in tropical rainforest areas where sustainable yield is a debated concept
   - environmental effects of expanding exotic pine plantations including the loss of natural habitats and nutrient cycling problems
   - environmental effects on forest clear-felling for wood-chips with consequent effects on wildlife habitats, soil erosion and the hydrological characteristics of forest catchments especially in the south-west of Western Australia and in southern NSW
   - fire and pest management to preserve forests

Agriculture

A   Land-use allocation issues
   - with urban-related uses for good farmland near cities
   - cultivation of marginal cereal lands which are subject to water and wind erosion
   - search for development options in the seasonally wet tropics which to date have not been successfully developed for agriculture

B   Land-use management issues
   - farm viability in the face of marketing problems
   - improvement of the nutrient status of naturally infertile soils
   - prevention of soil erosion especially on marginal farming lands in the cereals-producing regions
   - maximizing the efficiency of irrigation water use
   - salinity problems in irrigation areas due to rising saline water tables
   - control of pest flora and fauna
   - control of agricultural chemicals which have ecological side-effects

Mining

A Land-use allocation issues
- local conflict over quarries and sand extraction causing residential amenity and traffic problems and river channel degradation
- with conservation over the clearing of forests and the loss of wilderness values (e.g. SW., W. Australia), Myall Lakes, Fraser Island, Kakadu
- with Aboriginals over land rights, mining and royalties (e.g. Ranger, Shelbourne Bay)
- with agriculture for the use of land and water in the Hunter Valley coal-mining region

B Land-use management issues
- rehabilitation of open-cut mines
- controlling the quality of tailings water
- minimizing the use of water supplies and the effect of important watersheds

Aboriginal Lands

A Land-use allocation issues
- with pastoralists for land rights
- with white communities for services
- with mining for land rights and royalties

B Land-use management issues
- determining appropriate tenure and land rights
- determining management structures and planning principles for self-management of Aboriginal pastoral, coastal and urban fringe lands
- balancing economic and social development

Pastoral Lands

A Land-use allocation issues
- with Aboriginals for use of central and northern lands
- with conservationists about declaration of conservation reserves

B Land-use management issues
- prevention of dryland salinization resulting from over-clearing of land in sub-humid grazing lands of western Australia and to a lesser extent the Murray–Darling Basin of eastern Australia
- weed, vermin and disease control including brucellosis and TB
- maintaining adequate stock water supplies especially in artesian basins
- degradation of grazing lands and desertification resulting from overstocking

Geoffrey T. McDonald

Institutions

Management institutions

Australia is a federation of six states together with a number of territories administered by the Commonwealth. The states at federation gave to the Commonwealth power over a number of areas, including external trade, defence and foreign affairs, communications, and the financial system, retaining for themselves all other powers. The states have primary jurisdiction over urban development, land, water, minerals and forestry resources, the bulk of the subject matter of land-use planning.

Over the years since federation, the Commonwealth has increased its involvement in land-use and environmental planning by using its powers in traditionally accepted areas such as trade and finance to have far-reaching consequences on the cost of production of different rural activities and consequently upon land management and land use. Subsidies, bounties, taxation provisions, banking policy, foreign investment and export controls, have all been used to affect land use and production in Australian agriculture, mining, forestry and even urban development. No issue better illustrates the tension between the three levels of government in Australia than environmental decision-making, which lends itself to a philosophy of public involvement to achieve social goals of conservation of resources and ecosystems at the expense of narrow parochial interests or narrow development biases. The consequence is an increasing centralization of control over the environment despite the apparent lack of Commonwealth jurisdiction and increasing confusion and conflict over the extent of the states' rights over land matters.

The Commonwealth has used its financial controls over the State Grants Commission and Loans Council to influence the extent of government and semi-government borrowings and it provides tied grants to states for purposes such as forestry plantations, land development schemes, water storages, roads and other infrastructure. Some of the most overt recent actions of the Commonwealth include:

- It blocked the export of heavy minerals (rutile, zircon, illmenite) which were to be mined from the beaches and forested dunes of Fraser Island, Queensland by using its control over

trade matters (Customs (Prohibited Regulations) Act). Despite the Commonwealth providing compensation to the miners and local governments, the decision created a great deal of conflict, including an unsuccessful High Court challenge, and did not remove the possibility that the decision could be reversed.
- The Commonwealth effectively prevented the construction of a hydroelectric power station and dam on the Franklin River in Tasmania by creative use of its constitutional responsibility for foreign treaties, in this case the World Heritage Treaty which obliges signatory countries to protect registered sites. Again the substantial compensation paid by the Commonwealth did not stifle heated conflict and another unsuccessful High Court challenge.

This is not to say that relationships between the state and national governments are always uncooperative. The Commonwealth has attempted to provide a leadership and co-ordinating role between the states on land-use matters including playing host to a whole range of Ministerial Councils that deal with matters such as agriculture, forestry, water resources, environment, nature conservation, and so on. It has also attempted to stimulate research and the dissemination of new technologies through a wide range of research agencies most notably the CSIRO which has an enviable record of scientific research into land-use and management issues in the country.

Within the states there are 900 local governments. They did not originate from any grass-roots democracy but owe their existence to state government legislation which delegates local powers to them. Their powers are constrained by a relatively weak financial base (mainly land taxes which are low by world standards), by the routine requirement for state approval of many activities (including planning) and in the limit by the states' ability to sack them and call for new elections or abolish them altogether.

Land tenure

State government control over land and land tenure has been a central issue in Australian land policy and states still own 70% of the country held in the form of forest reserves, national parks and other special-purpose reserves and in particular land leased to pastoralists (see Table 9.3 and Fig. 9.3). The importance of state leasehold farmland should not be overstated since these leasehold tenures are virtually coincident with the semi-arid and arid zones of the country. Virtually all the cultivation and the majority of livestock are on private lands.

Leasehold lands are managed by a range of covenants that limit the time period and total area held, residency and lessee legal status, stocking rates and land management aspects such as fencing, disease and pest control. The states have used their absolute control over leasehold land to achieve various objectives including resource conservation, closer settlement and the maintenance of living areas. The retention of state ownership released pastoralists' capital for other investments although there is a gradual reduction in the leasehold area through conversion to freehold in several states.

Determining the size of 'living areas' of land has always created conflict between the objectives of maximizing the amount of farm settlement and production on the one hand and assuring reasonable incomes without grassland degradation on the other. Production potential is very low and variable, droughts are common, and there is a need for upward adjustments in the size of pastoral properties in most of Australia's arid and semi-arid zones. Such increases would allow for reduced grazing pressure and improved incomes (Young 1979).

Table 9.3 Land tenures in Australia c. 1983 (million hectares).

State	Private land	Crown Lease	NPs	Public forests	Crown Other	Total area
NSW	28.7	36.4	3.4	9.1	2.7	80.3
Victoria	14.0	0.9	1.3	3.5	4.9	22.8
Queensland	32.5	123.8	4.1	8.8	5.2	172.8
S. Australia	6.8	55.4	14.1	0.0	36.2	98.4
W. Australia	18.9	96.6	4.5	2.3	136.3	252.6
Tasmania	2.6	0.2	0.9	1.9	3.6	6.8
N. Territory	10.5	76.9	2.0	0.5	46.8	134.6
Australia	113.7	390.5	3.8	26.1	253.3	768.3

Sources: Bureau of Agricultural Economics 1983, Australia Department of Arts Heritage and Environmental 1986.

Planning and plans

Urban and regional planning

Along with English law and the Westminster system of parliamentary democracy, Australia has inherited much of the philosophy and apparatus of the United Kingdom's approach to town planning. The Australian inheritance includes the statutory form of rigid end-state planning based on zoning and land-use tables, subdivision controls and performance standards on specific uses (see Ledgar 1976). These are the customary bases for town planning in Australia and all states and most local authorities with significant land-use change have planning machinery to prepare, administer, amend and cope with appeals about land-use zoning in this way (see Bowman 1979, Bates 1983).

In reality the similarities between the states are greater than the differences although there are differences in the details of procedures as to scope for public participation, the strength of the role played by the state, and the terms used to label the various instruments. Over the past ten years, local land-use planning has been augmented by a whole battery of other devices of land-use control, including more broadly based and indicative strategic and policy-type plans applied at various levels from the state down through regional plans in some states and to the local authority level.

The case of New South Wales is worth special mention because it probably represents the current high-water mark in Australian land-use planning. The state government is responsible for coordinating and controlling development of regional and state importance. This level of planning has varied from overseeing development of areas of a few square kilometres to controlling specified categories of development throughout the state. The two principal tools are State Environmental Planning Policies and Regional Environmental Plans.

The Department of Environment and Planning prepares State Environmental Planning Policies and sets guidelines for specific issues of importance to the whole state. The policies cover a wide diversity of issues such as rainforest, coal mining, housing, multiple occupancy in rural areas, and planning standards for different types of development. Regional Environmental Plans cover matters of regional significance and give guidance to councils and developers in the region on issues such as transportation; protection of mineral, agricultural and agricultural resources; subdivision of land; protection of scenic areas; and tourist development.

Local Environmental Plans are prepared and administered in accordance with a hierarchy of issues as set at the other two levels and are very similar in form and content to local plans produced elsewhere in the country (see Fig. 9.4).

The other key attribute of the NSW system is that it integrates the planning and environmental assessment process. Applications for development approval that may cause undue environmental impacts could be required to produce environmental assessments. Planning approval can then be given without the need to follow parallel environmental assessment procedures (see Formby 1986). This is not the case in all states. Pollution control programmes are also administered by the same agency.

Regional economic planning has been part of the planning rhetoric in Australia especially since 1945 when the need was for postwar reconstruction. Resource development is a recurring theme focused on water resources and irrigation projects (the best example being the Snowy Mountains Hydro-Electric Scheme), mining (the Pilbara region, Fitzroy Basin, Latrobe Valley and Hunter Valleys) land development (Ord River and Brigalow schemes, plantation forestry) are the most important. 'Decentralization' was a strong theme in the 1960s and 1970s: a reaction against the inherent metropolitan dominance in all Australian states and to alleged inefficiencies in the large cities. It was a justification for a wide range of subsidized infrastructure (roads, freight rates and irrigation dams) and every town had to have an industrial estate. In the early 1970s the policies evolved into the more fashionable growth centres programme which lead to the selective encouragement of urban centres. A set of such centres was identified and in part established, but parochial interests in Australia would always ensure that positive discrimination never went too far. In the past few years the emphasis has shifted from growth management and the need to direct growth to one of coping with economic restructuring and lack of employment opportunities in rural centres and regional planning as now emphasizing 'local economic development'.

In all states, with the exception of Queensland (it often is an exception), regional plans have been prepared for officially recognized economic planning regions (see Conroy 1987). Most of these plans have a rural land-use planning dimension consisting of a mixture of economic development strategies, small area-specific sector plans and area land-use planning dimensions. Unfortunately the majority of these plans are weak in implementation:

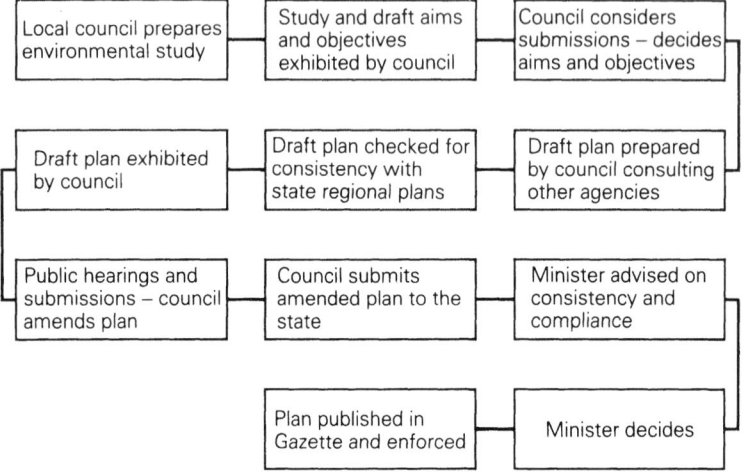

Figure 9.4 The planning process for local plans in New South Wales. Source: NSW Department of Environment and Planning 1980.

There has been a great deal of local economic inventory-taking, goal-setting and planning in Australia during the 1970s and 1980s. While it would be unreasonable to describe it as practice flourishing in the absence of theory, clearly much of this activity has taken place without its being grounded in coherent models of regional economic development, and without full appreciation of the broader national and international economic forces impinging on the local economy. Many studies have also lacked any real strategy element, in the sense of mapping out paths to be followed in the achievement of stated goals.

(Conroy 1987 p. 8)

Very many studies and reports have been prepared by government agencies to address regional land-use planning problems. These include land resource inventories, economic profiles, forecasts and 'strategy studies'. Collectively they may have some effect on land-use planning in that they raise consciousness about the problems or provide informal 'guidance' for the various local, state and national agencies with an interest in the region.

The problem arises due to the lack of any power at the regional level other than the discretionary power available to states to provide for regional administration. It depends upon the commitment of the various agencies of the states to carry through the recommendations and unfortunately there is no guarantee in Australia that agencies will co-operate even at one level of government nor that the political objectives will remain stable long enough to see any action. The main methods of implementation are management of infrastructure such as transport and piped services, land-use controls and industrial subsidies and promotions.

In some states, notably Victoria which has a state economic development strategy and a centralist planning philosophy, these regional plans have some chance of success. Some of the other states are more committed to receiving stimuli from the private sector.

Land and water management
Land and water mismanagement is a major land-use planning issue in rural Australia. A summary of the condition of the 1.5 million hectare Wimmera basin in Victoria is exemplary:

> Most of the upper catchment consists of highly erodible soils and is cleared. As a result, the upper catchment has severe erosion problems with extensive gullying and stream bank erosion. The harsh climate, heavy grazing pressure and saline flows combine to restrict re-establishment of plant growth once it has been lost.
>
> The Wimmera River itself in the upper region suffers from severe bank erosion problems and from substantial siltation and weed growth which aggravate erosion. In the lower Wimmera, bank erosion is significant with erosion on the outside of river bends existing along 20% of the river from Mount William Creek to the junction to Lake Hindmarsh. As in the upper reaches, blockages by siltation and weed growth cause much of the erosion problem diverting flows into the banks. These blockages also aggravate localised flooding.
>
> The upper reaches of many tributary streams are gullying and in the lower reaches of some of these tributaries severe bank erosion is common.
>
> Flooding within urban areas along the Wimmera River is a serious problem for the City of Horsham and the Town of Glenorchy. In the towns of Japarit and Dimboola artificial levees provide protection.
>
> (Victoria, Department of Water Resources 1987 p. 45)

The consequences are economic losses to farm productivity through lower yields, abandoned land, increased flooding, tree die-back, salinity under both dryland and irrigation conditions. To rectify these problems which are common to many Australian streams and here occur in just one basin, requires a programme costing $27 million to stabilize private lands, $5.2 million for stream management and $0.6 million for annual maintenance.

The most significant basin is the Murray which drains three states. The River Murray Commission has attempted without great success to provide a forum for interstate co-operation in the management of the River Murray, the allocation of its waters and land use in the catchment and floodplains of this vital river. The Commission lacks powers to coerce the states and depends on persuasion. (It is worth remembering in this context that at federation, Australian states had three different rail gauges.) Most of the efforts in land and water management have been intra-state efforts and river basin authorities or their equivalent have been created in a number of areas spread across the country (see Pigram 1986). Most states deal with land degradation on a farm-to-farm basis.

A recent initiative in the state of Victoria established an integrated approach to land and water management. It defines the catchment as the unit of planning for all the 38 catchments in the state. A 'Catchment Co-ordination Group' is responsible for the preparation of Catchment and Waterway Strategy Plans which will stabilize rivers and their frontages, stabilize catchments and reduce erosion, and improve the river environment. In effect these plans will be integrated regional rural land-use plans to be implemented in a range of ways.

- On *private lands* a range of programmes including whole-farm planning, weed and rabbit control, incentive grants to farmers and local agencies, tree planting schemes and finance to buy back farms in low-productivity hill country when they become available. The total cost of the programme on private lands will be $253 million, of which half will be paid by the state.
- On *public land* which includes conservation and forestry lands there are programmes to carry out land capability studies to identify erosion hazard zones and key areas for flora and fauna conservation, prepare codes of practices for land managers, and train staff.

All the Australian states have some programmes of river basin catchment management; Victoria has made the greatest progress with a rigorous implementation programme. New South Wales has recently adopted a policy of 'total catchment' (Cunningham 1986). Queensland has from time to time applied the principle of 'project plans' on a sub-catchment basis as set out in its soil conservation programme.

Forestry

Australia's potentially exploitable forests are situated in a discontinuous belt on the eastern margins of the continent, in Tasmania, and in the south-west corner of Western Australia. Only 42 million hectares of the total forest area of 140 million hectares is economically exploitable (less than 6% of the total land area). There is no timber production from national parks and similar reserves and relatively little private native forest left (it comprises less than 20%).

Each state has a forestry agency responsible for the management of the state's forests and there are strong ideological and organizational similarities between them (Carron 1979). There is no direct control over private forests. Conservationists argue forcefully that these agencies are too closely allied with the client commercial timber interests and that they are preoccupied with the 'wood' values of the forests to the detriment of conservation and recreation values. The early 20th century battle between farmers and foresters has been replaced by conflict between foresters and conservationists. This is somewhat ironic since many recently declared National Parks were previously managed in the forest estate, albeit in remote and low-productivity areas of it.

The overriding issue in Australia's forest planning is that the country has very little forest and hence there is strong competition for the use of forests. Australia is also a net importer of timber and pulp products and has adopted a policy of long-term self-sufficiency in these products, implemented by public investment in a large programme of exotic softwood plantation forests in all states. Self-sufficiency is also a foundation for planning activities, determining land requirements, and in defending forestry claims for land sought by other uses (McDonald 1985). This policy has been attacked, by economists on grounds of national economic efficiency, and by conservationists on grounds of the environmental effects of the plantations. Foresters point out the predicted long-term supply shortage in forest products and the substantial regional development benefits of the programme in depressed rural areas. Conservationists are somewhat ambivalent because the plantation programme is taking pressure off the ecologically more significant native forests.

The major land-use planning issues involving forestry in recent years have concerned nature conservation issues, especially:

- logging of small areas of remnant rainforests in Tasmania, New South Wales and Queensland, which conservationists believe will threaten the survival of the forest. In NSW, state government policy is to phase out rainforest logging and their rainforests have been nominated for the World Heritage List. No such policy exists in Queensland and at present there is a very hot debate about the future of the north Queensland rainforest: the state proposing to log it on a sustained yield basis and the conservationists arguing that there is no scientific evidence to support the feasibility of such management and that the risks to the scientific and tourist values are too high. The Commonwealth government is proposing to list them on the World Heritage List to protect them from further exploitation, but the political costs will be high and the compensation demanded from the local timber companies and the state government probably exorbitant.
- wood-chipping of Australian forests for short-fibre eucalypt pulp involving clear felling operations began on a large scale in New South Wales, Tasmania and Western Australia in the 1970s. Forestry interests argue that the clear felling of these degraded forests resembles wildfire in enabling regeneration of vigorous quality trees to provide the forests of the future. Opponents argue that there are questionable economic benefits to the country and that the environmental effects are so uncertain that the risks are not worth taking. The potentially serious side-effects are soil erosion, increased salinity in vulnerable catchments, sedimentation and hydrological change in streams affecting important floodplains and water supply catchment, and loss of flora and fauna. It is also argued that the long-terms productivity of the regenerated forests cannot be guaranteed.

Nature conservation

The area of land in conservation reserves in Australia has increased fourfold in the past 20 years and now about 4.4% of Australia is in National Parks and similar reserves. Total area by itself, however, is not a good guide to the adequacy of this system of reserves given that not all species and vegetation types are in the reserves. Since European settlement, 76 plant species,

1 bird and 12 mammals have become extinct; 203 plant species, 18 birds, 2 reptiles and 23 mammals have become endangered to the extent that they are likely to disappear from the wild in the next 10–20 years; and a further 612 species are vulnerable (Leigh et al. 1984 pp. 51–2). Furthermore, of the 203 endangered plant species, 156 are not found in parks or reserves, existing only on private land or Crown reserves with other functions such as forestry.

There is no national system for the declaration and management of protected natural areas, the matter being largely a state responsibility. Consequently, designations of conservation reserves vary markedly from state to state, though most states have variants of the following:

- National Parks (quaint misnomers since they are run by the states except in the case of the Commonwealth role in the territories). These are dedicated to preserve the natural values of an area and with few exceptions have no developments other than recreational or tourist services and are analogous to the North American National Parks. The whole or part of a park may be included in limited-use categories including primitive areas, recreational areas, scientific areas and historic areas. Many of the older more accessible parks are very small and suffer intensive use-pressure and degradation.
- Environmental Parks or State Parks are natural or near natural areas that are smaller in area or less outstanding in their natural values.
- Flora and fauna reserves and sanctuaries for the purposes of protecting the fauna and habitat. Some do not allow any public access, others merely prevent the taking of fauna.
- Designated areas which have natural values to be protected in the development process.

The Commonwealth administers the Australian Heritage Commission which identifies and catalogues places of special natural or cultural significance throughout the country. A majority of states also have heritage legislation but unlike the Commonwealth they also have the power to apply preservation orders and take any other necessary action. In most cases the states rely on public education programmes, moral suasion and provision of financial incentives – the only options available to the Commonwealth.

The Commonwealth also has the World Heritage Properties Conservation Act 1983 which specifies the form of Australia's participation in the World Heritage Convention. While seemingly rather innocuous this involvement has spawned some of the most far-reaching and divisive intervention by the Commonwealth in states' rights since federation. By making what the Commonwealth argues is an international treaty obligation it has been able to block development in the South-West Tasmania Wilderness (Franklin and Gordon rivers), Jacky's Marsh Forest, the North Queensland Rainforest and the Kakadu National Park in the Northern Territory. These are listed sites and protected by the Commonwealth legislation in this respect.

Aboriginal lands

It has taken almost 200 years for the European settlers of Australia to recognize the legitimate claim of the country's Aboriginal people to special treatment in the land. The reasons for this situation are many and complex. There was a period in Australian history during which it was believed the Aboriginal people would disappear as a race as a result of health and other factors. For the bulk of this century until the 1970s, the policy of most governments was for eventual assimilation into the Western culture and hence special land tenures were unnecessary and even counter to the prevailing philosophy. At the heart of the matter is land tenure:

> The European system of land ownership and rights that carry with it have no parallel under Aboriginal customary law. This situation has only recently begun to be challenged by Aboriginal groups. The Aboriginal's relationship with the land is more spiritual than proprietary. Land is inextricably interwoven with life itself; it is the beginning and end of life. It is not therefore possessed by any one person. It must sustain the traditional community needs within any particular area and it is in the truest sense therefore, 'community land'.
>
> (Bates 1983 p. 16)

Until very recently, Aboriginals did not have a basis in law that recognizes land they consider they have always been entitled to under customary law. The situation is rapidly changing but not before the Aboriginals were dispossessed of most of the more fertile and well-watered parts of the country and became a remnant population in the relatively inhospitable arid and northern regions.

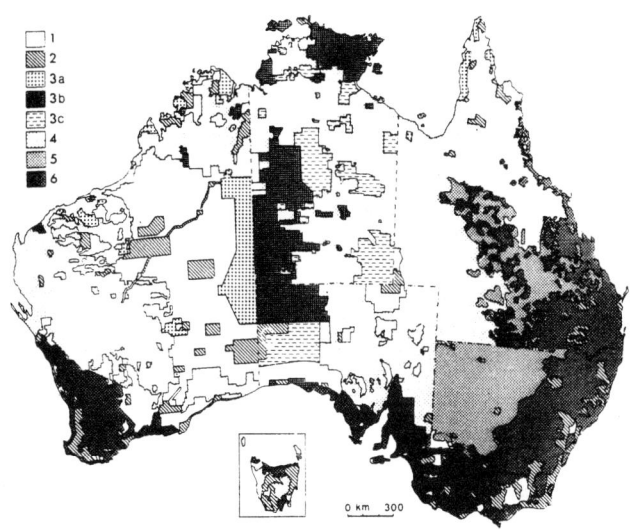

Figure 9.5 Land tenures in Australia, c. 1984
Key: 1 – Vacant Crown Land
    2 – Reserves (excluding Aboriginal reserves)
    3a – Aboriginal reserves
    3b – Aboriginal lands (alienated)
    3c – Lands claimed by Aborigines
    4 – Pastoral leases (extensive, i.e. few size or ownership controls)
    5 – Pastoral leases (intensive, i.e. strict size and ownership controls)
    6 – Alienated lands (excluding Aboriginal lands, but including perpetual leases
Note: because of the map scale details have been generalized
Sources: Heathcote 1977 and various.

Accordingly, it is in these areas where most of the current conflict over Aboriginal land tenure and land use are found (see Fig. 9.5).

The struggle for land tenure by Aboriginals began in earnest in the early 1970s with the Ranger Uranium Environmental Inquiry and the Aboriginal Lands Rights Commission (Justice Woodward) which reported in 1974. The Commission recommended, *inter alia*, the establishment of regional land councils, amendments to land law, establishment of an Aboriginal Land Commission to hear claims, legal support to persons making claims, and a land acquisition fund. These recommendations were followed by the Commonwealth government, which has jurisdiction over the Northern Territory, but state governments have been slow to follow this vital lead.

In the Northern Territory the result was the passage of the Aboriginal Lands Rights (Northern Territory) Act of 1976, the establishment of the Central and Northern Lands Councils to provide the administrative support to self-management and the dedication of large areas of Aboriginal-controlled land (see Fig. 9.5). In South Australia a similar piece of legislation was passed to provide for Aboriginal self-management for the Pitjantjatjara peoples in the north of that state by the Pitjantjatjara Land Rights Act of 1981. In New South Wales, a totally different approach has been adopted, eschewing special tenures but providing for expanded Aboriginal lands through the purchase of land through the normal freehold title system. In Queensland, the state government maintains a very antiquated system of Aboriginal 'reserves'. The government will eventually decide to convert that system to one based on Aboriginal self-management and expand the area under Aboriginal control.

Needless to say the acquisition of lands for Aboriginals has not been harmonious. Pastoral and mining organizations and in some cases state governments have attempted to block these claims and a very thorough legal process has been established to review the claims and make recommendations. The major challenge for the future is the design of community development, settlement, and land-use plans for the Aboriginal lands which can provide for a balance of traditional and Western commercial objectives of the people.

Even on the relatively secure Northern Territory lands, there remain conflicts about land use especially the rights of Aboriginals to participate in and even veto mining proposals on their lands. The response is evolving at present and the compromise may be a procedure that would guarantee the Aboriginal owners full rights of negotiation with development interests including the extent of royalties or compensation (see Coombs 1982). With the Land Councils at least, the Aboriginals now have the skills to participate in this argument in a way not at all possible only a decade ago.

On two National Parks in the Northern Territory, Uluru (Ayres Rock) and Kakadu, management by the Aboriginal people of the lands for multiple purposes in conjunction with other agencies sets a model for controlling access to Aboriginal lands of very high conservation value. Whether the rest of the community will allow them rights of veto over mining and National Park establishment not available to the rest of the community remains to be seen.

Aboriginal issues are important elsewhere in the country where land rights claims are not feasible, especially the protection of cultural remains. Sacred sites and land where cultural remains such as rock art exist are protected by special legislation in all states. Implementation of this legislation is not without conflict when protection may block development or access.

Conclusion

Australian planning practice has been pragmatic and reactive rather than ideological, and been less amenable to government interference with private property rights than in Europe, but more tolerant than in the USA.

Land-use planning is becoming important now as the *competition for the use of land* in Australia increases. This is unprecedented, the main problem in the past having been to find a use for land that would provide for permanent settlement at a level of living equivalent to that found in Europe where the majority of the population formed their expectations and cultural values.

There is *very little usable land left* that is not claimed by foresters, pastoralists, cultivators, recreationists, or miners and the image of limitless space in the country is fading.

The *impacts of development* are greater now too with very large mining projects, potentially toxic waste products from industry and agriculture and relatively greater population pressure on the land. There is increasing concern that the progress of European development has resulted in too many casualties in the natural environment and that therefore soil conservation and protection of a dwindling wilderness is important. There is now a greater interest in and need for the wise husbandry of existing resources rather than the expansion of exploitation. In general the country has realized that progress will result from making better use of resources already employed rather than seeking to exploit new resources – this is an important change for a new country.

Australians are developing a greater sense of place as the society matures, inspiring greater care for the land and promoting a land ethic that is so necessary if land-use planning is to proceed. Coupled with this, amenity values are gaining higher priority in the planning and management of all areas, especially the near-city regions. In rural areas people are participating more in recreational and cultural pursuits requiring more care in land-use planning and the protection of natural, aesthetic, historical and other heritage values in the landscape. Massive increases in tourism are magnifying the need for care and attention to these issues and even remote little communities in far north Queensland are preparing plans to maximize the tourist appeal of their districts.

The attitudes of Australian people and their planning agencies are rapidly changing to the needs of land use and environmental planning and to create a better balance between development pressures and the environment.

References

Aboriginal Land Rights Commission (Presiding Commissioner Justice A. E. Woodward, 1974. *Second Report*. Canberra: Australian Government Publishing Service.
Australia, Committee of Inquiry into the National Estate (Chairman, Justice R. M. Hope) 1974. Report. Canberra: Australian Government Publishing Service.
Australia, Department of Arts, Heritage and Environment 1986. *State of the environment in Australia: source book*. Canberra: Australian Government Publishing Service.
Australia, Department of Resources and Energy 1983. *Water 2000: a perspective on Australia's water resources to the year 2000*. Canberra: Australian Government Publishing Service.
Australia, Parliament Senate Standing Committee on Science, Technology and the Environment 1984. *Land use policy in Australia*. Canberra: Australian Government Publishing Service.
Australian Advisory Committee on the Environment 1975. *Land use in Australia*. Canberra: Australian Government Publishing Service.
Australian Environment Council 986. *Guide to environmental legislation and administrative arrangements in Australia*, 2nd edn. Canberra: Australian Government Publishing Service.
Australian Forestry Council 1986. *National forestry strategy for Australia*. Canberra: Australian Government Publishing Service.
Balderstone, J. S. (chair) 1982. Working Group Report to the Minister for Primary Industries, 1982: *Agricultural policy issues and options for the 1980s*. Canberra: Australian Government Publishing Service.
Bates, G. M. 1983. *Environmental law in Australia*. Sydney: Butterworth.
Bowman, M. 1979. *Environmental management in Australia – the response of the states*. Hobart: University of Tasmania.
Bureau of Agricultural Economics 1983. *Rural industry in Australia*. Canberra: Australian Government Publishing Service.
Carron, L. T. 1979. Forestry in the Australian environment – the background. *Australian Forestry* 42, 63–73.

Chittleborough, D. J. 1986. Loss of land. In *Australian soils: the human impact*, J. S. Russell & R. F. Isbell. Brisbane: University of Queensland Press.
Cocks, K. D., G. McConnell & P. A. Walker 1980. *Matters for concern. Tomorrow's land issues*. Canberra: CSIRO Division of Land Use Research, Divisional Report 80/1.
Conacher, A. J. 1979. Water quality and forests in south-western Australia. *Australian Geographer* 14 150–9.
Conroy, J. D. 1987. *An evaluation of local area economic strategy studies*. Canberra: Australian Government Publishing Service.
Coombs, H. C. 1982. How to balance the Aboriginal interest in resource development. In *Resource development and the future of Australian society*, S. Harris & G. Taylor (eds). Canberra: Australian National University, Centre for Resource and Environmental Studies.
Courtenay, P. P. 1978. Agriculture in North Queensland. *Australian Geographical Studies* 16, 29–42.
Cunningham, G. M. 1986. Total catchment management – Resource management for the future. *Journal of the Soil Conservation Service of NSW* 42 (1), 4–5.
Davidson, B. R. 1966. *The northern myth*. Melbourne: Melbourne University Press. 2nd edition.
Donald, C. M. 1965. The progress of Australian agriculture and the role of pastures in environmental change. *Australian Journal of Science* 27, 187–98.
FAO 1986. *FAO production yearbook*, vol. 38. Rome: Food and Agriculture Organization.
Formby, J. 1986. Environmental policies in Australia – climbing down the escalator. In *Environmental policies. An international review*, C. C. Park (ed.). London: Croom Helm.
FORWOOD 1974. *Forestry and Wood Based Industries Development Conference*. Canberra: Australian Government Publishing Service.
Gifford, R. M., J. D. Kalma, A. R. Aston & R. J. Millington 1975. Biophysical constraints in Australian food production: implications for Australian population policy. *Search* 6 (6), 212–23.
Hallsworth, E. G., A. E. Martin, R. J. Millington & R. A. Perry 1976. *Principles of a balanced land use policy for Australia*. Melbourne: Commonwealth Scientific and Industrial Research Organisation.
Heathcote, R. L. 1970. The visions of Australia 1770–1970. In *Australia as human setting*, A. Rapoport (ed.). Sydney: Angus & Robertson.
Heathcote, R. L. 1987. Images of a desert? Perceptions of arid Australia. *Australian Geographical Studies* 25, 3–25.
Isbell, R. F. 1986. The tropical and subtropical north and northeast. In *Australian soils: the human impact*, J. S. Russell & R. F. Isbell. Brisbane: University of Queensland Press.
Ledgar, F. 1976. Planning theory in the twentieth century: a story of successive imports. In *Man and the landscape in Australia*, G. Seddon & M. Davis (eds). Australian UNESCO Committee for Man and the Biosphere Publication no. 2. Canberra: Australian Government Publishing Service.

Leigh, J., R. Boden & J. Briggs 1984. *Extinct and endangered plants of Australia.* Melbourne: Macmillan.
McDonald, G. T. 1985. Rural land use planning and forestry in Australia. In *Managing the tropical forest*, K. R. Shepherd & H. V. Richter (eds). Canberra: Development Studies Centre, Australian National University.
McDonald, G. T. & R. E. Rickson 1987. Saving farmland from whom and for what purpose. In *Demands upon rural lands*, B. E. Smit & C. C. Cocklin (eds). Boulder, Colo.: Westview Press.
Meinig, D. W. 1962. *On the margins of the good earth.* Chicago: Rand McNally.
Miller, G. 1986. *The political economy of international agricultural policy reform.* Canberra: Australian Government Publishing Service.
Mosley, J. G. & J. Messer 1984. *Fighting for wilderness.* Sydney: Fontana Books.
New South Wales Department of Environment and Planning 1980. *A guide to the environment and planning legislation.* Sydney.
Pigram, J. J. J. 1986. *Issues in the management of Australia's water resources.* Melbourne: Longman Cheshire.
Powell, J. M. 1976. *Environmental management in Australia, 1788–1914.* Melbourne: Oxford University Press.
Powell, J. M. 1986. Approaching a dig tree: reflections on our endangerd expedition. *Australian Geographical Studies* **24**, 3–26.
Ranger Uranium Environmental Inquiry (Presiding Commissioner Justice R. W. Fox) 1977. Second Report, Canberra: Australian Government Publishing Service.
Rolls, E. C. 1985. *More a new planet than a new continent.* Canberra: Australian National University, Centre for Resource and Environmental Studies, Paper 3.
Russell, J. S. & R. F. Isbell 1986. *Australian soils. The human impact.* Brisbane: University of Queensland Press.
Seddon, G. & M. Davis 1976. *Man and the landscape in Australia.* Australian UNESCO Committee for Man and the Biosphere Publication no. 2. Canberra: Australian Government Publishing Service.
Slatyer, R. O. 1975. Ecological reserves: size, structure and management. In *A national system of ecological reserves in Australia*, F. Fenner (ed.). Canberra: Australian Academy of Science.
Victoria, Department of Water Resources 1987. *Better rivers and catchments.* Melbourne: Department of Conservation, Lands and Forests.
Webb, L. J. 1966. Preserving what's left of Australia's rainforests. *Habitat* **10**, 3, 3–17.
Wells, K. F., N. H. Hood & P. Laut 1984. *Loss of forests and woodlands in Australia.* Canberra: Commonwealth Scientific and Industrial Research Organization.
Weston, E. J. et al. 1981. *Assessment of the agricultural and pastoral potential of Queensland.* Brisbane: Queensland Department of Primary Industries Agriculture Branch Technical Report no. 27.

Wilson, J. L. (ed.) 1984. *Nature conservation reserves in Australia*. Occasional Paper no. 10. Australian National Parks and Wildlife Service.

Woods, L. E. 1983. *Land degradation in Australia*. Canberra: Australian Government Publishing Service.

Young, M. D. 1979. Influencing land use in pastoral Australia. *Journal of Arid Environment* **2**, 279–88.

10 Sectoral and statutory planning for rural New Zealand

Warren Moran

Introduction

Any analysis of planning for the rural sector in New Zealand must take account of six aspects of the nation's experience that together make it unique – the overwhelming importance of pastoral farming in the agricultural economy; the long-term reliance on rural exports to generate foreign exchange; the country's colonial experience; the nature of the political pressure groups generated by the dominance of rural production; the existence of a distinctive attitude to land and its use by Maori people; and the rapid, perhaps unprecedented, transformation of the New Zealand economic environment since 1984.

New Zealand farmers and agricultural scientists have spent a century and a half developing a system of pastoral farming that is among the most efficient in the world. Its efficiency depends on one family being able to manage a large area of land and large numbers of livestock. This is achieved by close subdivision using stock-proof fences and sophisticated methods of pasture management that are highly dependent on liberal applications of superphosphate. It also depends on intensive but selective mechanization, especially in the dairy industry. In the last decade other systems of rural production have begun to rival the importance of some of the pastoral industries. Horticulture has progressed rapidly and is now dominant in some regions and forestry based on *Pinus radiata* has continued its steady growth, as well as expanding into new regions.

Exports based on the pastoral industries – dairy products, meat, and wool, together with by-products – continue to earn more than 50% of New Zealand's foreign exchange. This proportion has decreased from almost 90% in the last two decades, and without major changes to the regulation of international trade in agricultural products is likely to decrease further in relative importance. Traditionally, New Zealand was a supplier of pastoral products in bulk to the British market. This too has changed. More diverse and more highly processed products are supplied to a much wider range of markets (Lewthwaite 1980), but the transformation took much longer to achieve than might have been expected and is still evolving. The adventitious roots of colonialism had penetrated deeper than expected.

New Zealand's colonial association with the UK was economically advantageous to both parties. Britain obtained reliable supplies of basic food and industrial products in bulk. New Zealand, through a simple but efficient agricultural system, was able to support the rest of its society at one of the highest and most evenly distributed standards of living in the world (Clark 1949). The association had its detrimental aspects from New Zealand's point of view. Economic complacency was deep-rooted, local industrial innovation for export stagnated in the first half of the 20th century, trade with other nations was stifled, and commercial associations developed that did not act in New Zealand's interest when circumstances changed. For example, much of the meat processing industry was controlled by British capital and its reluctance to maintain investment and to diversify markets and products as rapidly as the dairy industry cannot be divorced from this relationship. Moreover, planning itself was strongly influenced by the British experience. Planning teachers and professionals and the model of planning were imported from Britain and indigenous developments were constrained.

An economy structured in this way, and towards these ends, had its inevitable social and political ramifications. In comparison to its numbers, the rural farm lobby was as strong as anywhere in the world. Its strength partly explains the absence of a specific country political party for most of this century. No party could neglect pastoral farming. The primacy of agriculture in the economy had other more subtle influences on the unstated ethic of the nation. An intense commitment to pastoral farming became accepted in the community at large and even by scientists who had been intimately and successfully involved in its evolution. Rural county councils were almost always dominated by landowning farmers, because the system of local government was modelled on the original British system of separating town from country – municipality from county.

To Maoris, land is much more than a productive resource. The expressions *turangawaewae* – a place to stand – and *tangata whenua* – people of the land – capture something of the importance of association with land and lineage to Maori people (Stokes 1980). Traditionally, all land was held in communal ownership but alienation of land by Europeans – *Pakehas* – during the 19th century disrupted Maori society and involved bitter land wars. The Treaty of Waitangi of 1840 was meant to safeguard Maori rights to land and other resources but there are numerous examples of tis principles being disregarded by both European settlers and by the Crown. Only since the mid-1970s has sectoral and statutory planning formally recognized the range of Maori values and have procedures been established to correct some of the abuses of the Treaty. Ironically, the recent corporatization of some central government departments, and the tenurial distinction that it required between land to be used for production and land to be used for conservation, has forced a landmark Court of Appeal decision that it seems will ensure a continued legal support of Maori rights in sectoral and statutory planning (Court of Appel 1987).

The accession to power of the fourth Labour government in 1984 has resulted in changes to the economic environment that are probably more profound than in any other period of similar length. Planning must be seen in relation to these. Deregulation of the economy, floating the exchange rate, the progressive removal of all subsidies to rural producers and creating a set of state-owned corporations are four major developments, but it is the philosophy behind these that is important for planning. The current government has aspirations to create a much less regulated economy and to distinguish more clearly its social expenditure. The role that local and regional planning will assume in this distinction is not yet clear but some suggestions of the likely outcome are made at the end of the chapter. Of specific relevance to planning is the reorganization of the responsibilities of a number of government departments, which includes the creation of a Department of Conservation (DOC) and Ministry for the Environment. At the moment, town and country planning remains a responsibility of the Ministry of Works and Development (MOWD), which may reflect the regulatory role planning is expected to play (Figure 10.1).

New Zealand has a unitary system of government with devolution of power to local and special-purpose authorities through Acts of Parliament. The two main Acts which cede power to territorial

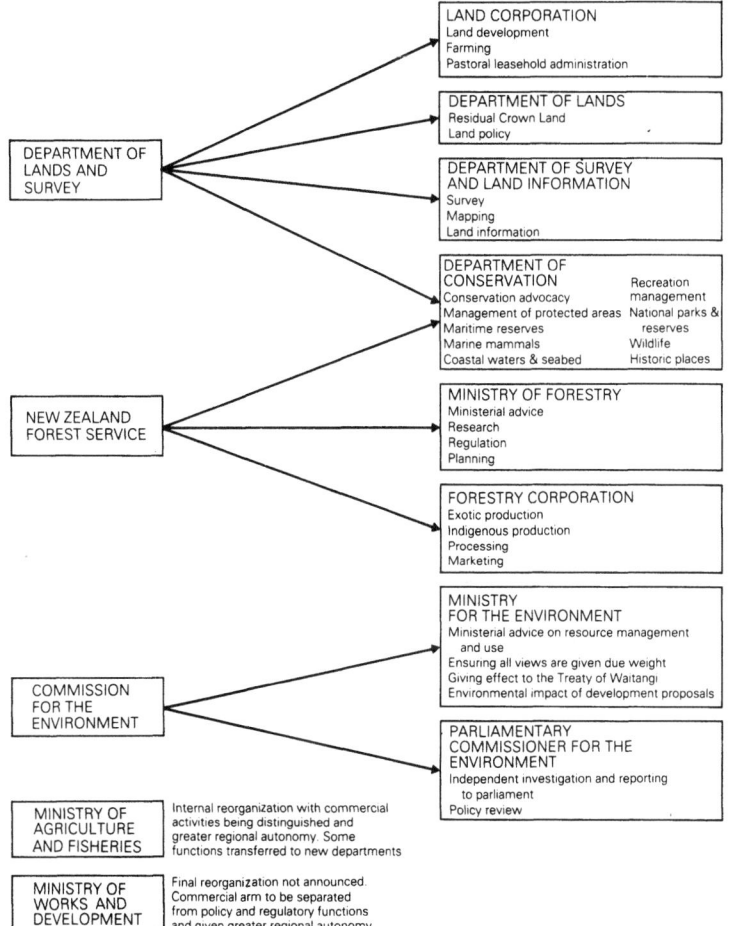

Figure 10.1 The structure and responsibilities of the main central government departments involved in planning for rural New Zealand after their reorganization in 1986 and 1987.

authorities and control planning, in the narrow sense of the word, are the Local Government Act 1974 (LGA) and the Town and Country Planning Act 1977 (TCPA). It can be convincingly argued that many other agencies, all of which operate under their own legislation, are more influential in the wider meaning of the term planning. These include the plethora of special-purpose authorities, often called *ad hoc* authorities, and the sectoral departments of central government itself, which are frequently highly influential in their expenditure and planning for their own sector. This chapter adopts the point of view that the activities of *ad hoc* authorities and the sectoral departments of central government must be included in any discussion of rural planning.

Local and regional statutory planning

The Town and Country Planning Act and Local Government Act were both revised in the 1970s. During their revisions, it was intended that they be compatible and mutually supportive. In particular, the LGA was written to encourage, and indeed demand, a substantial reduction in the number of *ad hoc* authorities and their consolidation into regional bodies with a more comprehensive range of functions (Auburn 1979, Norwood 1981). Subsequent changes of central government resulted in a dilution of these aims and the retention of most of the *ad hoc* authorities, all with their different powers and boundaries, and a less definite move towards stronger regions. The result is a TCPA that assumes strong regional structures and government without such structures.

For a country of its size, New Zealand has strong regional identities (Cumberland & Fox 1958). They exist because of the variability in terrain and resources, the coastal settlement pattern, the differentiation of regional economies, and the attenuation of the country which has helped to create a functional regionalization. Until the abolition of the provinces in 1876, regional affiliation had an even stronger political identity. Only in the last 25 years has this begun to re-emerge. Recent economic restructuring has increased the differentiation, clarified some of the influences at work and suggested useful avenues for explaining the variable regional performance (Britton & Le Heron 1987).

One model for regional administration in New Zealand is the Auckland Regional Authority which was created under its own Act in 1963 (Rankin 1979). It has responsibility for regional planning and a range of regional services such as bus transport, bulk water reticulation, and sewage and refuse disposal, as well as administering the soil and water legislation in the region. In hindsight, its existence is a minor triumph for co-operation and consensus considering the long-term difficulty of successfully completing any reform of local government in New Zealand (Sutch, 1956, Auburn 1979). In general, the Auckland Regional Authority has to be judged as highly successful. It has effectively promulgated a regional view and avoided the worst excesses of local authority parochialism. During the preparation of the two regional schemes that have been gazetted, it has raised the level of debate and understanding of regional issues in a variety of forums that it has organized. Its performance in bringing a high level of professionalism to rural and environmental planning is especially noteworthy. It has been less successful in advancing a coherent and united regional opinion to central government, partly because of the parochialism of local authority politicians who have concurrently been members of the Authority.

The 1977 TCPA strengthened regional planning. Under this Act, regional planning schemes took precedence over local planning. In writing their schemes, local authorities have to comply with approved regional schemes, as do departments of central government. It seems as though the legislators had in mind a suite of regional authorities, similar to the Auckland example. Unfortunately, subsequent amendments to the 1974 LGA weakened regionalism. It was no longer mandatory to have regional authorities. Instead, local authorities were given the option of deciding whether they would prefer to form United Councils. These are a weaker form of regional body because their politicians are appointed from members of the constituent local authorities rather than being elected directly to the regional body. Most local authorities opted to form United Councils and the majority came into existence in the late 1970s and early 1980s.

The processes of local, sometimes called district statutory planning in New Zealand are similar to those in other Western nations. Published district schemes contain two parts – the planning scheme and a code of ordinances (Palmer 1984, New Zealand Official Yearbook 1984, 1987, Williams 1985). The scheme sets out the objectives of the authority together with supporting evidence, and the ordinances provide the legal statements to achieve the objectives. Consultation with individuals and interest groups in the community is mandatory. At various stages in the process people and organizations have the right to object to aspects of the scheme.

In the early stages, when the scheme is proposed, these objections are heard by the council. Appeals of the council's decision must be heard by the Planning Tribunal, a judicial body headed by a judge of District Court status, before the scheme becomes operative. If the appellant is dissatisfied on matters of law with the outcome of this appeal, the full hierarchy of the courts is available – High Court, Court of Appeal, and Privy Council.

Regional schemes are produced under slightly different procedures. Any person or body may make a submission to the draft scheme but because local authorities are bound by the approved scheme they have the right to question its content when it is at the proposal stage and may request an inquiry into its policies before the Planning Tribunal. When the scheme has passed this regional scrutiny, it is lodged with central government which may request or demand changes before it becomes approved.

Existing alongside local and regional authorities are a powerful set of *ad hoc* authorities (Scott 1979). Organizations such as electricity supply authorities, water boards and especially harbour boards, gain their power from being suppliers of goods and services which raise revenue. In this way, and over a long period, some have been able to acquire considerable assets, including land as well as power. The acquisition frequently occurred at times when environmental controls and other public restrictions were much more liberal. The same opportunity does not exist for modern authorities, which makes some of the special-purpose authorities relatively more powerful, although their role is being questioned and modified by the current central government.

The role of central government agencies

Agencies of central government have been pre-eminent in planning for rural society in New Zealand. From New Zealand Post, which maintains a heavily subsidized rural mail delivery, to the Ministry of Agriculture and Fisheries (MAF), which is a technical, research and servicing agency, these central government agencies have been much more influential in rural planning than local government. The sole exception, in the case of local government, may be its function as the agency responsible for local roading, the original reason for its institution. Discussion of the role of central agencies is complicated by their recent reorganization. However, no functions will disappear in the reorganization. They will be redistributed so that like functions are grouped and some agencies will be given much greater autonomy and flexibility, which will make those even more powerful and less directly influenced by central government (Fig. 10.1).

Four main functions of past and present central government agencies that are directly involved in planning are distinguishable: development and production; regulation and servicing of rural industries; administration of public lands; and research. In the past, these functions have been spread across many departments with almost all of them having something of each. The reorganization of central government attempts to bring similar functions together, as well as distinguishing commercial operations.

Lands and Survey and the New Zealand Forest Service (NZFS) are the two best examples of departments that were directly involved in rural development and production. In the reorganization of central government, the commercial branches of these two departments have become state-owned corporations – Landcorp for all former Crown commercial land including rural land that it is developing, Forestry Corporation for management of commercial forests, and their processing and marketing. Under the State-Owned Enterprise Act 1986 a total of 14 such commercial agencies are being created. The philosophy behind their creation is clear and consistent. Government's commercial activities are to be competitively neutral businesses using private sector management structures and methods with the aim of making these enterprises commercially successful. Considerable controversy has arisen over the valuation of their assets and central government funding for them is being reduced progressively. In its second term the fourth Labour government has moved quickly to privatize these agencies. During 1988 guidelines have been prepared to sell forest and perhaps land assets to private sector firms.

The Ministry of Works and Development (MOWD), as well as being the major state agency for roading and other infrastructural development such as power plants, administers the TCPA and, probably more importantly for rural planning, the soil and water legislation. In the reorganization of departments the development arm of the MOWD will be separated and compete for commercial contracts with the private sector. The administrative destiny of its regulatory branches is unclear, although it seems that they could become separate agencies or incorporated in the Ministry for the Environment. MAF also has an important regulatory function in setting standards for veterinary and other animal services, but it is through its direct advice to farmers based on its considerable research capacity, and in its planning for the agricultural sector, that it mainly affects rural people. All of the other central government agencies influential in rural planning also have some research capacity.

In the past, numerous government departments have been concerned with the administration of natural areas such as National Parks, coastal reserves, and other parcels of indigenous vegetation and reserves. In the reorganization, these functions are consolidated into DOC. With responsibilities for the management of historic and natural land held in the national estate, it will be the largest of the government agencies concerned with environmental matters. It has a specific brief for the advocacy of conservation. A separate agency, the Ministry for the Environment, will implement a system for the environmental impact assessment of development proposals. Establishment of an independent Commissioner for the Environment, directly responsible, in a similar manner to the Ombudsman, to Parliament rather than the government of the day, further strengthens the environmental legislation.

As in most unitary systems of government, the central government departments are represented in the regions by their field service units (Paddison 1983). Each agency has established its own regional boundaries that often reflect past conditions and its own sectoral needs. New Zealand is, therefore, carved up into a plethora of field service regions, some of which are unique to a single government department (Marshall & Kelly 1986). Their hierarchy often bears little relationship with the intra-regional hierarchy of central places. Such balkanization of administration does little to foster communication between central government departments and the regional authorities and United Councils. Unfortunately, no greater uniformity is to be found among the boundaries of the newly created central government agencies, so that an excellent opportunity to strengthen central–regional government co-operation has been neglected.

Development and production operations

Both Lands and Survey and the NZFS have had considerable impact on the development of New Zealand, although the impact has varied regionally and temporally. Lands and Survey has been responsible for developing for settlement Crown land, much of which was residual. In preparing this land for sale, in consultation and collaboration with MAF and MOWD, it has undertaken all stages of the development process. It has cleared the land from bush or scrub, prepared the ground, sown the pasture, fenced the properties, run the first livestock, farmed the property until it is ready for settlement and selected the settlers. By deciding such things as farm size and layout, roading and settlement pattern it has a considerable impact on the locality and region. The landscape of many parts of the country bears the stamp of Lands and Survey development.

State farm settlement was most intense after both world wars, when provision was made for many returning servicemen who wished to farm, although the state has continued to maintain an active land development programme and settled civilians on farms until the mid–1980s. The regional impact of state farm settlement is most noticeable in the central North Island which in the 1930s was virtually unpopulated. Land development that was initiated in the 1930s was rapidly increased after 1945 and most of the region developed and settled by the state (Ward 1956, Campbell 1970, 1979). Elsewhere, its impact has been much more localized, but all regions have examples of state-settled farms. Research in the central North Island (Wood 1984) has demonstrated that the land market quite quickly transforms the size and arrangement of holdings until they are very similar to like parts of the country. Other evidence of the origin of the farms remains, such as the uniformity of house types and the similar appearance of the landscape.

Development projects of the NFZS are also most evident in the central North Island. Here, the state, together with private sector companies, has planted one of the largest areas of managed forest in the world. The state plantings of *Pinus radiata* began in the 1920s and continued in the 1930s to combat unemployment but soon developed a momentum in their own right, especially as New Zealand was rapidly running out of indigenous timber. The region is now highly dependent on the production of pulp and paper and other timber products and the state has been heavily involved in all phases of developing the industry. It has since relinquished most of the processing plants to the private sector but continues to provide more than half of the raw material. The NZFS has supported the private sector in many other ways. Timber has been sold at much below costs of production and the Forest Research Institute at Rotorua has provided a stream of information that has been the foundation of many industry developments. With the formation of a state forestry corporation these services will be charged at closer to their costs. The corporation is also likely to become more heavily involved in processing once again.

The forestry industry has maintained a strong commitment to sectoral planning, with the state and the forest companies both involved, some would suggest mainly to the advantage of the corporations (Le Heron 1985). Since the 1960s, quinquennial conferences have established annual planting targets which include the regional proportions to be planted by the state and private sectors (Kirkland 1981). This setting of targets has occurred without significant consultation with regional or local authorities, another procedure which highlights the origins of tensions between sectoral and regional rural planning. Since the late 1960s, forest plantings have begun to disperse as the land available for forestry in the central North Island diminishes and the forest industry continues its policy of attempting to attain regional self-sufficiency. The impact of forestry on rural communities has, therefore widened and more local and regional authorities have become concerned at the effect of forestry on roading and on agriculture (Storey 1981, Fowler 1983, Fowler & Meister 1983). This pressure has lessened as planting rates have slowed with the abolition of subsidies to forestry after 1984.

Service, research and planning organizations of central government

Despite its name, the Ministry of Agriculture and Fisheries has played a less direct role in planning for New Zealand agriculture than the NZFS has for forestry. Certainly, in advising government over the sector and in advocating economic policy favourable to agriculture, it has been influential, but it has had little direct influence on the regional distribution of agricultural production. In general, farmers have made the decisions about which crops and livestock to produce and where. The contrast with forestry arises because of the much larger number of producers and the variety of products, which makes any attempt to influence supply or its regional distribution, much more complex and unacceptable to many farmers. Under the reorganization of central government the MAF loses few functions. Its internal reorganization emphasizes commercial objectives and it is charging for many of its services.

New Zealand's agricultural policy has, until very recently, been driven by the philosophy of increasing production (McLean 1978). MAF has advised government on the means by which higher production can be achieved, but it has left the results of these nation-wide policies to influence individual producers, regardless of their location. Until 1986, these policies maintained subsidies to agriculture that by international standards were modest but influential. They included subsidies on the price and transportation of fertilizer, supplementary price support for meat and wool, low interest rates from the reserve bank to producer boards, subsidized interest rates to farmers from the rural bank, land development encouragement loans, and virtually free extension advice to individual producers from farm advisory officers. These subsidies have been abolished or are being reduced rapidly. Producers of agricultural products in New Zealand are now fully exposed to the market, although most of the products that they produce have limited access to the markets of all other nations.

A further reason for the less direct influence of MAF compared with the NZFS has been the intervening role of producer boards. They were established in the 1930s at the time of depressed international prices to market and control the quality of New Zealand meat, dairy products and wool (Belshaw *et al.* 1936). The Dairy Board, in particular, has successfully fulfilled these roles, but all of the boards have experienced adjustment difficulties as markets have diversified and their requirements become more diverse. The Apple and Pear Marketing Board is also a single desk agency with sole rights to the local and international marketing of apples and pears, but kiwifruit have until 1988 been marketed by a group of licensed companies. From the 1989 season a Kiwifruit Marketing Authority will have statutory responsibility to market all kiwifruit internationally.

Regional development

Considering the importance of rural production to New Zealand, it is ironical that regional development policy originally included nothing about production from agriculture or forestry. Elements of the policy, which was introduced in the early 1970s, were influenced by European experience. Responsibility for regional development was given to the Department of Trade and Industry with manufacturing as the main sector to receive assistance (Franklin 1978). Regional Development Councils were formed in priority regions of the nation with their membership dominated by accountants, lawyers, and business people of the small towns servicing the rural communities. Central government serviced the councils and provided a variety of monetary and other assistance for existing and nascent industries. Assessment of the policy have been variable, and they have not included the opportunity costs of the capital that has been employed (Le Heron 1979, Creagh 1986).

In the late 1970s, some non-traditional forms of agriculture were included under regional development as eligible for assistance, but no studies have been made of the effectiveness of these grants and loans. Central government has been reviewing regional development policy and has attempted to align it more closely with United Councils and regional authorities, an approach which has been advocated for some time. The exact form that any relationship will take is not known, partly because the Local Government

Commission is currently attempting to convince local authorities to reduce their numbers and rationalize their boundaries. The outcome of this dialogue and debate will have an inevitable influence on the number of regional bodies.

Administration of planning and soil and water legislation

In the reorganization of government departments the TCPA and the soil and water legislation are, for the meantime, left as the responsibility of the MOWD. In rural areas of New Zealand, the soil and water legislation is frequently more important, and certainly less maligned. The problems of soil erosion and flooding have a visibility and public acceptance that supports community intervention to correct them. New Zealand became fully aware of soil erosion problems during the 1930s (Cumberland 1944, McCaskill 1973). The Soil Conservation and Rivers Control Act 1941 enabled the creation of catchment boards for all regions of the country. The function of this new set of *ad hoc* authorities was to advise landowners on the prevention and treatment of soil erosion and river control problems and if necessary to take firmer action. Subsequent legislation, the Water and Soil Conservation Act 1967, has emphasized the allocation of water rights and the control of water quality under Regional Water Boards. These Acts are currently being revised and integrated with other planning and environmental legislation.

The MOWD has also responded to local requests for the initiation of community irrigation schemes. In this role it has been an extremely influential rural planning agency. Although in theory it is the community which requests an irrigation scheme, the potential for irrigation had frequently been established by the Soil and Water Division of the MOWD, MAF, or some other agency. Once the request had been made, and the feasibility confirmed, the MOWD liaised with other government departments such as MAF, as well as local authorities, and planned the scheme. Such irrigation projects have the potential to transform the rural society and economy of a region, especially during a period of horticultural expansion as has recently occurred in New Zealand (Evans & Cant 1981, Kearns & Moran 1985). Until 1985, they too were heavily subsidized by central government and have provided windfall profits to those lucky, or far-sighted, enough to own land within them.

Administering the TCPA gives the MOWD a much less direct and less powerful day-to-day role. The Ministry can, and of course does, object to the planning documents of local and regional authorities. These objections sometimes reach the Planning Tribunal. But, apart from suggestions for changes to the Act, it has less opportunity to initiate on-the-ground proposals than it does when involved in planning for an irrigation scheme.

An appraisal of rural planning in New Zealand

With the wide definition of rural planning adopted here, statutory planning under the TCPA must be distinguished from the role of other agencies. Rural statutory planning is very young in New Zealand. Until the late 1970s, it consisted mainly of confirming on zoning maps the existing land use of the local authority and controls over the siting of buildings. The rural sections of most district schemes were a series of inadequate tables of production statistics, tentatively analysed and frequently out of date, with no integrated suggestions of possible rural development. Even today, very few local authorities are prepared to identify tracts of land for rural uses other than those that already exist on contiguous parcels of land, or to engage in comprehensive development planning by identifying the rural production options and potentials of their jurisdictions.

Rural planning has also been dominated by the perceived need to react to specific problems. Two such problems have dominated New Zealand rural statutory planning in the 1970s and early 1980s – the influence of urban centres on agricultural land and the competition of forestry for agricultural land. The first was responsible for a significant revision to the TCPA in 1973, the present Section 3 on matters of national importance, while the second has resulted in local authorities grappling with mechanisms to satisfy the demands of forestry corporations for more land, while placating pastoral farmers who see the competition as unfair. A third issue, the need to incorporate Maori cultural values and attitudes into decisions over rural resources, is much more fundamental to New Zealand society. It has been addressed in statutory planning and through the less conventional Waitangi Tribunal. All three issues illustrate aspects of planning in New Zealand and the influence on it of the structures discussed in the introduction and in the body of this paper.

Urban centres and agricultural land

Section 3 of the TCPA 1977 lists the following as matters of national importance which are relevant to this discussion:

(d) The avoidance of encroachment of urban development on, and the protection of, land having a high actual or potential value for the production food.
(e) The prevention of sporadic subdivision and urban development in rural areas.
(f) The avoidance of unnecessary expansion of urban areas into rural areas in or adjoining cities.

These clauses were introduced from 1973 to provide legislative support to curb the subdivision of pastoral farms into smallholdings of 4 hectares (10 acres), mainly in counties on the periphery of urban areas. The amendment to the Act received widespread support from organizations of agricultural scientists and it was largely as a result of their support that it was introduced (New Zealand Institute of Agricultural Science 1974). It has since become one of the most utilized part of the Act, often for reasons far beyond its original intent. The limited debate surrounding its inclusion was based mainly on assumptions about the undesirability of holdings smaller than pastoral farms on land of high quality near cities and neglected almost entirely the productive potential of horticultural intensification and such important social issues as the legislation's potential for decreasing the supply of urban land for housing and the effect of this on lower socio-economic groups. Its uncritical acceptance illustrates the all-pervading influence of the pastoral farming ethic on both professionals and the public at large. Subsequent research and the success of intensive agriculture on properties of this size have demonstrated the potential of smallholdings to stimulate intensification and diversification of land use (Chiu 1975, Ward 1978, Stokes 1982). Even holdings occupied by commuters and grazing livestock are, in the Auckland Region, as productive on average as pastoral farms occupying land of similar quality (Moran *et al.* 1980).

Dispersal of exotic forestry

Until the early 1970s, exotic forestry in New Zealand was concentrated in the central North Island. Most forests outside this area were in state ownership. Stimulated by generous government subsidies, export incentives and taxation advantages, forest plantings have become much more dispersed. Some of the major companies involved in forestry have purchased additional land in new areas, and individuals and groups of investors, as well as the state have also planted trees. As a result, many more parts of rural New

Zealand have come directly into contact with forestry and the forest companies (Campbell 1986, Fowler & Meister 1983). The development has exposed the limitations of the accepted mechanisms used in planning and the attitudes from which they derive.

The regional dispersion of forestry was influenced by the policies of central government, notably its Forestry Encouragement Grants, but it was the local and regional organizations which had to respond on the ground and in face-to-face meetings with their constituents. Communities of pastoral farmers recognized the possible impact of an expansion of forestry on the distribution and density of rural populations and ultimately on rural service centres. Corporate forestry was identified as being of most concern (Smith & Wilson 1980). The reaction of many local planning authorities was to institute some zoning limitation on forestry by making it a conditional use, frequently accompanied by a statement on a minimum area of trees that could be planted as of right. Any occupier who wanted to plant larger areas had to make a special case to the local council. Normally, such restrictions were applied to land of higher potential for agriculture – classes 1 to 4 on a land capability classification of seven classes.

The two assumptions behind these planning approaches are revealing. The restriction of production forestry to land of lower capability reflects the strong influence that soil conservators have had on New Zealand thinking. The place for trees is hilly land. This is the message that soil conservators have been giving to New Zealand farmers, albeit in reverse; solve problems of accelerated soil erosion by planting trees. In introducing the zoning ordinances, little thought was given to the difficulties of harvesting the mature crop, or indeed, of the possibility that better quality land close to the processing plants might be the place where trees provide best returns (Fairgray 1981, 1983). The limitations of zoning as a technique for rural planning was also exposed by this experience. Definitive zoning requires knowledge of the outcome of comparative advantage, a question that has not yet been solved in real-world circumstances. Unless the area of land required to meet national production is known, and competition from alternative uses in each region is also known, it is impossible to zone in any definitive way for specific rural activities.

Maori cultural values and planning

The incorporation of Maori values and attitudes into statutory and sectoral planning has been very recent and incomplete, although it is gathering momentum in the 1980s. It has been effected in four main ways. Amendments have been incorporated into the main Acts which govern the use of resources, various local regional and *ad hoc* bodies have been advised or required to appoint a Maori member, the Waitangi Tribunal has been created to hear and to make recommendations on Maori grievances, and the courts have made judgements which define more clearly the rights of Maori in New Zealand law.

In Section 3 of the TCPA 1977, clause 1(g) provides for 'the relationship of the Maori people and their culture and traditions with their ancestral land'. This clause has provided statutory avenues to encourage territorial authorities to plan for Maori values and cultural attitudes, although some commentators present evidence that its effects have been limited (Tamihere 1985). At the very least, territorial authorities must be aware of the distribution of Maori land in their jurisdiction and the sites and cultural features of importance to the Maori community. This requirement is strengthened by Section 36 of the Act which requires the District Scheme to provide 'for marae and ancillary uses, urupa reserves, pa, and other traditional and cultural uses'. Similar principles have been used to introduce appropriate clauses into Acts that govern the use of other resources such as the Fisheries Act and the Mining Act and will be included in the Water and Soil Bill that is now under discussion as a consolidation and extension of existing legislation (Patrick 1987).

The tensions in reconciling different cultural attitudes within statutory planning are illustrated by the juxtaposition of clause 3 (1)g in the TCPA 1977 alongside clauses to control the perceived impacts of unplanned and dispersed urban development that were discussed earlier. Traditional Maori settlement is loosely clustered around the marae, or meeting place. Such settlement is itself a form of sporadic urban settlement that other clauses in the same section of the Act are designed to prevent. The internal contradiction in this section of the Act is clear. Although forces such as high urban unemployment, a desire for former rural–urban migrants to return to their ancestral land, and the involvement of Maoris in rural land-use intensification, have stimulated demand for accommodation in the vicinity of some rural maraes, legal deterrents from other clauses in the same section of the TCPA Act have to be overcome before this can be achieved.

Powerful affirmation of the need to provide for the distinctive Maori view of resources has derived from the findings of the Waitangi Tribunal. Legislation was introduced as the Treaty of

Waitangi Act in 1975 to provide a type of permanent Commission of Enquiry in which Maori grievances over land and other resources can be heard, particularly where Crown policy is involved. It is chaired by a Judge and makes recommendations to government as well as finding of fact and interpretation (Durie 1986). Specific grievances have been brought before the Tribunal by tribal groups, and, although its findings are not legally binding, both central government and local and regional organizations have responded to meet its recommendations. Hearings are held on a local marae and Maori protocol is observed. Until 1988 it had only seven members and is staffed by a small research team.

Some of the claims brought before the Tribunal are actionable in the courts, but the grievances heard by it often have a much wider significance for New Zealand society. As Durie (1986 p. 236) points out:

> It needs to be borne in mind that the Treaty of Waitangi was not directed to the cession of land or the sale of rights, but rather to assuring the place of Maori people in the life of the country as a fundamental basis for annexation and European settlement. On that basis the Treaty is not just a potential source of particular legal rights for the indigenous people, but a political statement of policy.

The Waitangi Tribunal's approach and findings lie easily with the 1987 Court of Appeal judgement over the allocation of land to the reorganized agencies under the State-Owned Enterprises Act 1986 (Court of Appel 1987). This decision is being acclaimed by the legal professions as a landmark in New Zealand law as it sets the Treaty of Waitangi 'within the core or our legal system for the first time and ... shifts decisively the ground for debate on Maori/Pakeha legal relations' (Taylor 1987). As part of the restructuring of central government departments some Crown assets, in the terms of this discussion mainly land, are being allocated from multi-purpose central government departments to the state-owned enterprises and new departments. For instance, land formerly administered by the Department of Lands and Survey is being allocated mainly between the new Land Corporation and Department of Conservation (Fig. 10.1).

The State-Owned Enterprises Act 1986 includes a clause stating that the Crown cannot act inconsistently with the principles of the Treaty of Waitangi and suggests a procedure by which claims lodged with the Waitangi Tribunal after 1986 should be dealt with.

The New Zealand Maori Council, which brought the case, argued that under the legislation the Crown would not be able to recover land which had been transferred to the state-owned enterprises and subsequently sold by them. In effect, the Maori Council was successful. The Court of Appeal ruled, in a unanimous judgement, that transfer of assets could not take place until a scheme was in place which ensured that the principles of the Treaty were being adhered to. It instructed the Crown to prepare such a scheme within 21 days and gave a similar time for the Maori Council to comment on it before it was filed with the Court for its consideration and approval. The judgement implies that the courts should continue to be involved in the case of infringements.

One commentator summarizes these recent developments by suggesting that: 'It is now recognised that in our society, laws should allow Maori to be Maori and do things in their way unless there is an overwhelming imperative against it. The Maori Council decision caps this in a most authoritative way' (Taylor 1987). Many aspects of resource allocation, development and planning will be affected by the decision.

In summary, New Zealand statutory rural planning has used a limited number of planning mechanisms, such as limiting subdivision, insistence on economic units, and conformation of activities through zoning. It has been mainly concerned with planning for land use and, therefore, economic rather than social issues, although at times social concerns have stimulated planning action. In responding to issues of the moment, the dominance of pastoral farmers, their strong political position, and their thinking derived from the pastoral farming experience, have influenced the approach to planning. Maori attitudes and values have been very slowly incorporated into statutory or sectoral planning, although recent statutes and court decisions ensure stronger recognition of the bicultural basis of New Zealand society. Rural planners in local and regional authorities have, in all of these events, often found themselves reacting to situations resulting from central government policy; recent changes in economic policy will heighten the tensions.

Central government agencies and planning

Rural planning by central government departments in New Zealand is much older and has had much greater influence than local statutory planning. It too, however, has always been stimulated by a mixture of social and economic motives, although, since the early 1970s, economic objectives have been paramount. For much of New Zealand's past, the primary motive of increasing agricultural production has been in harmony with settling as many people on pastoral farms as there was land available. Socially inspired projects, such as the creation of employment by planting forests in the central North Island during the 1920s and 1930s, have usually appeared to have desirable economic outcomes, or their real costs have been submerged in the complexities of central government accounting.

In the last decade, however, it has become increasingly obvious that the type of uncoordinated rural planning that has been accepted for the tail-end of New Zealand's period of rural settlement is not longer appropriate. Further development of rural parts of the country will derive from intensification of land use and from demand from urban dwellers for land as well as for urban-based activities such as tourism. It seems inevitable that demand for land for these purposes will be highly localized and greater variability in the economic wealth of different parts of New Zealand will emerge, although locally it will continue to be unevenly distributed. Evidence of greater polarization between rural regions is already apparent with the emergence of specialized horticultural regions such as the Bay of Plenty (Stokes 1982) and the adverse effect of depressed international markets and changes in government policy on hill country farming (Taylor 1985). Increased competition for land will place much greater pressure on the planning system.

Polarization between regions will also focus more sharply some of the assumptions about the spatial distribution of opportunity that have been taken for granted for most of New Zealand's European history. Equality of opportunity for education and for health services, regardless of location, as well as regionally uniform pricing of almost all government services and many commodities, have been practised since New Zealand adopted a unitary system of government in 1876. In the last few years, some of these have been eroded and it seems highly likely that increased regional differentiation, together with current government philosophy and policy, will erode them further. Catchment authorities, for instance, now have to fund a higher proportion of their activities from local sources. Yet those regions most in need of catchment expenditure are frequently those with lower incomes.

Central government rural planning has demonstrated considerable sectoral independence. Planning for agriculture and for forestry have proceeded as if they occupied completely different territory. It is not surprising, therefore, that the potential of such combinations as grazing and forests took so long to realize. Effective dialogue and joint experiments between the two groups of scientists did not occur until the late 1960s (McQueen et al. 1976). At the same time, the role of some central government departments in planning rural development for parts of New Zealand has been as comprehensive as in any country, including centrally planned economies. The experience exists for a renewed emphasis on rural development planning to help realize the considerable potential of many regions of the nation. In many regions, the process of rural intensification has hardly begun.

For this experience to be realized, and a type of development planning put in place that is appropriate for the next stage of New Zealand's evolution, a number of structural changes are required. No longer can development planning, of the type conducted by Lands and Survey or MOWD in conjunction with other government departments, be the prerogative of central government alone. Now that all parts of the country are settled, the residents of the regions must be fully involved. For this to occur at least two structural changes must be instituted. Stronger and more comprehensive regional organizations must exist and central government departments must be given greater regional autonomy.

The prospect is not remote from realization. The folly of having two separate bodies for regional planning and regional development has been realized, and simultaneously the demands of the Seventh Local Government Commission have been receiving some surprising responses. A grass-roots regionalism appears to be emerging. In Northland, for example, the catchment board and United Council have combined to form much stronger regional organizations. The political problems of the Auckland Regional Authority have been averted and the continuing strong and committed performance of the Canterbury United Council and Wellington Region provide encouragement.

It remains to be seen whether the philosophy and policy of the present government will accommodate these developments. On one hand the present administration has been encouraging the rationalization of regional and local government, but, on the other, its economic policy and reorganization of central government departments appears to leave little room for more comprehensive development planning by the state in co-operation with regional and local bodies. At the core of the present government's economic policy is the wish to interfere as little as possible in entrepreneurial decisions and to allow the market to allocate resources. The extent to which it is prepared to intervene in the case of market failure, or where markets do not exist, or when markets are an inadequate method of allocating resources, is not yet clear.

The reorganization of government departments highlights the paradox. The two state trading corporations are to operate using similar principles to private sector organizations. Profit and growth will become the primary objectives. The creation of the Forestry Corporation has had more clear-cut regional effects than the separation of any of the other state-owned enterprises. Rural processing and servicing towns in peripheral regions have lost population and jobs as the corporation gives autonomy to regional managers and they respond by shedding labour, closing establishments, and substituting contract for wage labour.

In the past, of course, these arms of central government have had different roles to play. From a rural regional planning perspective, they have been linchpins in limiting regional disparities, in stimulating development where the private sector was not prepared to invest, and in providing employment and opportunity in less developed regions. That they have operated on different principles from the private sector has been their strength. Indeed it may be incompatible for state land development or forestry organizations to be expected to function as competitors with private sector firms. With their size and probably favourable debt-to-asset ratios they are unequal competitors, and in some regions are sufficiently large to act in an oligopolistic fashion.

In the reorganization of central government departments and corporatization of state trading agencies sectoral and regional/local planning have assumed a different relationship. Sectoral planning for rural productive activities has been weakened. Central government departments, such as the Ministry of Forestry, no longer have control over productive activities so that the state must use less-direct mechanisms to influence production. At the moment, it is assuming that the market will suffice. Concomitantly, Landcorp and Forestry Corporation no longer have the privilege of the Crown under the TCPA 1977 and similar legislation so that they will experience some of the disadvantages, as well as the assumed advantages, of their new status.

The reorganization and economic restructuring has also had differential regional effects with the peripheral rural regions, it seems, bearing a disproportionate share of private and public disinvestment, as indicated by their generally higher level of unemployment. These widening regional disparities may force regions to take a stronger stance over planning for their own destiny, thereby encouraging alliances among the territorial and *ad hoc* regional bodies and resulting in more powerful regional pressure groups. It is not surprising that regional development has again become a political issue in the late 1980s. The ballot box may demand that political parties give much more attention to their rural regional policies.

Acknowledgement

The assistance of Dr G. H. Campbell, Principal Planner, Auckland Regional Authority, in constructing Figure 10.1 and in discussing the paper is gratefully acknowledged.

References

Auburn, A. A. 1979. Regional government, regional planning and the local government Act, 1974. *New Zealand Geographer* 35 (2), 83–4.

Belshaw, H. D. W. Williams & F. B. Stephens (eds) 1936. *Agricultural organisation in New Zealand*. Melbourne: University of Melbourne Press.

Britton, S. G. & R. B. Le Heron 1987. Regions and restructuring in New Zealand: issues in the 1980s. *New Zealand Geographer*, 43 (3), 129–38.

Bush, G. W. A. 1980. *Local government and politics in New Zealand*. Auckland: Allen & Unwin.

Campbell, G. H. 1970. *The family farm and farm development on the Volcanic Plateau*. MA thesis, Department of Geography, University of Auckland.

Campbell, G. H. 1979. *Rural land use in the Taupo region*. PhD Thesis, Department of Geography, University of Auckland.

Campbell, G. H. 1986. *Planning perspectives on social impact assessment and exotic afforestation in New Zealand*. DipTP Research Essay, Department of Town Planning, University of Auckland.

Chiu, B. K. 1975. *The economic implications associated with part-time farming on rural subdivisions: a case study of Manawatu*. MAgSc Thesis, Massey University, Palmerston North.

Clarke, C. 1940. *Conditions of economic progress*. London: Macmillan.

Court of Appeal 1987. *New Zealand Maori Council and Anor v. Attorney-General and Ors*, CA 54/87, 29 June 1987.

Creagh, H. 1986. *Employment effects of regional development policy in New Zealand: an example of the effects of capital subsidy on the firm's demand for labour*. MA Thesis, Department of Geography, University of Auckland.

Cumberland, K. B. 1944. *Soil erosion in New Zealand, a geographic reconnaissance*. Soil Conservation and Rivers Control Council, Wellington.

Cumberland, K. B. & J. W. Fox 1958. *New Zealand: a regional view*. Wellington: Whitcombe & Tombs.
Durie, E. T. J. 1986. The Waitangi tribunal: its relationship with the judicial system. *New Zealand Law Journal*, 235–8.
Evans, M. & G. Cant 1981. The effect of irrigation on farm production and rural settlement in Mid-Canterbury. *New Zealand Geographer* 37 (2), 58–65.
Fairgray, J. D. M. 1981. *Regional afforestation issues*. Technical report no. 2, Central North Island forestry and transportation study, McDermott-Associates and Ministry of Works and Development, Wellington.
Fairgray, J. D. M. 1983. *Central north Island forestry and transportation study: afforestation directions*. Project report no. 2, McDermott-Associates and Ministry of Works and Development, Wellington.
Fowler, D. W. 1983. *Rural planning and forestry*. Dip.Ag. Economics dissertation, Massey University, Palmerston North.
Fowler, D. W. & A. D. Meister 1983. *Rural planning and forestry: formulation of policy at county level*. Department of Agricultural Economics and Farm Management, Massey University, Palmerston North.
Franklin, H. 1978. *Trade, growth and anxiety: New Zealand beyond the welfare state*. Wellington: Methuen.
Kearns, R. & W. Moran 1984. *Irrigation proposals and land use intensification at Maungatapere*. Department of Geography, University of Auckland.
Kirkland, A. 1981. *Needs and opportunities for future planting*. Keynote paper, 1981, New Zealand Forestry Conference, Wellington.
Le Heron, R. B. 1979. A round of growth: the verdict on New Zealand's programme of regional development? *New Zealand Geographer* 35 (2), 71–9.
Le Heron, R. B. 1985. Expanding exotic forestry and the extension of a competing use for rural land in New Zealand. *Journal of Rural Studies* 1 (3), 211–29.
Lewthwaite, G. R. 1980. New Zealand milk on the map. *Annals of the Association of American Geographers* 70 (4), 475–9.
McCaskill, L. W. 1973. *Hold this land: a history of soil conservation in New Zealand*. Wellington: Reed.
McLean, I. 1978. *The future for New Zealand agriculture: economic strategies for the 1980s*. Agricultural strategy paper no. 2, Massey University, Palmerston North.
McQueen, I. P. M., R. L. Knowles & M. F. Hawke 1976. Evaluating forest farming. *Proceedings of the New Zealand Grassland Association* 37 (2), 303–7.
Marshall, B. W. & J. Kelly 1986. *Atlas of New Zealand boundaries*. Department of Geography, University of Auckland, Auckland.
Moran, W. 1974. Systems of agriculture: regional patterns and locational influences. In *Society and Environment in New Zealand*. R. J. Johnston (ed.), 123–49. Whitcombe & Tombs and New Zealand Geographical Society, Christchurch.

Moran, W. 1987. *Farm size and government policy in New Zealand.* Paper presented at the AAG Annual Meeting, Portland, Oregon.

Moran, W., W. Neville & D. G. Rankin 1980. *Rural smallholdings in the Auckland region: agriculture and productivity.* Auckland Regional Authority, Auckland.

New Zealand Institute of Agricultural Science 1974. *New Zealand Agricultural Science* **8**. The issue is devoted to land use in the urban periphery.

New Zealand Official Yearbook 1984, 1987. Wellington Government Printer.

Norwood 1981. Rural planning in New Zealand: the political dimension. *New Zealand Geographer* **37** (2), 79–82.

Paddison, R. 1983. *The fragmented state: the political geography of power.* Oxford: Basil Blackwell.

Palmer, K. A. 1984. *Planning and development law in New Zealand.* Sydney: The Law Book Company.

Patrick, M. 1987. Maori values of soil and water. *Soil and Water,* Autumn, 23–30.

Polaschek, R. J. (ed.) 1956. *Local government in New Zealand.* New Zealand Institute of Public Administration and Oxford University Press, Wellington.

Rankin, D. G. 1979. Auckland Regional Authority 1963–1978. *New Zealand Geographer* **35** (1), 41–3.

Scott, C. D. 1979. *Local and regional government in New Zealand: function and finance.* Auckland: Allen & Unwin.

Smith, B. N. P. & P. A. Wilson 1980. *Rural attitudes and sector growth: a case study.* Unpublished paper presented to the New Zealand Sociology Conference, Hamilton.

Stokes, E. 1980. The effects of land use policies on rural communities: some Maori perspectives. In *Towards a land use policy for rural New Zealand,* G. R. Cant & A. O'Neill (eds). Land Use Advisory Council, Wellington.

Stokes, E. J. 1982. *The impact of horticultural development in the Tauranga district.* Ministry of Works and Development, Wellington.

Storey, W. R. 1981. Forestry development – the farmers view. *People and Planning* **20**, 5–7.

Sutch, W. B. 1956. Local government in New Zealand: a history of defeat. In *Local government in New Zealand,* R. J. Polaschek (ed.), 12–43. New Zealand Institute of Public Administration.

Tamihere, J. (1985). Te Take Maori: a Maori perspective of legislation and its interpretation with an emphasis on planning law. *Auckland University Law Review* **5**, 137–43.

Taylor, G. T. 1987. Higher status for Treaty of Waitangi. *National Business Review,* 10 July.

Taylor, N. W. 1985. *Some aspects of the sheep and beef industry, 1985.* New Zealand Meat and Wool Board, Wellington.

Ward, A. B. 1978. Smallholder farming and rural lots. *New Zealand Journal of Agriculture* **138**, 24–5.

Ward, R. G. 1956. Land development in the Taupo County. *New Zealand Geographer* **12** (2), 115–32.

Williams, B. 1985. *District planning in New Zealand.* New Zealand Planning Institute, Auckland.

Wood, A. 1984. *Changes in farm size, farm ownership and land use on state-settled farms, Taupo County.* MA thesis, Department of Geography, University of Auckland.

11 *Land-use regulation in deregulatory times*

PAUL CLOKE

Introduction

One of the objectives of this book (see Chapter 1) was to present a range of case studies of rural land-use planning in different nations. In so doing, some of the parochialism which has beset the understanding of planning and policy-making in this sector may prove slightly less of a barrier. It is also important, however, that strands of comparison and contrast be brought out of these national case studies. Perhaps the most immediate impression of the different accounts of rural land-use planning presented here is the sheer diversity of locations, problems, mechanisms and outcomes. Nevertheless, by stripping away the façade of locality, crucially important though that is in many instances, insights can be gained of more structural issues which underpin problems, policies and planning in many of the nations discussed.

The difficulties of such fundamental comparisons should not be underestimated. Obvious geographical factors such as the diversity of scale, climate and terrain, as well as the political differences between federal states and smaller nation states, will all lay serious claim to the explanation of rural land-use change and the response of planners and policy-makers at different levels (Cloke 1988). MacDonald sees Australia, for example, as dominated by a colonial past, a remote location and low rainfall, and there would be a legitimate expectation that these phenomena will influence the form of planning involved. Furthermore, Canada's 7.5% of rural land in agriculture contrasts markedly with the situation in smaller European states such as the UK, the Netherlands and West Germany; and the oriental rice economy in Japan has distinct rural land-use characteristics compared with occidental rural economies.

Yet these difficulties in bringing together comparative themes should not be accepted as just cause for not attempting to break out from national-scale parochialism. The material presented in the preceding chapters gives clear evidence of important bonding themes in rural land-use studies, and these themes in turn reflect some of the conceptual issues raised in Chapter 1. In this concluding chapter these communalities will be discussed under the headings of 'problems', 'policies' and 'political context', although it is realized that such a classification represents an artificial division of the topic. Before proceeding in this direction, however, it is interesting to note that the case-study chapters have revealed striking and important similarities in some of the underlying conditions for land-use planning in rural areas:

(a) the policies and plans reviewed reveal a fundamental adherence to the rights of land and property owners. Although some alternative prescriptions for state intervention in land-use issues have attacked this basic premise (for example, the Community Land Act in Britain) the political imperative of protecting property rights has stood firm. Recognition of this factor limits the scope of interventionary planning and reduces the 'art of the possible' in land-use policy. The ingrained support for property rights has also led to important issues involving the land rights of indigenous cultural groups such as the New Zealand Maori and the Australian Aborigine.

(b) linked with (a), most nations have historically been (and many currently are) highly dependent on agricultural exports. Thereby, agricultural producers, and more specifically the owners of agricultural land, have received very favourable treatment from governments. Farm policies have dominated the rural arena, and the requirements of increasing agricultural production have often overridden other considerations in the use and abuse of rural land.

(c) following on from (a) and (b), the political strength of farm lobbies has been an important factor in the determination of rural policies. Certainly until recently, farmers and landowners have enjoyed disproportionate access to power in both the central and local states, and therefore other rural land users have been effectively blocked or steered into unconflicting areas by the dominance of the farming voice. One clear pointer to future change will be a diminution of farmer power. Deregulation of agricultural support policies

will only occur in circumstances where farming votes become for some reason or other less important. This is an interesting feature of deregulation in New Zealand and is beginning to happen elsewhere. Nevertheless most contemporary rural policies have been founded on the historical dominance of the farming lobby.
(d) it is also clear from these accounts that rural people tend to be conservative both in nature and in politics. There is a strong tendency therefore to eschew any policy which suggests radical intervention into market-led systems *unless* such intervention is for the benefit of farmers. Thus where farming is strong, outside interference can be resisted, but where farming is in trouble, intervention to promote economic development receives the backing of the conservative farm-oriented populace. Elsewhere, where rural areas have been infiltrated by the urbanite middle classes, many of these conservative values are maintained although a greater emphasis on conservation often emerges.
(e) planning for rural areas faces a struggle for political acceptance and societal legitimacy. Planning is often viewed as unwarranted interference in the affairs of country people, and there is no strong local political backing for a potent local planning presence. In some nations, such as the USA, local planners are directly responsible to their electorate, a circumstance which represents a direct opportunity for subservience to current social and economic relations rather than legitimate intervention on behalf of other interests.
(f) following on from (e), rural areas lack funds, not only because of the conservative nature of people, but also because of the low population thresholds in each administrative unit. In some cases, resource deficiencies can lead to an inability to monitor and enforce existing planning mechanisms; in others there is a basic lack of database information on which to found any planning proposals; and elsewhere rural planning suffers from a lack of local expertise or may be carried out by urban-based consultants.

These characteristics result in what MacDonald in the case of Australia describes as the paradox between free enterprise and agrarian socialism. Local planning is required as a defensive rampart in the fortress of agricultural protection and support, but is constrained in its operation by underlying political values favouring landowners, freedom of choice and the market mechanism (except where this can be bettered by state support). In illustration of this point, Rex Honey of the Department of Geography, University of Iowa, once described to me a political meeting in rural Iowa, where local people were drawing together their 'manifesto' during the run-up to a presidential election. Two of the major planks in the proposed platform were: no government interference in agriculture; and government security of minimum prices for agriculture. This political acceptance of the contradiction of 'no interference unless it is of direct benefit' is the local arena in which much of rural land-use planning takes place.

Inevitably, then, more radical land-use planning proposals emanate from the centre rather than the locality. Here the agricultural power base is set against other major interests: conservation, recreation, mineral exploitation, housing construction, and so on. Here, political attitudes to rural land are worked out. Here the form and function of planning (see Ch. 1) is translated into negotiative mechanisms for implementation; the structural constraints for policy are set, and within these bargaining procedures over particular rural spaces can commence.

Rural land-use problems

The range of rural land-use issues which emerge from the case-study chapters reflects the diversity of the different nations concerned. Nevertheless, a series of common 'conflicts' emerges from these accounts. Perhaps the term conflict is over-used in this context, but it is adopted here so as briefly to delineate various types of land-use problem occurring in the rural areas of the developed world.

Four main types of conflict appear to be common in the case studies of this book. No all are assessed to have equal priority in each nation. Indeed the cultural mores of a particular nation may exclude a particular problem, a case in point being the lack of appreciation of 'wild' area in Japan which negates any need to preserve wildness. Neither are conflicts consistent over time, with the degree to which an issue is perceived (by governments and by researchers) as problematic varying historically. Yet these four themes arise sufficiently frequently in the case studies to warrant mention here. In each, conflict is viewed as occurring between agricultural use of land and other uses. Given the primacy of agricultural *policy* (if not land use in some nations) in rural areas, other potential land users will often have to contest the agricultural status quo in those specific parts of rural areas where conflict occurs.

Conflict with urban uses

The most obvious aspect of the conflict between agricultural land use and urbanization comes at the fringe of metropolitan growth. All chapters highlight this tension between city decentralization and surrounding agricultural land uses, although different degrees of landowner adhesion to their land, and varying levels of state control over development (despite landowner willingness to accede to development pressure) produce a range of resulting land-use patterns. Hebbert's account of the situation in Japan, for example, highlights the tenacity of landowners in retaining the ownership of their small plots of agricultural land as an investment despite the fact that cities such as Tokyo are spreading out beyond them. The resultant patchwork of small farming areas interspersed with urban development contrasts markedly with the land-use segregation sought after in, for example, Britain's green belts or the green heart of the Randstad in The Netherlands. Even in the most expansive nations, urban fringe conflicts are of importance because of the potential loss of good quality agricultural land from the nation's budget.

Some land-use conflicts arising from the decentralization of urban functions are less visible than at these fringe locations. Many deeper rural areas are now being 'opened up' to residential and economic development by the development of highways and by the processes underlying counter-urbanization (Cloke 1985). In some cases these areas lie beyond the daily urban systems of metropolitan centres and so it is trends of deconcentration (rather than decentralization – see Robert & Randolph 1983) which are bringing new economic developments into previously agricultural areas.

A third spread of urban land use is somewhat more sinister. Daniels *et al.* in their chapter stress the problem of dumping hazardous waste in rural areas of the USA, and this transfer of urban materials clearly poses severe problems of pollution, particularly of ground-water supplies. Rural areas are sparsely populated, inexpensive to buy into, and lacking in political clout with which to resist dumping. The same features lend rural areas 'credibility' as sites for nuclear power generation, nuclear waste reprocessing, and other potentially pollutant enterprises.

This grouping of conflicts poses clear questions of rural land-use planning. Should the transfer of land from agricultural to urban use be regulated despite the fact that this process may overrule landowner rights? What controls can be exerted over undesirable urban uses of rural sites? To what degree should agriculture be protected from the outcomes of deconcentration regardless of market forces? The rationality (or otherwise) of planning responses to these issues is discussed in the next section.

Conflict with conservation and/or recreation

The occurrence of rural land-use issues of this type is more variable. In the densely populated, smaller nations, conflicts between agriculture, conservation and recreation are the subject of considerable political concern and debate. In other nations there has been a common perception that so much rural land exists that there is no need for conservation. Particularly the expansive nations have not developed sophisticated policies for conservation because it is perceived that the use of land for agriculture, conservation and recreation can easily be segregated. However, there are clear signals that the 'problem' of conservation in expansive nations does exist but has not yet received political legitimation. Thus Daniels *et al.* point to the problems caused, for example, by overgrazing of state-owned ranchland in the USA, leading to soil erosion, over-trampling and damage to wildlife habitats from herbicide spraying. This land is considered unsuitable for mainstream agriculture, but the farming processes adopted there are clearly in conflict with other rural land-use objectives. Bryant suggests that Canada is still at the stage of needing to increase awareness of conservation issues and MacDonald claims that an over-optimistic appraisal of the rural resources in Australia has led to the destruction of forests, over-use of water supplies, overstocking of semi-arid grassland areas, and erosion of areas of steep terrain and thin soils.

The major conflict between agriculture and conservation occurs where the methods of achieving required levels of agricultural productivity offend characteristics of landscape, wildlife and amenity. This is not only a question of whether the scale of the rural land mass is sufficient to permit either a clear segregation of land uses or a compatible form of multiple land use, but also a question of the political weight given to conservation and recreation issues. In many cases, specific locations become microcosmic showcases for land-use competition – mixed-use national parks, watershed protection areas, wilderness areas, shoreline zones, and so on. It would be wrong to suggest that the confluence of agricultural, conservation and recreational land uses lead to inevitable conflict, but equally, some of the old ideas of there being so much rural land that disputes over use need not be critical are also misleading. The case-study chapters have repeatedly reported on key aspects of the landscape where these three land uses can be incompatible and where regulation is required in order to prioritize one or other of them. Again, the use of rural planning mechanisms to administer political priorities will be a key theme in the next section.

Conflict with forestry

A further area of land-use competition revealed in the foregoing chapters is that between agriculture and forestry. As with other conflicts, there has been a conventional wisdom of how forestry uses of rural land should be managed so as to avoid clashes with the productive needs of agriculture. At a basic level, forestry has been seen as a land use which should be restricted to areas of poor soil, usually in upland areas. Such segregation of 'good' agricultural land and land used for forestry is, however, subject to pressure from the economics of forestry. If forestry is merely viewed by policy-makers as use for land which is not required for other purposes, then this model of segregation can be used with relative impunity. If, however, forestry is required to make a substantial contribution to the national export production, the requirements of productivity and easy harvesting (see Moran's account of exotic forestry in New Zealand) are such that better quality land close to processing centres will represent the market-led location for planting. Thus strategic and macro-economic factors are likely to govern the regulation of conflicts between the agricultural and forestry industries in their demand for land.

Conflict over tenure

Rural land-use planners are not only concerned with potential or actual disputes over the most appropriate utilization of particular stretches of land. In many nations there have arisen important questions over the rights of certain social or cultural groups to control the use of rural land. Some nations with colonial histories have had to deal with claims of indigenous peoples for land which was annexed by conquering invaders. In New Zealand, for example, the Maori people maintain a strong cultural tradition associated with their ancestral land and have mounted steady pressure over recent years to regain some of their rights to control land currently owned by the Crown and other landowners.

Elsewhere, the struggle for control is being waged between 'local' sections of the population and the increasing tendency for non-farmers and non-residents to own agricultural land. Bryant's account of rural land-use problems in Canada stresses the way in which opposition to these outside interests has gained political support and thereby found a place on the policy-making agenda.

This rather simple listing of land-use conflicts is unsurprising, and serves to mask the more fundamental processes which underpin decisions over rural land in developed nations. In particular, the notion of issues being perceived as 'problems' or 'conflicts' needs attention. Many questions arise from this notion including 'perceived by whom', 'on behalf of whom', and 'with what aims in mind?' Consider the following alternative scenarios which might be suggested of the state in regulating such change:

- one dominant fraction of capital (which can be corporate or dispersed as in the case of family-farm agriculture) claims the dominant use of the rural land in question. No 'conflict' arises if the state is content to give support to this fraction of capital either by issuing no regulation over land use or by implementing protective regulations which benefit the dominant fraction.
- two or more capital fractions (for example agriculture, forestry, or construction) compete in market conditions for the same land. There is no 'conflict' in an unregulated market since the highest rent bid will succeed. The outcome will only stem from conflict if the state owes higher allegiance to one or other of the unsuccessful bidders than to the market leader, or if it judges that the consumption of a broader value from the land (for example, conservation, amenity, and so on) is politically expedient or ideologically necessary.
- conflict can also arise where the political requirements of the central and local states collide over land-use issues. For example, the strategic requirement for agricultural productivity and consequent profitability for large-scale agricultural producers may require central state policy to ignore questions of local ownership which achieve high political profile at the local level.

The idea of planning as a neutral arbitrator between competing land-use bidders ignorers these political allegiances. Even if such structural determinants of state policy direction are unacceptable to some rural researchers, it should still be acknowledged that decisions relating to the 'public good' or the 'common good' pervade rural planning in developed nations. These decisions appear to be politically value-laden in most of the cases discussed in this book. Equally, it is these political decisions which legitimate the idea of 'problematic conflicts', and it follows that the perception of conflict which is talked about very often represents conflict *between capital and the state* over land as well as between *competing use bidders*.

What, might be asked, about the 'natural' conflict between say agricultural intensification and the conservation of valuable habitats? Surely in this case there is use conflict, not political conflict? Again such an issue might be seen to depend on the political credence given by the state either to production or to conservation in any society. Planning conflicts, as such, will only arise where there are divided political loyalties or where there is political opposition to the dominant economic use. The planning response to the conflicts outlined in this section, then, will depend on the power relations between different land-use interests and the role of the state in the interpretation of these power relations. Out of this political arena have arisen the policy mechanisms for regulating rural land use.

One further factor in the political nature of conflict over land use concerns the overall view taken of national land budgets. From the traditional position where expansive nations were thought to have no problem over the quantity of rural land, the suggestion is now that the extent of high-quality accessible land is sufficiently small for greater care to be taken over regulatory controls. Yet from the traditional position where intensive smaller nations were thought to be in crisis over the loss of agricultural land, the suggestion is now (certainly in EEC nations such as Britain, France, West Germany and The Netherlands) that transnational agricultural trade policies have led to the opportunity to take considerable slices of land out of agriculture production, thus easing the requirement for regulatory controls. State–capital conflict over interventionary land-use policies will therefore depend to an extent on the political discretion available to offer substitute benefit to disadvantaged land uses within a flexible overall land budget.

Policies for the regulation of rural land use

Given this array of rural land-use conflicts which have been ascribed varying political importance in the nations described in the case-study chapters, it would be anticipated that governments would in response use a variety of planning mechanisms. The introductory chapter highlighted a number of fundamental issues concerning the role of planning in its state context. Two of these questions are useful in understanding the land-use planning responses of various nations. First (and certainly more straightforwardly), have 'standard' planning policies emerged in different contexts? And secondly, is it possible to assess whether land-use policies have a function of legitimating other government activities in support of fractions of production capital in rural areas rather than (or as well as) presenting *in their own right* a rational response to perceived problems centring on rural land use? This section offers a brief summary in relation to the first of these questions, and the following section tackles the issue of problem-response and legitimation in the context of the changing nature of the political arena in the various nations reported in this book.

Superficially, strong threads of similarity can be seen weaving through the land-use policies described in the case-study chapters. At a more detailed level of analysis, however, significant local variations are apparent and it would therefore be unwise to suggest sweeping generalizations. Nevertheless the different policies may be summarized within a threefold categorization of the ability of governments to influence land-use issues.

State ownership

In some cases, the main attention given by governments to rural land use occurs where they have direct control through ownership. In Canada, for example, the *federal* level of government has little impact on rural land use outside of its own landholdings north of the 60° parallel and in the Northwest Territories and the Yukon. It follows that because of this spatial structure of land ownership, direct federal government control is limited to specific types of rural environment, away from, for example, the pressures and conflicts of agriculture and urban land uses. Similarly, MacDonald's account of Australia notes that state governments' control over land covers some 70% of the country, including land leased to pastoral farmers, but that such landholdings are coincident with the semi-arid and arid zones of the country and that virtually all land-use conflicts over land used for cultivation (and most over that for livestock) occur in a context of private ownership. Most of the case-study nations do hold land in public ownership for productive use. For example, state-owned forestry holdings are variously reported, and state schemes to initiate settlement and agricultural production in marginal rural areas in nations such as New Zealand occur on government-owned land. It is worth noting here, however, that these productive holdings are now becoming increasingly susceptible to ideological trends towards privatization (see pp. 281-3).

State ownership of land tends to be historically determined and geographically peripheral. Historical determination means that governments will work with the land that has been passed down to them, but have been reluctant in recent decades to extend their land ownership as a response to conflicts occurring on privately owned rural land. Indeed the opposite trend towards privatizing state-owned productive land is becoming prevalent. Geographical peripherality means that only certain types of land-use issues are being dealt with under conditions of full tenure control. Thus national parks in many nations enjoy policies which are predicated on decision-making freedoms which would be unattainable given private ownership of land. Conflicts can still arise in this cushioned land-use arena – witness for example the clashes between conservation interests and the booming use of off-road recreational vehicles in some remote rural areas (Webb & Wilshire 1983). Nevertheless, the purchase of land by the public sector continues to be a favoured policy prescription amongst various resource interests, particularly those concerned with conservation, and particularly in areas where historic state ownership of rural land is at a low level. Governments, however, are tending towards increasing support for the rights of private landowners and for the market mechanism, and so such prescriptions are politically unrealistic in the present climate of New Right governments.

Expenditure

A second mechanism for regulating rural land use is by attaching conditions to the financial benefits offered through rural development programmes. In most cases the most prominent programmes have been to support agricultural production in the interests of national self-sufficiency or of export requirements. In all cases agricultural support policies have been fuelled by the political power exerted by farming and landowning lobbies. These development programmes tend to be umbrella schemes, implemented in a top-down manner thereby reducing the sensitivity to local land-use issues. Thus the chapters on France, West Germany, The Netherlands and the UK show that rural land-use issues are inextricably bound up with the provisions of the Common Agricultural Policy of the EEC. Equally, the larger federal nations have also established hefty agricultural support programmes, with that in the USA, for example, costing $26 billion in 1986. As Daniels *et al.* note in their chapter, these umbrella policies tend to throw money at unspecified problems rather than allocating specific funds to specific areas in order to resolve interrelated problems such as lack of infrastructure, the need to improve land and upgrade productivity, and the need to prevent the despoliation of natural resources. In other words their purpose is unidirectional in support of farming interests, and although conditions could be attached to these financial provisions in order to specify particular forms of husbandry or to maintain particular landscape features or to prevent the erosion of precious land resources (Bowers & Cheshire 1983), the political thrust of these programmes tends to prioritize agricultural interests over others. An exception to this trend is found in the 'sodbuster' and 'swampbuster' schemes in the United States to prevent valued grasslands and swamplands from being drained and ploughed up for crop production. Here, the penalty for improving designated land is ineligibility to receive federal subsidies.

Having established the initial principle of support for farmers, it is politically difficult to avoid the secondary principle that they should be compensated for not undertaking production which would yield them maximum economic benefit. Thus schemes to take land out of production on environmental grounds have to be founded on the expensive premise of ensuring financial compensation. This situation may change rapidly, however, in those nations where the state's ideological preference for deregulation is able to overcome the political lobby of farmers and is therefore extended to the agricultural sector through a dismantling of subsidies (see Moran's chapter on New Zealand).

There is some evidence to suggest that expenditure on farm support has actually been responsible for some of the rural land-use conflicts suggested in the previous section. The drive for productivity which has been sponsored by state subsidy has caused significant landscape damage and raised the level of use of pollutant chemical fertilizers and herbicides. It is only at the local level that concerns over these conservation issues have gained any headway towards a more integrated form of rural development. Regulation of rural land use through centralized expenditure programmes has tended to be a policy prescription which has proved largely untenable given the distribution of power in most rural areas.

Legislation

If state land ownership has not found approval as a contemporary means of controlling land use, and if the moderation of landscape damage and other conflicts is not to be achieved by conditional granting of economic support for agricultural production, then nation states wishing to regulate rural land use have had little option but to legislate for a system of planning controls over land-use change. There are three common components to such systems:

Zones and ordinances Most of the case-study nations have established a system of land-use planning control which combines the designation of zones in an overall land-use plan with some ordinance or regulation with which to implement the intended land use of the zones. Each nation has developed its peculiar version of this scheme and it is not intended here to restate the detailed descriptions of the case-study chapter. Nevertheless certain key variations are worthy of note. First, the varying power of local land-use plans reflects the degree to which governments have been prepared to sanction legally binding documents detailing rural zones. In the USA, for example, there has been relatively little zoning because the strength of America's constitution of rights tradition is such that state and local governments cannot use zoning if a landowner's rights are subsequently unreasonably restricted merely because of a public policy. So, if land is zoned for agriculture, and farming in that location is not profitable, the zoning regulation may impose a burden on the landowner without any compensation and could therefore be judged as unconstitutional. There is an evident and significant contrast between this reluctance to introduce legally tested plans in the USA, and the statutory plans in the UK where policy directives are backed up by the legal requirement that changes in the use of land be approved by the local authority. Such a requirement affords significant advantages in maintaining regional-scale land-use policies such as those relating to green belts in areas of severe urban pressure. Even so, it should be made clear that not only do these UK provisions exclude changes within a land-use type (so one type of agricultural production may be swapped for another without recourse to planning permission) but it is also the case that planning decisions can be appealed against in law, and so central government by allowing appeals can achieve some flexibility within seemingly restrictive legislation which has its roots in the 1940s. Variations in land-use plans also vary within federal nations, as the differences between British

Columbia, Québec and Ontario amply demonstrate (see Bryant's chapter on Canada).

Also worthy of comment are the different types of zones used in the case of rural land. Some nations tend towards the establishment of a minimum lot size within an agricultural zone, so as to prevent the break-up of viable farm units through subdivision. Others require that the designated land use (for example, agriculture) be exclusive in that zone. Some countries (for example, Japan) use both types of zoning according to locality, and in France, the initial distinction between urban (U) and natural (N) zones is further divided into:

NA – where urban development will take place in the future
NB – where diffuse urbanization is permitted
NC – where there is a strong presumption against non-rural development
ND – where protection of sites, habitats and landscapes is of uppermost priority.

Zoning is also used to denote land for forestry and as a mechanism for further conservation and recreation objectives (see below under *designation*).

The evidence of the case-study chapters suggests that zoning and cognate procedures have been most strongly and successfully implemented in urban fringe zones where the political will to stem the tide of urban expansion has generally been strong. Throughout the case-study accounts, however, there are clear suggestions that the implementation of zoning has become increasingly problematic. In the USA, where ideological attachment to negative planning controls is weak, there is a tendency for zoning objectives to be frustrated by localized amendments and exceptions. Zones are notoriously temporary. Decisions are made by politically vulnerable local planners, who are particularly susceptible to local demands for an expanded tax base. Moreover there is little co-ordination between local authorities, thus rendering any idea of regional zoning strategies unworkable in many cases. Other problems with zoning are noted in the cases of Japan and New Zealand. In the former, overlaps have occurred between incongruous zonings, with Hebbert noting that 4% of the land area is simultaneously classified as city planning area, forest zone and agricultural zone. In New Zealand, Moran suggests that the use of zoning to dedicate land for national production is limited both because definitive zoning requires foreknowledge of comparative advantage relating to potential land uses in the region (which is often not available) and because the area of land needed to meet national production targets is also usually an unknown quantity.

Zoning procedures, then, have been found to be weak because of rational difficulties in attempting to piece together the various parts of a national land budget jigsaw, because of local political negotiations, and because of lax mechanisms for implementation and monitoring. There is also an underlying constraint in that the practical outcome of zoning has been to leave room for flexibility for governments to negotiate with various national and local interests. The constraint is therefore that governments have ben unwilling to be boxed in by binding planning systems which preclude the broad maintenance of political support for landowning and farming groups. This structural constraint appears to have prevented the utilization of legally binding forms of negative control over rural land. Even where the most regulatory mechanisms have been introduced such as in the UK and The Netherlands, the current political economy is shifting through national government ideology away from the existing commitment to strong regulatory control. This shift is further discussed in the next section of the chapter, which deals with changing political context.

Designation The second component of most attempts to legislate for land-use objectives may be met. There is some overlap here between control through ownership, and negative control on land-use change through zoning, but this category covers designations of land areas where control is attempted through persuasion rather than by binding. Thus West Germany has 4 National Parks, 64 Nature Parks, 23 480 Nature Reserves and 20 wetland reserves covering some 22% of the land area. Similarly France has legislated for issues of landscapes and habitat protection by designating a series of reserves. Most nations have extensive national parks and are becoming more conscious of the need for specific reserves surrounding and including habitats for valuable flora and fauna. It has now become almost chic to have a version of the Environmentally Sensitive Area so as to flag to increasingly important conservation lobbies that the political response to their concerns has been unequivocal.

The efficacy of these designations, however, depends on the methods of control or positive persuasion which underpin them. State-owned national parks suffer only from lack of financial provision and the constitutional 'rights' of those engaging in potentially conflicting recreation practices. However, designation of a national park, the land of which is largely in private ownership as in the

UK, inherently constrains land-use planning and requires further mechanisms to bring about required objectives. As MacDonald notes in the case of Australia, the total area of land in conservation reserves is not *per se* a good indicator of the adequacy of planning for conservation. Whether planning is effectively implemented within designated reserves and whether designations cover the habitats of endangered species or susceptible landscapes are much more pertinent questions in the evaluation of designated rural areas. In the current political climate, much depends on whether finance is made available from the state or from the voluntary sector to bring designated areas into a controlling ownership, or whether sufficient inducements can be offered to persuade landowners to comply with conservation planning requirements. Again, the designation of special areas, permitting high-profile lines to be drawn on land maps, has become a favoured political response to pressure from various lobbies. Designation has been like a talisman; designate and all will be well. Clearly, however, if designation is not to be thought of as merely pragmatic or a technique of legitimation, then it must be accompanied by appropriate carrots or sticks so as to ensure ground-level responses to planning objectives.

Management by agreement The favoured carrot has come from legislation which seeks to establish a form of compensated partnership between rural landowners and rural resource agencies. The 1981 Wildlife and Countryside Act in the UK set up the idea of management agreements in which a landowner's compliance over matters of land management practice would be purchased by compensation payments from quasi-government conservation agencies. A similar mechanism exists in The Netherlands, and landscape management programmes requiring the co-operation of local communities prevail in each of the European case studies. Here, the suggestion is that governments have wished to make some policy move so as to appease the growing political support for the conservation movement, but have not wished to exert new levels of control over their traditional political constituency of farmers and landowners. Thus management by agreement represents the pragmatic response of a political juggler attempting to keep all the balls in the air at the same time.

Management by agreement also crops up in non-European settings, for instance in the USA where co-operative agreements and conservation easements mark a move in this direction. Moreover, with the growing recognition that agricultural land in many nations is no longer sacrosanct because of the excesses of subsidized overproduction, the motivation to transfer land from agriculture into other uses, particularly those with an emphasis on conservation, is becoming irresistible. The USA already has a set-aside scheme with its Conservation Reserve Program. This aims to remove from production cropland which is highly susceptible to erosion. Eighteen million hectares are targeted in the first 5-year period. The ALURE proposals in the UK also represent the beginnings of an attempt to agree countryside policies for agriculturally redundant land. These changes could lead to a windfall success for conservation interests if sufficient compensation funding is available for a widespread implementation of new schemes.

Policy comparisons?

Compared to an equivalent analysis of the policies and plans used to respond to issues of rural society and economy (Cloke 1988), these land-use policies are far more varied in terms of their localized detail. At a more structural level, however, this brief summary analysis shows that similar fundamental decisions are being grappled with in the political arena of land-use planning. How far are policies able to exert direct controls over landowners? How do governments maintain their traditional support for agricultural and landowning interests while paying at least lip-service and some heart-service to the increasingly important conservation interests? There are variations, but in general similar power relations appear dominant. The exception concerns recent deregulatory developments in New Zealand and to a lesser extent in other nations, and it is to this type of change in the political inputs to rural land-use planning that the chapter now turns.

The changing political context

Following the issue of whether standard policies have emerged in different contexts, we turn to the second question of the *function* of these policies in their political context. Some would see them as rational responses to perceived problems; others as pragmatic attempts to do *something* about important conflicts; and yet others as legitimations of other government activities which are more directly performing the function of supporting capitalist production in rural areas. All of these views are value-laden, and readers will bring their own ideological preconceptions to the question, which is not suited to verification or falsification by the information presented in the case-study chapters. What the evidence of this book does demonstrate, however, is that the governmental relations which underlie policy-making for rural areas are changing, and it is possible that the direction of change will give some indication of the function of rural land-use policies, either reflecting their importance *per se* or indicating that they are rather more like representative holograms of the state–society relationship, changing as the relationship changes.

Three sets of governmental relations were discussed in the introductory chapter, and the changes evidenced in this book can be summarized under these three headings.

Central–local relations

Those states with a longer tradition of planning, and these are largely European, have undergone very significant changes in the role of the central state in land-use planning. In order to establish planning regulations which were to some extent instrumental in restricting the powers of landowners to do what they liked with their land, central governments were responding at least to an extent to the postwar visionary fervour of idealist planners and politicians. Regulation of land use for the 'common good' was a radical central policy stance which appears to be a real (in the sense of not being artificial) attempt to address environmental issues in rural areas. Certainly it can be argued (see Ambrose 1986) that powerful interests were bought off in the process – agricultural capital by the exemptions of agricultural land-use change from planning and by systems of economic support, and construction capital by the alternative opportunities for profit afforded by new and expanded town initiatives and by high-rise urban developments. Certainly, it can also be stressed (see Reade 1987) that the establishment of a 'neutral' planning system acted as some kind of cover for the very profitable and political operations of the land market. But nevertheless, the early planning systems did represent a high point in the interference of central states in land-use changes. Subsequent attempts to introduce greater interference, for example, through the very temporary centralized land agencies in the UK and in Japan were quickly rebuffed. It is possible to recognize a steady retreat by central governments from these earlier more radical positions on land-use regulation.

Other nations did not go through this earlier radical stage, but (sometimes grudgingly) accepted the need for a less rigorous system of control!. Here it is noticeable that in several of the case-study nations, responsibility for land-use planning has been increasingly devolved to local government agencies. Although, in cases such as France, this devolution has provided an impetus for integrated planning at the local level, elsewhere there is evidence that planning in the hands of local authorities suffers because of financial restrictions, lack of powers with which to implement policies, and political vulnerability. In fact, the decentralization of planning mechanisms has been matched in most nations by a centralization (and even internationalization) of political control through budgetary restrictions and legislation inspired by ideology. These characteristics are compatible with the political objectives of the New Right administrations currently in power throughout the developed world. It is worth noting, however, that another such characteristic is an attack on planning itself. Market-oriented policies require less government interference and not more. Thus the central domination of the locality in most nations provides a fruitful arena for the demise of planning due to changes in the relations between the public and private sectors.

Inter-agency relations

Inter-agency relations are dominated by a lack of co-ordination and a fragmentation of power. Most case-study chapters report of proliferation of *ad hoc* agencies and a balkanization of spatial units. Explanation of this phenomenon will also be value-laden. Does the profusion of agencies, acting within a plethora of laws and regulatory instruments, and suffering from mutually overlapping yet divergent interests reflect a parentage of pragmatism or ideology? Authors in this book adopt differing views. One sees the problem as planning being beset by a presumption with symptoms and not causes; pragmatic responses to perceived crisis have led to short-term responsive action which proves to be long-lasting especially when the next round of 'temporary' measures are grafted on. Another suggests that the development of a series of integrated co-ordinating agencies with strong powers of planning and policy-making would run contrary to the requirements of central states whose aim is to decentralize responsibility but to centralize power; fragmentation of implementing agencies is compatible with a sophisticated divide-and-rule tactic by the state.

These views are not necessarily mutually exclusive. The 'blunder' and 'conspiracy' theories greatly over-simplify the realities of how agencies evolve, stake out territory, and react with each other. What is clear is that in most cases there has not been a rational move towards single powerful agencies of rural resource management and therefore those who suggest that problems of policy co-ordination would be overcome by the establishment of such agencies should first seek to understand the political context which appears to mediate against local forms of integrated response.

Public–private sector relations

Perhaps the most important changes in governmental relations are those which involve a transfer of functions from the public to the private sector. The themes of privatization and deregulation represent fundamental planks in the platform of contemporary New Right governments and although the impact of these changes are only just beginning to be experienced in rural areas it seems likely that the widespread deployment of deregulatory legislation will force a radical re-evaluation of the role of planning in rural land use. Aside from the broader impacts of the economic deregulation which has occurred in most nations, three areas of change can be foreseen:

(a) New Zealand is the first developed nation to take radical steps to extend deregulation to the agricultural sector. By removing subsidies and by raising farm-sector lending rates to market levels, the Lange government has hastened the kind of debt crisis which is also seen in other nations such as in the US Midwest. Similar moves elsewhere are currently being delayed or prevented by the friction of the political power of farming interests – a factor which is present in most nations and particularly deeply enmeshed within the EEC. Yet there are indications of a relative waning in the level of influence of farmers, and so deregulation or not, it seem likely that government insistence on the protection of agricultural land from competing uses may become less strong than has been the case in the past. This change is being hastened by government policies of restraining public expenditure, which will collide with costly agricultural support systems during times of over-production. The net result of these changes may be an unexpected boost to conservation objectives provided that land coming out of agriculture can be matched with land where landscape or habitat vulnerability requires sympathetic management practices. This matching procedure may prove to be unacceptably costly for the public expenditure requirements of the very governments whose deregulatory attitudes have brought the opportunity about in the first place.

(b) Associated with deregulation of agriculture and detachment from agricultural land protection is the threat to planning processes and procedure themselves. The reduction of government interference to the market mechanism is another important facet of New Right ideology. In the UK there have been wide-ranging discussions over how to 'simplify' town and country planning, and the resultant Green Paper on the future of development plans proposes a reduction in the role of county councils in what will be a much more localized process of development control decision-making. It is important to note, however, that these proposals also afford the opportunity for central government input into the flexibility or otherwise with which planning controls are imposed. Their input so far during the 1980s has been one favouring private-sector applicants over local authority restrictions in a significantly increased number of cases. Certainly the slide from early radicalism to contemporary political functionalism is noticeable in some European nations, and elsewhere there simply has not been the tradition of land-use intervention from which to slide. It seems likely that contemporary transfers of emphasis from the public sector to the private sector will lead to further declines in the rigour of land-use planning mechanisms.

(c) A further result of changing public-private sector relations has been the trend towards privatization of state assets. In forestry, for example, state agencies have been directed towards increasingly commercial attitudes during recent years. In Australia it is suggested that state forestry agencies have been too closely allied to commercial timber interests for the comfort of conservationists. The preoccupations with timber values of the forests has overshadowed conservation and recreation values. In New Zealand the state forest service has already relinquished its publicly owned processing plants to the private sector, and has sold timber to private interests well below the cost of production. Now with the Lange government's policy of *corporatization* – requiring state industries to be run along commercial lines – the new Forestcorp appears at least half-way to being privatized. Clearly any further moves towards the privatization of state-owned resources will lead to a substitution of amenity-oriented objectives by the market ethic of capital accumulation. Neither is it only forest resources that are at risk. The British government is currently said to be investigating the privatization of land owned by local authorities, and of state-owned nature reserves, probably looking to transfer the latter to voluntary-sector agencies and charities. Equally, the high-profile deliberations over policies of charging for use of state-owned or state-controlled recreational facilities indicate the same direction of change in public–private sector relations. If the dominance of New Right governments continues, it appears likely that privatization of state assets will become widespread, and that current practices in the selling off of state-run infrastructural services such as those in the energy and telecommunications fields, will be extended to areas of direct state control over rural land use.

These changing sets of governmental relations appear to be derived, at least in part, from the ideological moves of the New Right governments of the 1980s. Although it could be argued that they are merely changing the nature of their response to total land-use issues so as to achieve greater economic efficiency, the net result of changing relations is to weaken the land-use planning systems in many nations. Such a conclusion again brings into question the function of planning in the context of the state's provision of appropriate environments for capital accumulation.

Planning regulation within state deregulation

A traditional conclusion for any analysis of rural land-use planning would be a call for stronger, more powerful and more comprehensive planning agencies within which land-use monitoring and regulation could be integrated yet achieve the necessary flexible response for the differing needs of different localities. Indeed, some of these themes emerge from case-study chapters with significant validity as responses to the ground-level failure of planning. Yet the arrival of a New Right political context for rural land-use planning has heralded a move away from, rather than towards, strongly implemented regulatory intervention by state agencies.

So, the major conclusion to arise from the evidence presented here tends to echo Dylan's 'The times they are a-changing'. Thus far the developed world has approached rural land-use planning with particular state functions to the fore. In the sphere of *production* the needs of major capital interests (particularly those connected with agriculture) have been served by *regulatory support* of economic restructuring. Thereby, the mechanization of agriculture, the introduction of and reliance upon chemical fertilizers and herbicides, and the guarantee of income levels have all been facilitated by state subsidy, the end result being good conditions for capital accumulation by the larger farming enterprises and by agro-support capital in, for example, the chemical and machinery sectors. A strong agricultural lobby has been maintained within both central and local states, which has reinforced the structural support for rural resource capital. With this production environment, state policies for the *consumption* of environmental welfare have not been subject to the kind of strong political opposition from capital interests which, for example, ensured the demise of policies for public-sector land acquisition agencies in Britain. The protection of agricultural land from urban intrusion through regulatory planning procedures was tolerated by the interests concerned as was the establishment of designated areas for conservation and recreation. A restriction of market forces was the price to pay for the facilitation by the state of capital accumulation in other sectors.

It can be argued that the state is responding to very different requirements of capital interest during current rounds of economic restructuring which are impacting on rural areas. It appears that *deregulation* is the contemporary requirement for some pertinent fractions of capital whose overall interests may be better served by low inflation, lower interest rates, lower taxes, and greater market freedom, than by direct financial support. Thus many areas of consumption previously serviced by the public sector are shifting, partly or in full, to the private sector. Alongside privatization, there are the beginnings of deregulation, even in the agricultural sector, where farmer lobbies find themselves less powerful than before. Such deregulation pressures seem likely to increase. Rural land-use planning thus stands as a process of regulation in a deregulatory age and may well come under increasing attack from ideologically inspired governments with anti-planning tendencies.

Yet in many ways the need for an efficient and equitable rural land-use planning mechanism remains undiminished and may indeed be made more important by the spatial and social divisions which will result in detachment of governments from policies of strictly preserving agricultural land. More than ever pressures on rural land will occur at the various interfaces between urban decentralization, deconcentration and rural areas. In depressed regions, however, land unwanted for commercial agriculture will pose novel problems. Minority cultural groups and local landowners are lobbying for policies of positive discrimination to maintain their own connections with rural land. On the surface, then, land-use planning will face the task of finding new uses for rural land, or arbitrating between new competing uses. In depth, taken at face value, this represents an exciting role for planning in the contemporary rural areas of the developed world. Yet, the ideological climate of anti-planning which is emerging in many nations may mean that rural land-use planning will become increasingly a *token* function of a state which recognizes that the current needs for capital restructuring are best served by deregulatory measures. There is therefore an important and urgent need for rural researchers to gain a full and detailed understanding of the contemporary links between capital, the state and rural land. Only by appreciating rural areas as arenas of accumulation by different fractions of capital will we understand the dynamics of rural land use in a period of accelerating deregulation. Equally, such links will only exposed if research relating to rural land-use planning becomes more theoretically informed. It is this theoretical underdevelopment which currently most hinders the development of thriving international and multidisciplinary studies in rural land-use planning.

References

Ambrose, P. 1986. *Whatever happened to planning?* London: Methuen.
Bowers, J. & P. Cheshire 1983. *Agriculture, the countryside and land use* London: Methuen.
Cloke, P. 1985. Counterurbanisation: a rural perspective. *Geography* 70, 13–23.
Cloke, P. 1988. Rural policies: responses to problems or problematic responses? In *Policies and plans for rural people*, P. Cloke (ed.). London: Allen & Unwin.
Reade, E. 1987. *British town and country planning*. Milton Keynes: Open University Press.
Robert, S. & W. Randolph 1983. Beyond decentralisation: the evolution of population distribution in England and Wales, 1961–1981. *Geoforum* 14, 75–102.
Webb, R. & H. Wilshire 1983. *Environmental effects of off-road vehicles*. New York: Springer.

Index

abandonment 98, 111, 113ff, 185
Aboriginal land 207, 230ff, 265
acid rain 2, 122
AGLV 30
alternative lifestyles 2
ALURE 38, 40, 43, 280
AONB 9, 30, 39, 40

bargaining 8
Barlow Report 19
basin management 226ff
betterment 24, 25, 32, 33, 37
bucolic idyll 19
buffer zones 58, 68

CAP 22, 36, 39, 41, 107, 275
capital 9, 12, 14, 20, 21, 29, 32, 35, 130, 184, 209, 239, 271, 272, 273, 280, 281, 285ff
central local relations 16, 281ff
class 8, 9, 11, 12
common good 6, 8, 9, 15, 19, 271, 281
Community Land Act 25, 265
Compact City 57, 58
compensation 22, 24, 32, 37, 44, 86, 98, 276
compulsory purchase 25
conservation 1, 21, 33, 37, 41, 43, 48, 56ff, 62, 85, 89ff, 124ff, 137, 148, 165ff, 194ff, 228ff, 269ff
consolidation 47, 62, 65, 85, 108ff, 140, 242
counterurbanization 2, 76, 153, 163, 268
Country Landowners Association 22, 26
Countryside Commission 33
critical planning theory 7
crown land 7, 256

depopulation 77, 141
deprivation 19
deregulation 12, 19, 149, 150, 240, 265, 266, 280, 283ff
development plans 26, 63, 65, 79ff, 93, 118, 198, 223
diversification 39, 40, 41, 78, 79, 252

economic growth 131, 162
EEC 22, 39, 48, 49, 86, 98, 107, 114, 208, 211, 272, 275
elitism 8
enterprise zones 9
environmental impact statements 158, 223
Environmentally Sensitive Areas 30, 38, 39, 278
espaces convoités 78
espaces délaissés 78
espaces marginaux 78
Exmoor 38
extensification 65, 185, 196

farmers 21, 23, 28, 32, 36, 40, 61, 64, 83ff, 100, 107ff, 140ff, 149, 156, 173, 248, 253
federal land 153ff, 189
forestry 20, 39, 48, 54ff, 82, 87ff, 100, 115, 121, 136ff, 154ff, 167ff, 173, 184, 213, 226, 227ff, 247ff, 252ff, 270, 273, 277
fragmentation 114, 140, 187
Friends of the Earth 23

General Development Order 9
gentry 21, 22, 28
green belts 26, 27, 28, 30, 39, 40, 268
Green Party 104
Greenpeace 23

Halvergate 37
heritage 1, 229, 230
hobby farms 173
horticulture 52, 53, 250, 252, 257
hunting 122

Ijsselmeer 48, 54
industrial waste 2, 158ff, 268
instrumentalism 8

Index

intensification 48, 62, 86, 107, 108, 148, 252, 257

key settlements 26

landowners 3, 21, 23, 28, 35, 36, 59, 84, 92, 115, 137ff, 152, 168, 195, 209, 239, 265, 266, 279
land prices 86, 141, 187
land reform 140
landscape plans 117
less favoured areas 83, 86, 98
littoral 94ff

management agreements 37, 65, 67, 279ff
managerialism 8
manufacturing 21, 141
Maori land 238, 240, 251, 253ff, 265, 270
mechanisation 2, 238
modernisation 83, 85, 107, 108, 141

National Farmers' Union 22, 26
national parks 9, 29, 30, 37, 39, 40, 92, 121, 126, 137, 148, 154, 156, 220, 228, 230, 233, 246, 269, 278
National Trust 23
Nature Conservancy Council 30, 33
nature reserves 30, 32, 60, 64, 66, 90, 91, 97, 121, 278
new towns 24, 26, 27
Norfolk Broads 37, 38

OECD 131, 132, 142, 150

paddy fields 132, 145
part-time farming 53, 100
permits 59
planning appeals 41
planning gain 9, 23
pluralism 8, 11
pollution 2, 5, 37, 44, 48, 51, 86, 89, 122, 158, 163, 197, 223, 268, 275
population density 20, 47, 95, 130, 131, 142
post-industrial society 2
power relations 3, 41, 43, 162, 265, 275, 282
pressure groups 189, 238
producer boards 249

Randstad 56, 57, 58, 268
rational decision-making 6, 14
rationalization 78, 117
reclaimed land 47, 143ff
recreation 1, 47, 48, 50, 55ff, 107, 113, 115, 122, 124ff, 138ff, 172, 186, 269ff
redevelopment 63, 65
regional planning 243ff
regulation 12, 96, 148, 190ff, 209, 245, 271, 274, 275, 278
remembrement 82, 85
restructuring 20, 48, 74, 113, 242, 259, 285
retirement 84, 170

Section 52 Agreements 1
self-help 32
self-sufficiency 1, 22, 227, 274
set-aside 28, 165, 280
simplified planning zones 9
sodbuster 165, 275
special development order 42
SSSI 30, 32, 33, 37, 40, 91
state farm settlement 247
state land 220ff, 273ff, 278
state owned corporations 240, 245, 255, 259
state theory 10ff
structuralism 8
structure plans 26
subdivision 153, 166, 169, 172ff, 193, 223, 238, 252, 277
subsidies 7, 32, 33, 54, 83, 150, 160ff, 225, 240, 248, 274, 275, 279
swampbuster 165, 275

Thatcherism 19, 24, 33ff, 38ff, 44
tourism 83, 95, 98, 124, 174, 234, 257

urban fringe 1, 152, 153, 166, 176, 215, 268
urbanisation 18, 57ff, 147ff, 178, 192, 268ff
Uthwatt report 19, 24, 25

wasteland 83
wetland 85, 156
wilderness 2, 152, 154ff
woodland 39, 106, 116, 121